Nineteenth-Century French Drawings
from the Museum Boymans-van Beuningen

A.F.W.M. Meij
Jurriaan A. Poot

Translated by
CHARLOTTE I. LOEB

INTERNATIONAL EXHIBITIONS FOUNDATION

This exhibition is organized and circulated by the International Exhibitions Foundation, Washington, D.C.

The exhibition is made possible by a grant from the National Endowment for the Arts, and an indemnity awarded through the Federal Council on the Arts and Humanities

This catalogue is underwritten in part by The Andrew W. Mellon Foundation

Designed by Polly Sexton, Washington, D.C.
Typeset by Carver PhotoComposition, Inc., Arlington, Virginia
Produced by Garamond/Pridemark Press, Baltimore, Maryland
Printed on 80 lb. Mohawk Superfine text; 80 lb. matching cover.

Cover: *View of L'Estaque,* Paul Cézanne (cat. no. 10).

Frontispiece: *Dancing Moroccan,* Eugène Delacroix (cat. no. 45).

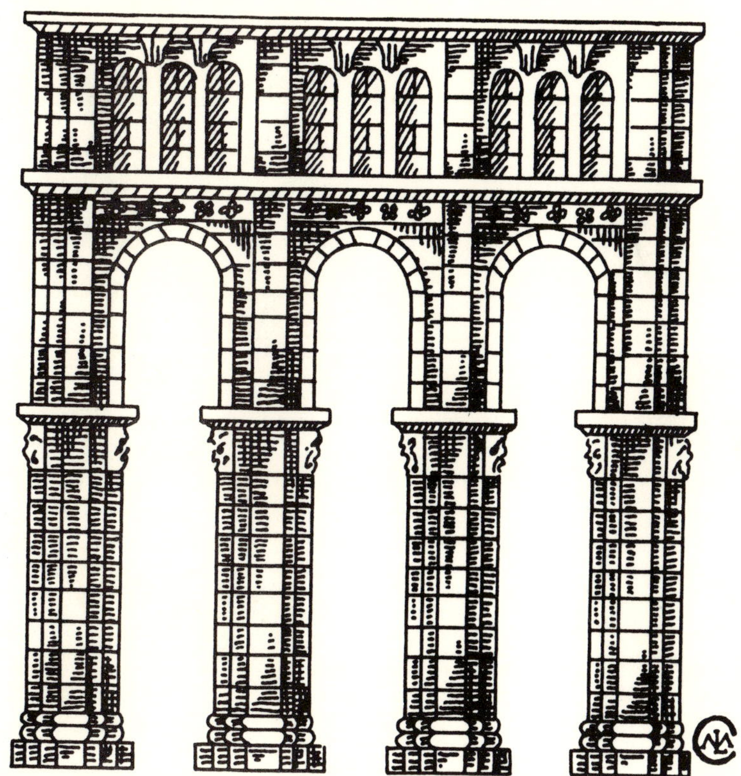

IN PRINCIPIVM ERAT VERBVM
EX LIBRVS STEVEN MOFFSON

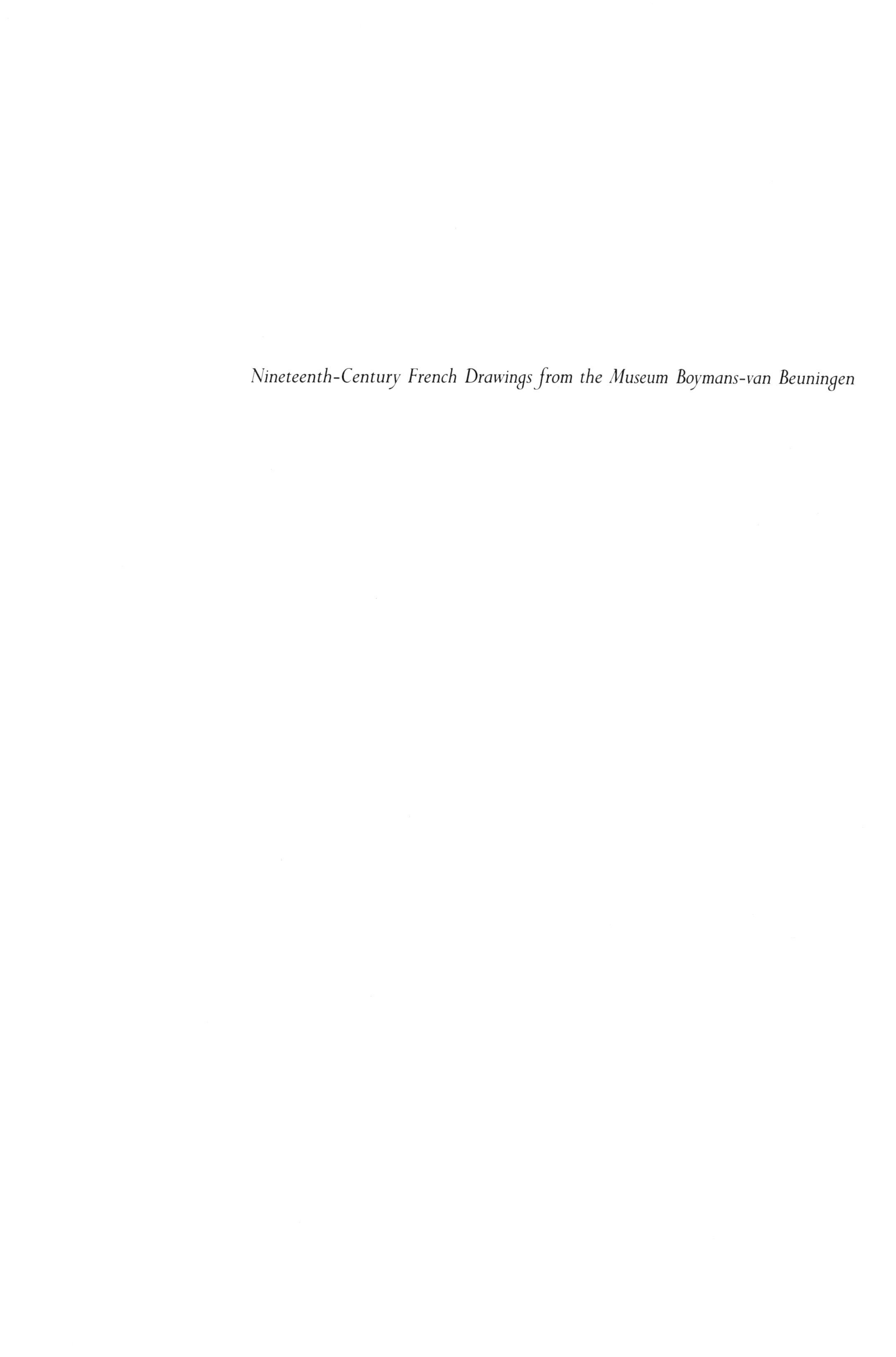

Nineteenth-Century French Drawings from the Museum Boymans-van Beuningen

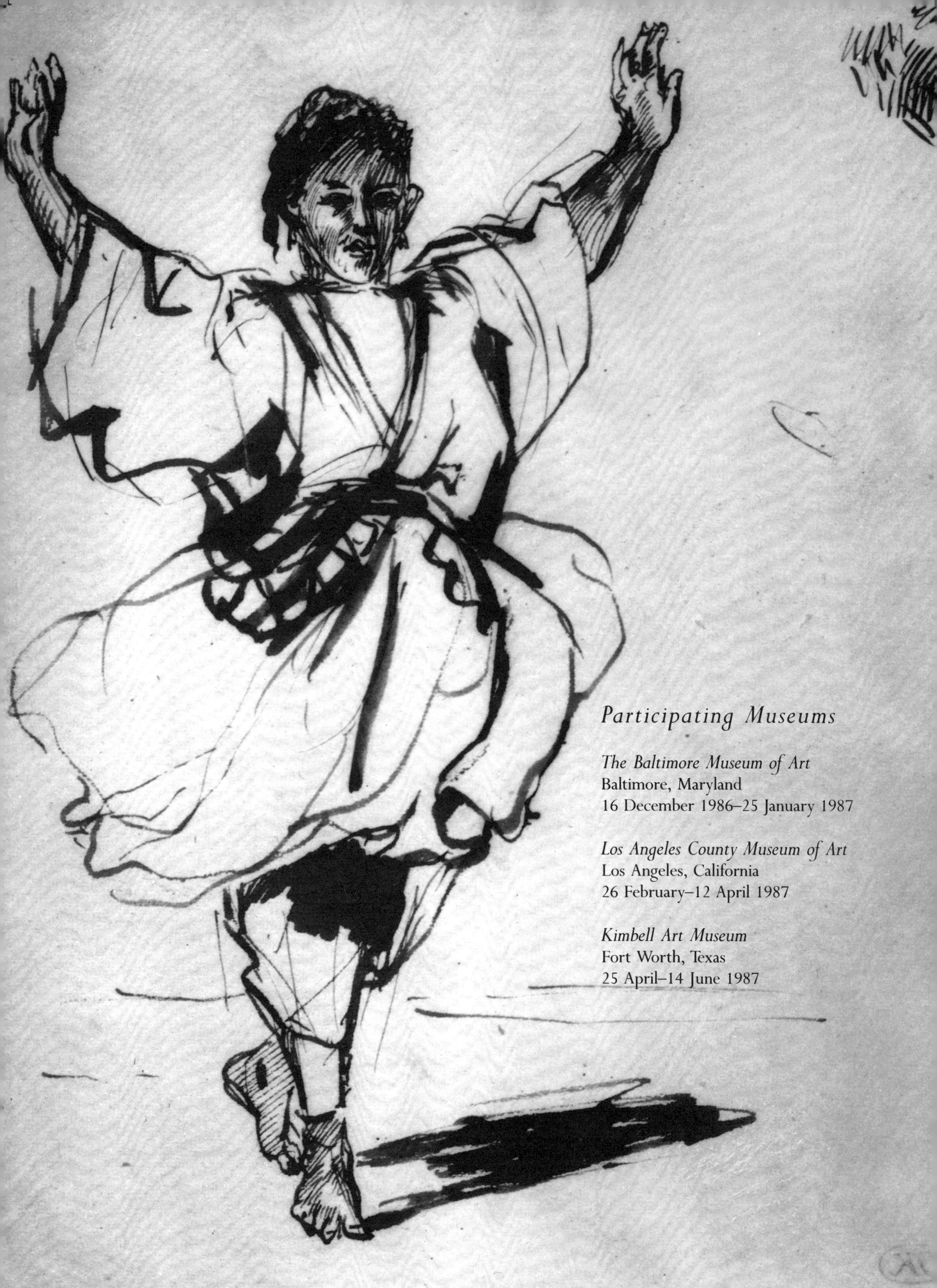

Participating Museums

The Baltimore Museum of Art
Baltimore, Maryland
16 December 1986–25 January 1987

Los Angeles County Museum of Art
Los Angeles, California
26 February–12 April 1987

Kimbell Art Museum
Fort Worth, Texas
25 April–14 June 1987

CONTENTS

The International Exhibitions Foundation takes great pleasure in presenting this superb exhibition of "Nineteenth-Century French Drawings from the Museum Boymans-van Beuningen" for its first American tour. The exhibition features ninety-eight drawings by the most influential artists of the period, including Ingres, Cézanne, Degas, Daumier, and Delacroix. These magnificent drawings place the Rotterdam holdings among the finest in the world.

Organizing an exhibition of this breadth and quality requires the cooperation and support of many people. First and foremost, we would like to thank guest director Mr. A.W. F. M. Meij, curator of drawings at the Museum Boymans-van Beuningen, for choosing the works and preparing the accompanying catalogue. Dr. W.A.L. Beeren, former director of the Museum and present director of the Stedelijk Museum in Amsterdam, provided valuable guidance in the early stages of planning this exhibition. Mr. Jurriaan A. Poot, formerly assistant curator of prints and drawings at the museum in Rotterdam and now at the Stedelijk Museum, co-authored the catalogue. To both of these scholars we extend special thanks. We would also like to express our sincere appreciation to the Museum Boymans-van Beuningen and its present director, Mr. W. H. Crouwel, for the generous loan of these splendid drawings to the three museums on the American tour.

His Excellency Richard H. Fein, the Ambassador of the Netherlands, has graciously agreed to serve as the honorary patron of the exhibition during its tour. We are grateful for his warm interest in this important project. Our thanks are also due Pierre Collombert, cultural attaché at the French Embassy, who has provided continuing assistance for our traveling exhibition program.

We have been most fortunate to receive a grant in support of this exhibition from the National Endowment for the Arts, and an indemnity from the Federal Council for the Arts and Humanities. We are extremely grateful for the invaluable help that these institutions have provided. It is a pleasure, once again, to thank The Andrew W. Mellon Foundation for partially underwriting the publication of this catalogue.

Mr. Julian Stock and Mr. Max Rutherston of Sotheby's have most kindly proffered their expert advice. Mr. Charles Tanguy, director of the Netherlands America Amity Trust, and Mrs. Tanguy have been exceptionally helpful.

In acknowledging the contribution of translator Charlotte I. Loeb, we cannot fail to mention the speed and dedication she brought to the project. Catalogue designer Polly Sexton likewise accomplished her work with great skill and sensitivity. Alan Abrams of Garamond/Pridemark Press oversaw the dependably high quality of the printing operation. It has been a privilege to work with such professionals in producing this beautiful catalogue.

Our thanks go to the directors of the museums participating in the tour of the exhibition: Dr. Arnold Lehman of The Baltimore Museum of Art; Dr. Earl A. Powell III of The Los Angeles County Museum of Art; and Dr. Edmund P. Pillsbury of the Kimbell Art Museum in Fort Worth, Texas.

Finally, I would like to express my gratitude to the staff of the International Exhibitions Foundation for their many contributions to this endeavor, especially to Gregory Allgire Smith, Executive Vice President; Linda Bell, Exhibitions Coordinator; Lynn Berg, Registrar; S. Stanley Dawson, Controller; Ingeborg A. Schweiger, Staff Assistant; and Joseph Saunders, who has framed all the drawings for exhibition. Tam Curry, our Editor, has prepared the catalogue for publication with the very able assistance of Sarah Tanguy, Diane Stewart, and Bridget Goodbody.

ANNEMARIE H. POPE
President
International Exhibitions Foundation

The collection of drawings and paintings in the Museum Boymans-van Beuningen in Rotterdam has its origin in the art collection bequeathed by F. J.O. Boymans to the city of Rotterdam in 1847. Nearly half of the Boymans drawings were lost in a fire that ravaged the museum in 1864, among them all of the French and Italian and many of the Dutch and Flemish drawings from the sixteenth, seventeenth, and eighteenth centuries. Attempts were made during the remaining period of the nineteenth century and the first quarter of the twentieth century to compensate for this loss; an example is the spectacular acquisition in 1866 of about six hundred drawings by the seventeenth-century Netherlandish seascape painter Willem van de Velde. But because of lack of funds, further purchases were made only on a small scale, and the collection was expanded mainly through bequests and donations, or through assumption of complete collections on special terms. As a matter of course, the latter type of acquisition reflected the particular interest of the original collector. An important group of German nineteenth-century drawings accompanied the collection of Domela Nieuwenhuis in 1923, its highlight being a series of watercolors by the Nazarene J. A. Koch. And the bequest of Montauban van Swijndrecht in 1929 brought to the museum a significant collection of Netherlandish drawings and watercolors from the eighteenth and early nineteenth centuries. Despite these important acquisitions, the museum's department of drawings was clearly below national and international standards.

The year 1935 brought a dramatic change in this situation, when Franz Wilhelm Koenigs gave his collection of drawings on loan to the Museum Boymans. Koenigs, born in Cologne in 1881, came from a family of merchant-bankers who had made their fortunes on the left bank of the lower Rhine at the start of the industrial revolution. The family had a strong interest in the visual arts, and young Koenigs was educated in this spirit primarily by his uncle Felix, a banker from Berlin who was a fervent collector of nineteenth-century German paintings, which he bequeathed to the National Galerie in Berlin. Koenigs's parents also had a small collection of paintings by old masters.

After a brief, and incomplete, period of study at the law school in Munich, Franz Koenigs went to work as an apprentice in a wool spinning mill in the German town of Dülken. In the following years, he was employed by several commercial firms in Antwerp and Paris—where he came to know the work of Toulouse-Lautrec and Degas—and in London, where he bought his first drawing, a landscape by Millet, probably the sheet described in cat. no. 73. Koenigs must have acquired a solid business reputation during those years, for in 1907 he was given the responsibility, at the age of twenty-six, for overseeing the sale of the Regatul Roman oil company (French and German) to the Astra Romana (Shell) in Rumania. His extreme youth led the French negotiators to report to Paris, "We regret the appointment of the Koenigs child," whereas his extraordinary tact caused the English to lament, "What will we go through with this Mephisto!"

Koenigs spent the next several years in Rumania as the president of the oil company, then departed in 1911 on an extended trip to India and Indonesia. In 1913 he succeeded his uncle Felix as president of the bank in Berlin. That same year, he married Anna, Countess von Kalckreuth, a daughter of the well-known symbolist painter, Leopold, Count von Kalckreuth, whom he had met in 1906 when the Koenigs family gave Leopold a large portrait commission (see next page). Anna, raised in an artistic, noble family, was one of the first women in Germany to be awarded the title of "Master Bookbinder."

In 1920 Koenigs, at the age of thirty-nine, joined his cousin Rhodius in founding the Rhodius-Koenigs Handelmaatschappij in Amsterdam, an international business and banking association in which the wool trade played a prominent part. From its inception, Koenigs operated this new business venture very profitably on foreign exchange and commodity markets, often with a certain speculative approach. He moved to Haarlem, near Amsterdam, in 1922, but one of his most successful business strategies was to make frequent trips abroad, which enabled him to conclude the most unexpected contracts.

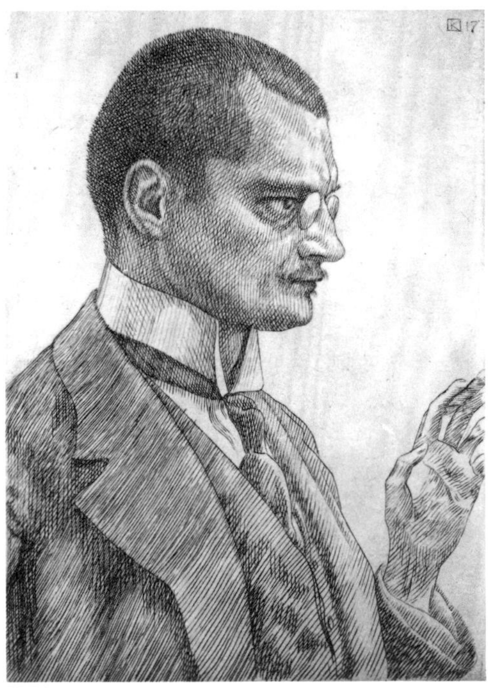

Portrait of Franz Wilhelm Koenigs, by Leopold,
Count von Kalckreuth, 1906

At this time Koenigs, in addition to his preoccupation with his business, began in earnest to collect old master drawings. He had already been actively acquiring paintings, several of which now belong to the Museum Boymans-van Beuningen, but collecting drawings became his passion; and the examples that he was able to assemble in little more than a decade assured him a place among the greatest collectors of old master drawings. Because of his innate feeling for quality, his inexhaustible energy, and his willingness to make personal sacrifices if necessary, his collection—although not extensive—was distinguished by solid connoisseurship and great breadth.

Koenigs's collection came to include more than two thousand sheets by French, German, Italian, Netherlandish, and Flemish artists from the fifteenth through the eighteenth century. But with respect to nineteenth-century drawings, Koenigs concentrated on French artists, whose work he had become acquainted with at an early age in Paris. Therefore, the roughly three hundred drawings by nineteenth-century French masters—of which almost one hundred are exhibited here—form a special group within this collection. They do not constitute a scholarly survey of the styles of the period, but reflect the preference of the collector almost exclusively, as evidenced by the numerous drawings by, for instance, Cézanne, Degas, Daumier, and Millet.

The international financial crisis of 1935 forced Koenigs to give his collection as collateral to the Jewish bank Lisser and Rosencranz in Amsterdam, but the bank fortunately accepted his condition that the collection be deposited in the Museum Boymans. Thus the director of the museum at that time, Dr. D. Hannema, could proudly announce at the opening of the new building of the museum in 1935, that the Koenigs collection had been given on loan to the department of drawings of the museum.

The survival of the Koenigs collection was in serious jeopardy in the beginning of 1940. In view of the approaching German invasion, the bank to which Koenigs had given his collection as collateral decided to liquidate and told the museum director to prepare the drawings for shipment to the United States. Although the collection had first been offered to the museum, in accordance with previous agreements, the museum did not have sufficient monies to meet the conditions. Hannema is to be credited, however, with finding two patrons of the arts in Rotterdam, Messrs. van der Vorm and van Beuningen, who were willing in principle to furnish the necessary funds. Then according to Hannema, matters took another turn, and in April 1940, one month before the Germans invaded the Netherlands, van Beuningen purchased the entire collection. A few months later Hans Posse, a German art historian and director of the museum in Dresden, bought part of the Koenigs collection: he had been charged by

Hitler with the founding of the "Germanisches Museum" in Linz, Hitler's birthplace. This sale comprised all of the early German drawings and part of the other schools as well. But the group of nineteenth-century French drawings remained intact, and toward the end of 1940 van Beuningen donated the Koenigs collection to the Museum Boymans Foundation, which is still the owner today.

In the years following World War II, the museum's collection of nineteenth-century French drawings has been modestly augmented. Of these additions, the nine drawings from the Vitale Bloch bequest in 1976 are the most important.

Franz Koenigs, who before 1940 had acquired Dutch citizenship because of his aversion to Nazism, assembled another collection of drawings between 1935 and his death in May 1941 in a train accident at the station in Cologne. This second collection comprised around 240 drawings by old masters and nineteenth-century masters, which passed on to his heirs after his death. Apparently his love of collecting drawings remained unquenchable even in the difficult years of the second world war.

In 1923 Koenigs presented his deputy manager, H. J. Abs, with a drawing by the seventeenth-century Netherlandish artist Jan Lievens, a pupil of Rembrandt's, with the words, "In order to poison you," meaning to excite in Abs the same passion for collecting drawings as he had himself. This has also been the motivating force behind the present exhibition; and the organizers hope that it will be effective.

We would like to thank the following persons for their help in preparing the catalogue and the exhibition: Helen Marres, for additional research; Carlos van Hasselt, Paris; The Rijksbureau voor Kunsthistorische Documentatie, The Hague; Ir. F.F.R. Koenigs, Bennekom; Anke Y. Smit, secretary; and Louis Damen, paper conservator.

A.W. F. M. MEIJ
Curator of Drawings
Museum Boymans-van Beuningen

Sources: Dr. Ir. F.F.R. Koenigs, son of Franz Koenigs; H. J. Abs, Frankfurt am Main; F. Lugt, *Les Marques de Collections de Dessins et d'Estampes,* The Hague, 1956, pp. 149, 150; J. C. Ebbinge Wubben, "Van Museum Boymans tot Museum Boymans-van Beuningen: Herinneringen aan enkele verzamelaars," in *Essays in Northern European Art,* 1983, p. 78.

COLOR PLATES

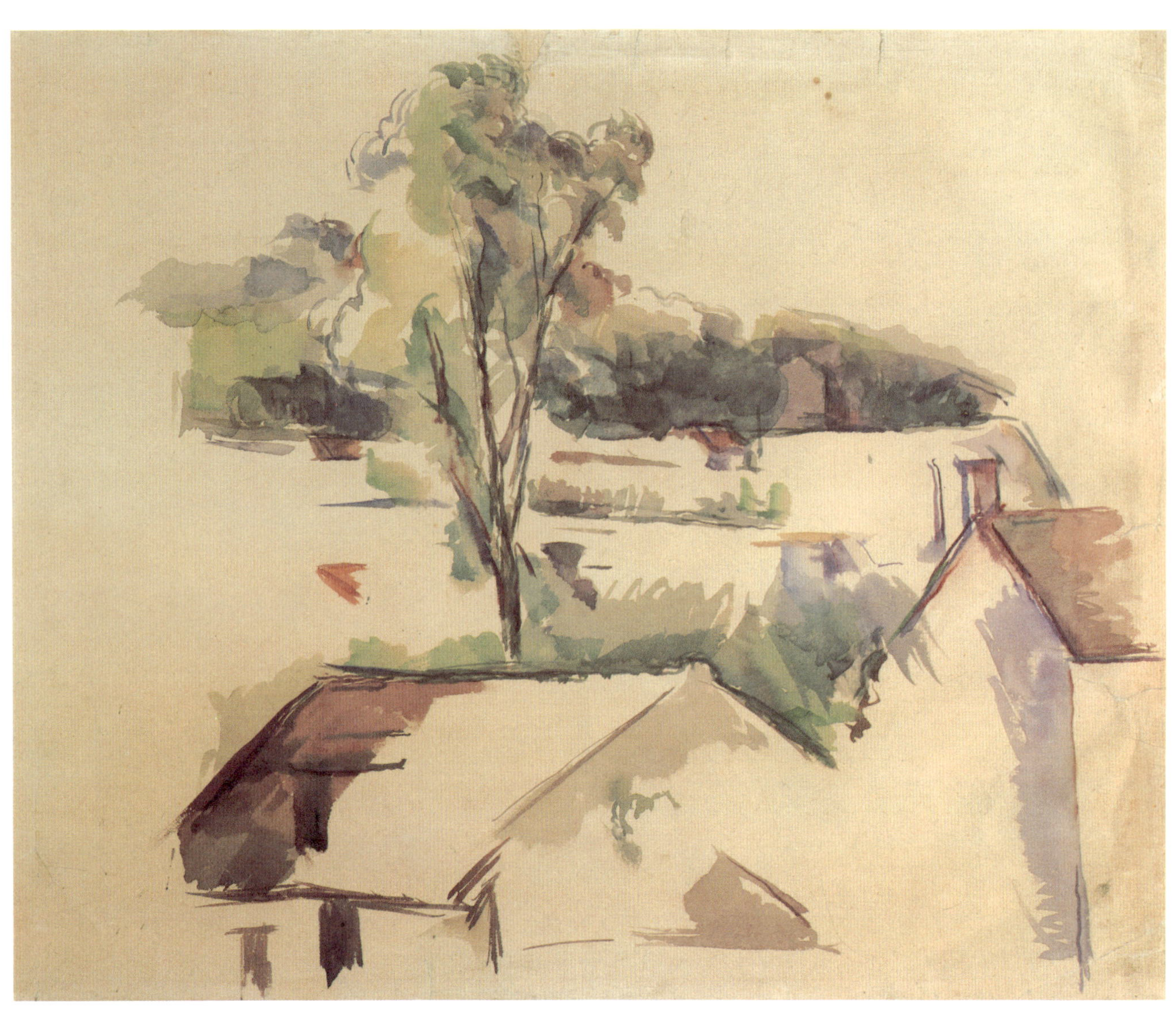

PLATE 1
View of Roofs and a Landscape with Mountains in the Background (cat. no. 17)
Paul Cézanne

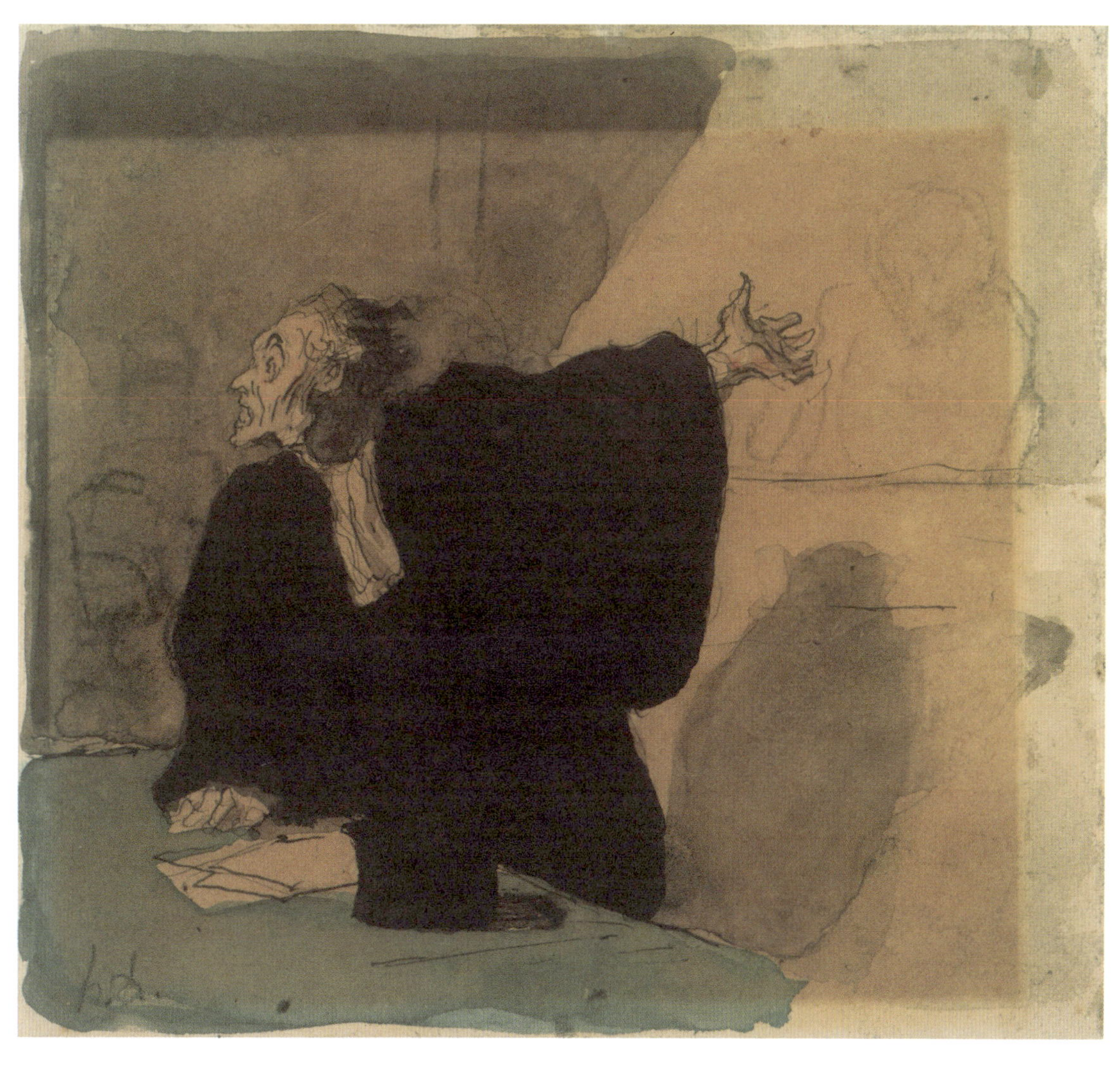

PLATE 2
A Pleading Lawyer (cat. no. 32)
Honoré Daumier

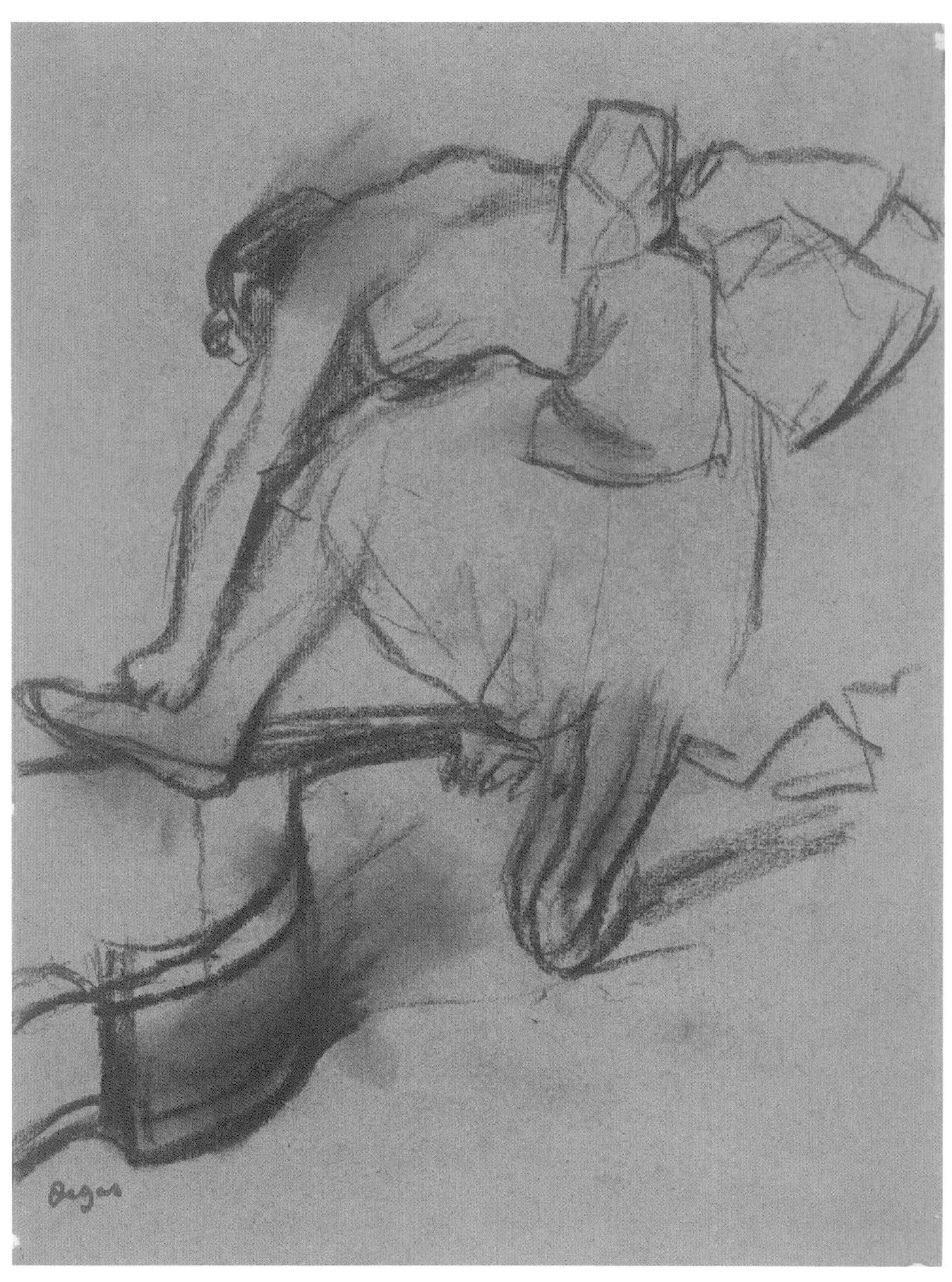

PLATE 3
Female Dancer (cat. no. 41)
Edgar Degas

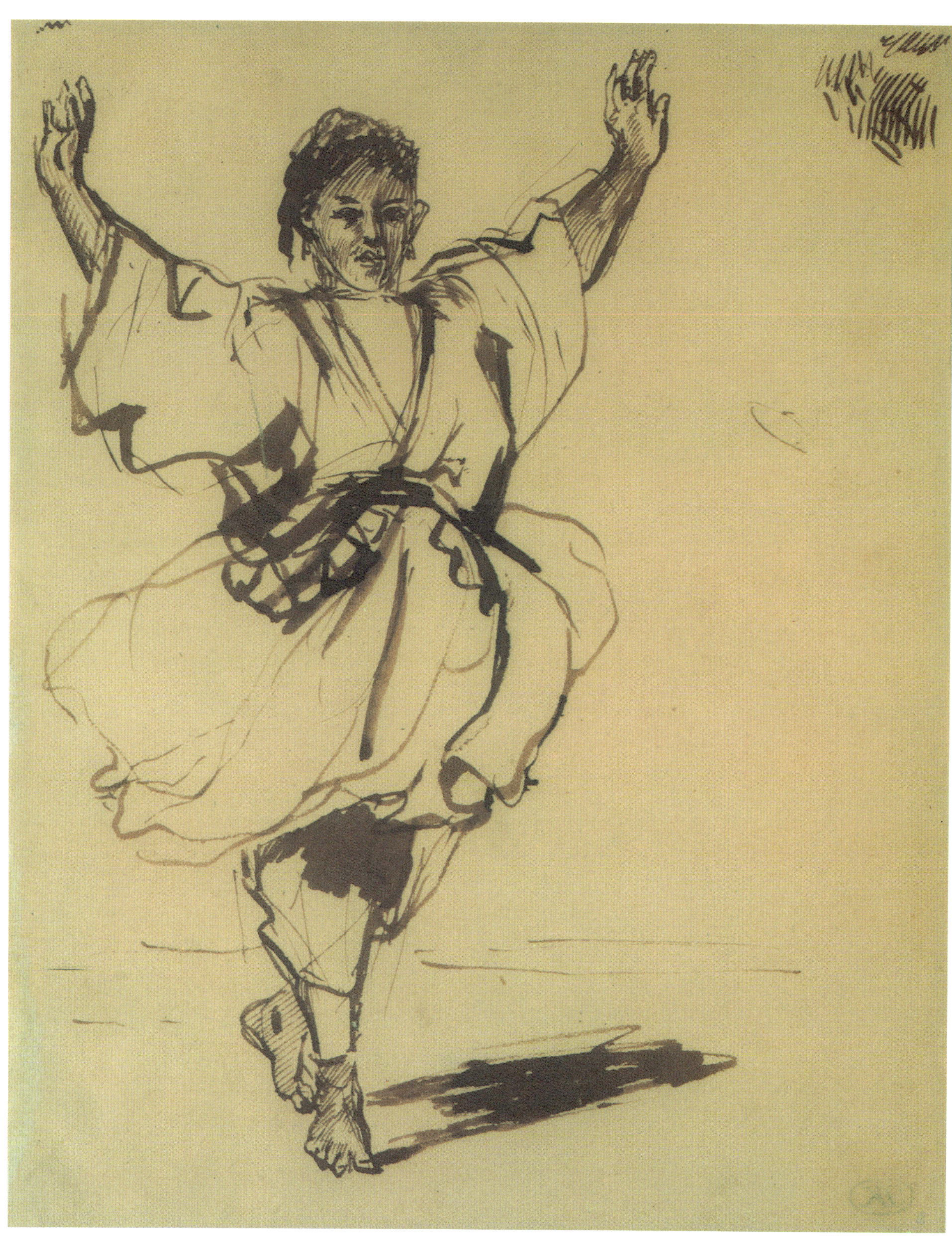

PLATE 4
Dancing Moroccan (cat. no. 45)
Eugène Delacroix

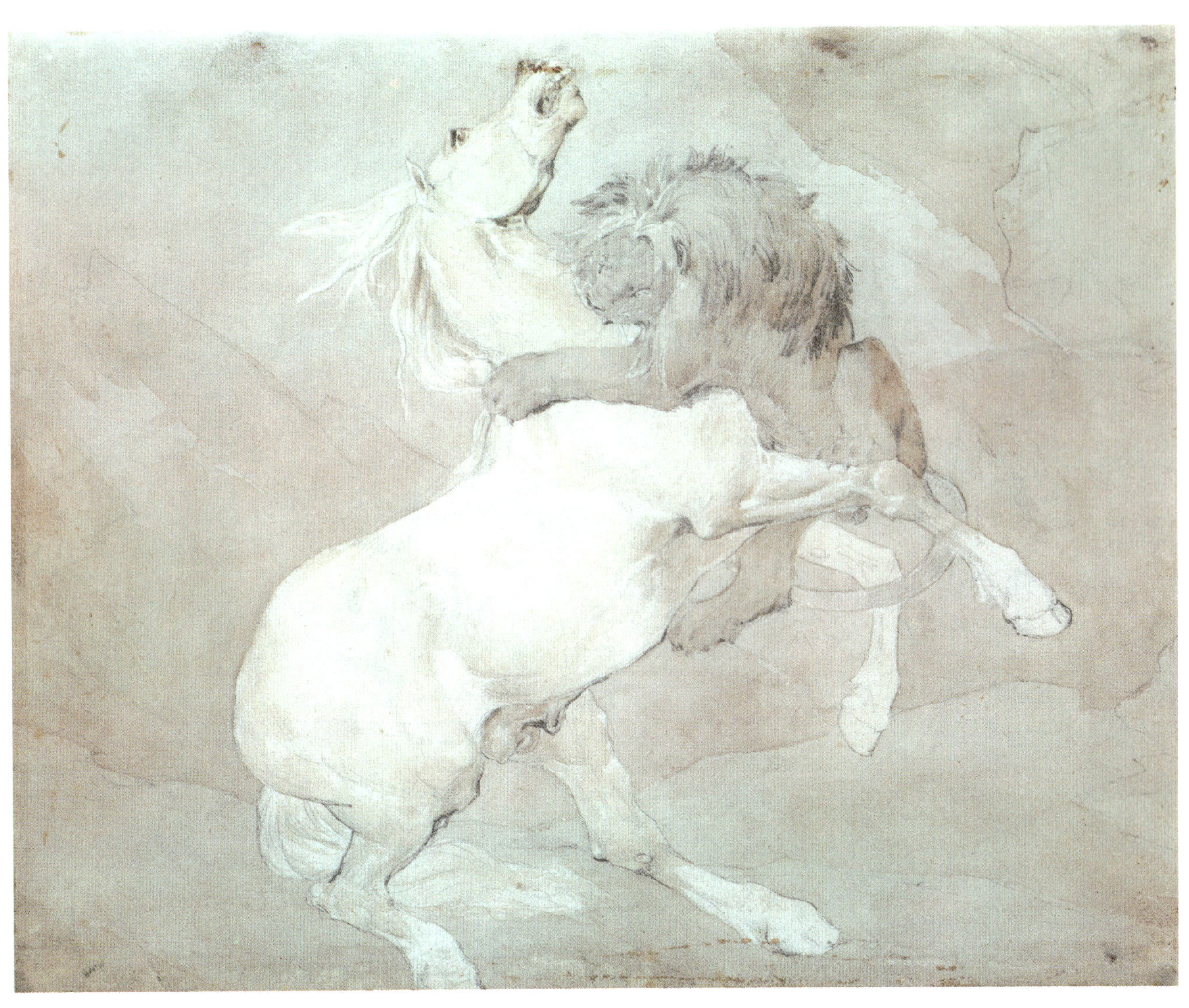

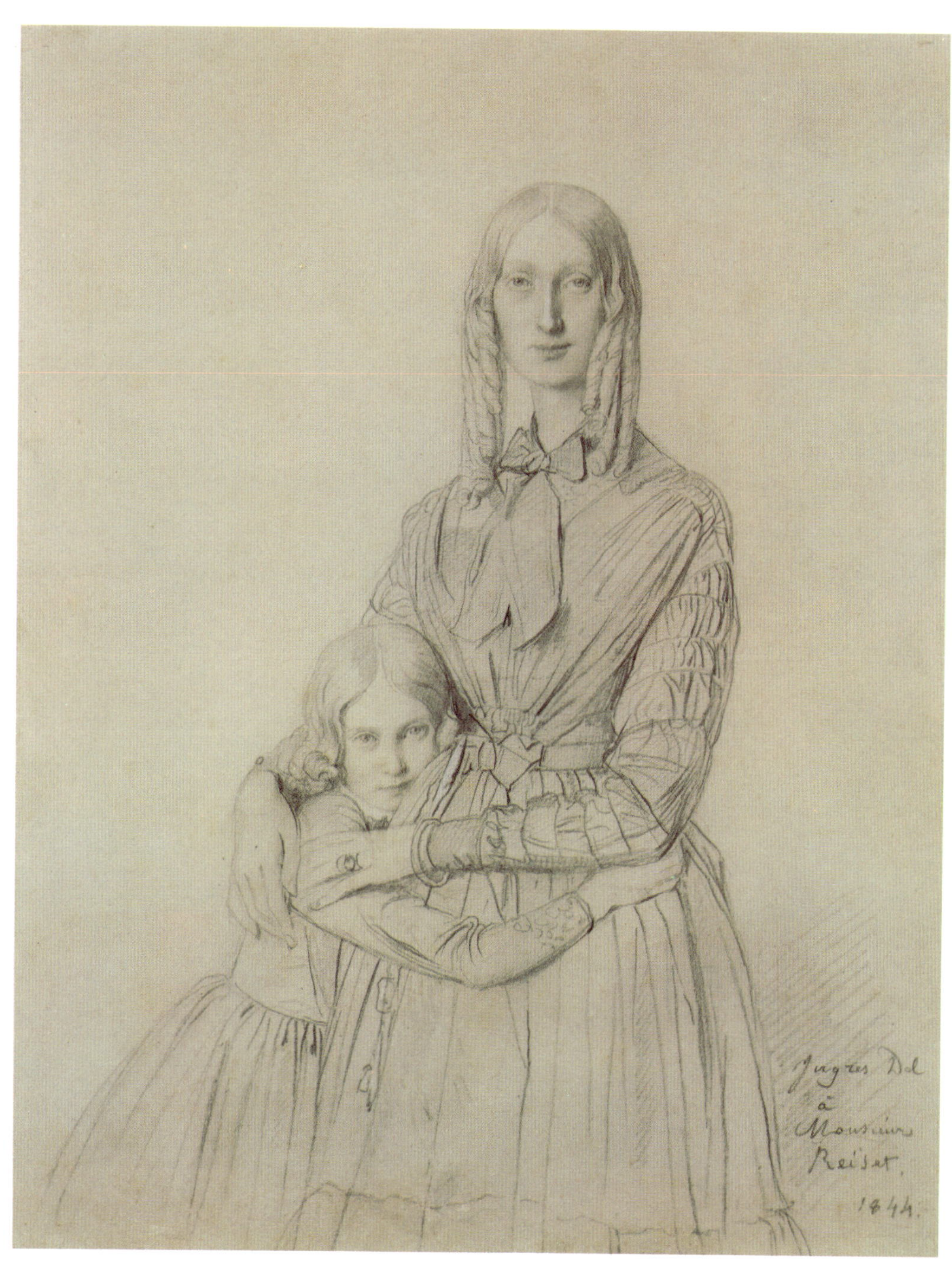

PLATE 6
Portrait of Mme Hortense Reiset and Her Daughter Marie (cat. no. 59)
Jean-Auguste-Dominique Ingres

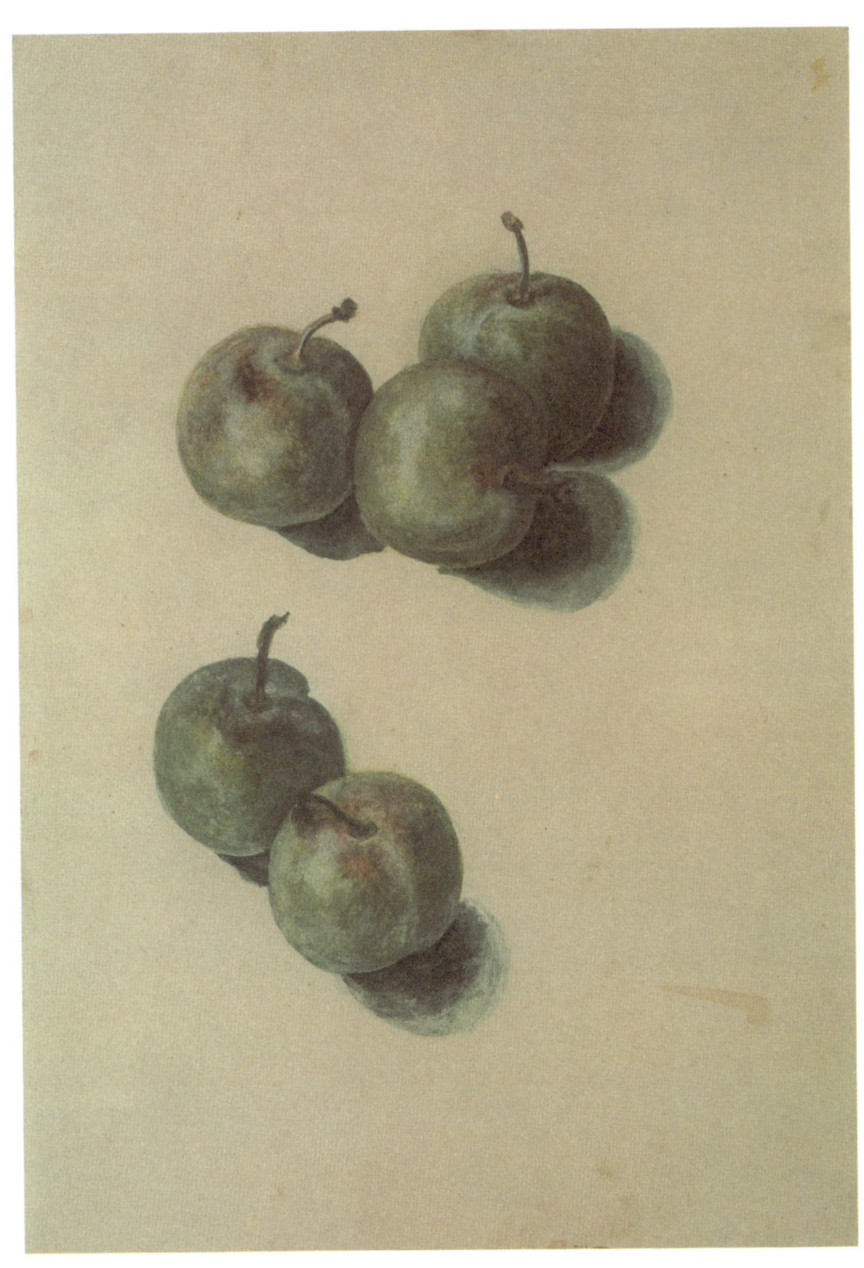

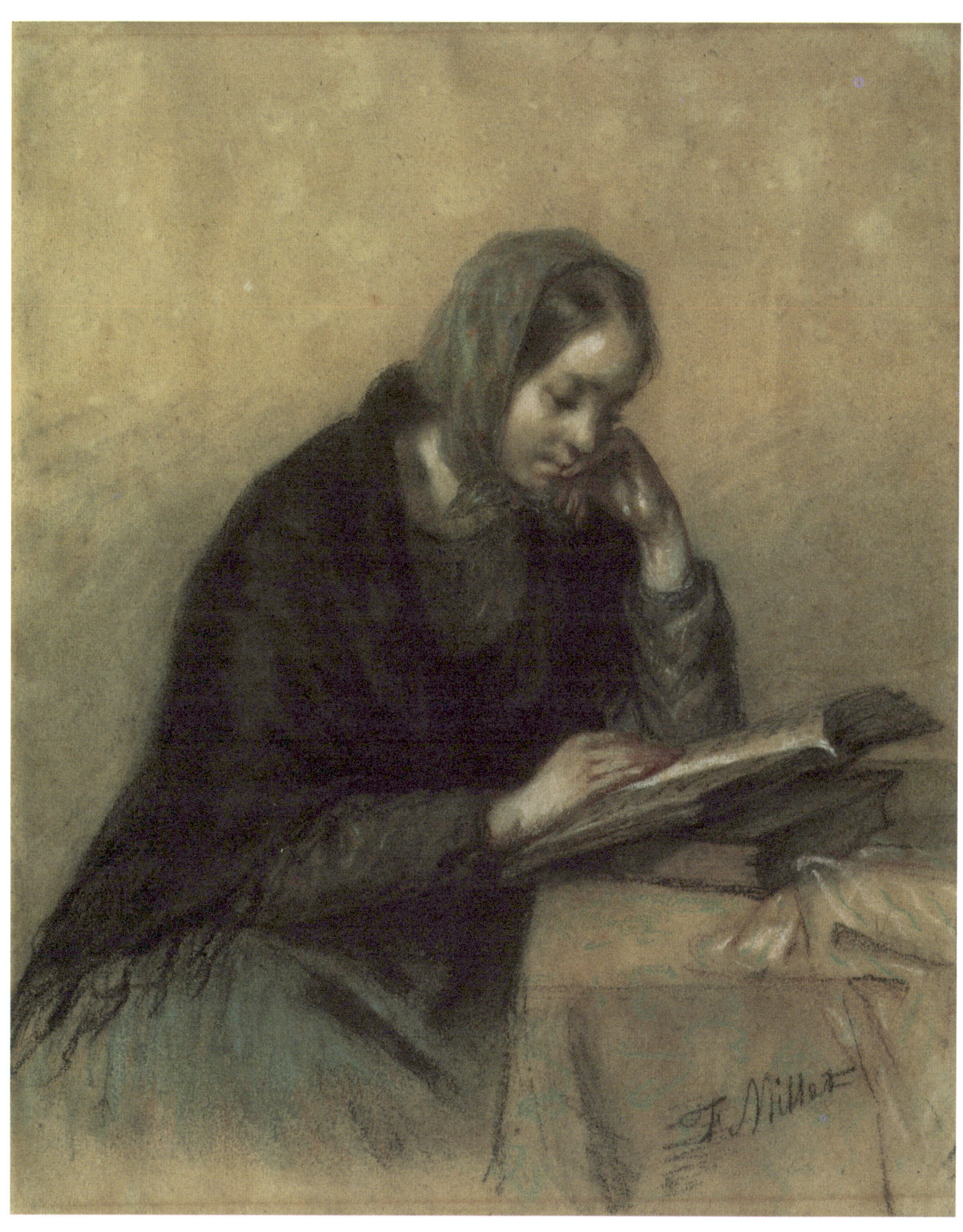

PLATE 8
Woman Sitting at a Table (cat. no. 69)
Jean-François Millet

Note to the Catalogue

For bibliographical details prior to 1968 and for the provenances prior to the Koenigs collection, readers are referred to the Museum Boymans-van Beuningen's 1968 catalogue, *Franse tekeningen uit de 19e eeuw,* by Hans R. Hoetink. Likewise, the bibliography before 1978 and provenances before the Vitale Bloch bequest can be found in the museum's 1978 catalogue, *Legaat Vitale Bloch.* Abbreviated bibliographical references in the text are defined in the Select Bibliography at the end of the catalogue.

The authors are identified following each catalogue entry with the initials *A.M.* for A.W.F.M. Meij or *J.P.* for Jurriaan A. Poot.

All drawings from the Koenigs collection are stamped with the collection mark *FK* (in monogram), Lugt 1023a.

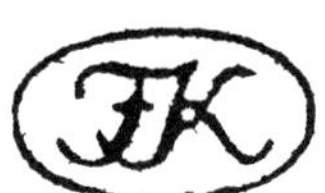

PIERRE BONNARD

Fontenay-aux-Roses 1867–La Cannet 1947

1

Female Nude on a Sofa

MB 1976/T13
Black chalk on transparent paper; 21.6 × 26.9 cm
Signed with black chalk: *PB*
Provenance: Vitale Bloch bequest, 1976
Literature: Rotterdam 1978, cat. no. 4 (ill.)

On the left side of this drawing a nude woman is sitting on a sofa, bent over her left foot. The walls of the room are defined in only a few quick lines, and a small table and chair can be seen in the background on the right. The entire scene seems to have been very sketchily drawn, with only the body of the woman accented by bolder contours.

Bonnard did a great many drawings in this genre, and the model was usually young and slender, with long legs and firm breasts. In his treatment of this subject—a nude young woman grooming her body—Bonnard proved himself a worthy successor to Edgar Degas. Bonnard's sketches are even more intimate, the woman's posture more graceful and more natural. This can perhaps be explained by the fact that Bonnard found the ideal model in his immediate environment, namely in his wife, Marthe (see Ch. Kunstler, "Bonnard, Painter and Lithographer," in *Pierre Bonnard, 1867–1947,* exhib. cat., National Gallery of Victoria, Melbourne 1971, pp. 10–16).

It is not entirely clear what the woman in the Rotterdam drawing is doing. She seems to be grooming her left foot. Another young woman in a painting from around 1908/1910 in Milan is portrayed in a similar pose; she is seated on a sofa putting on her stocking (see J. Dauberville and H. Dauberville, *Bonnard,* Paris, n.d., vol. II, no. 485 [ill.]).

J.P.

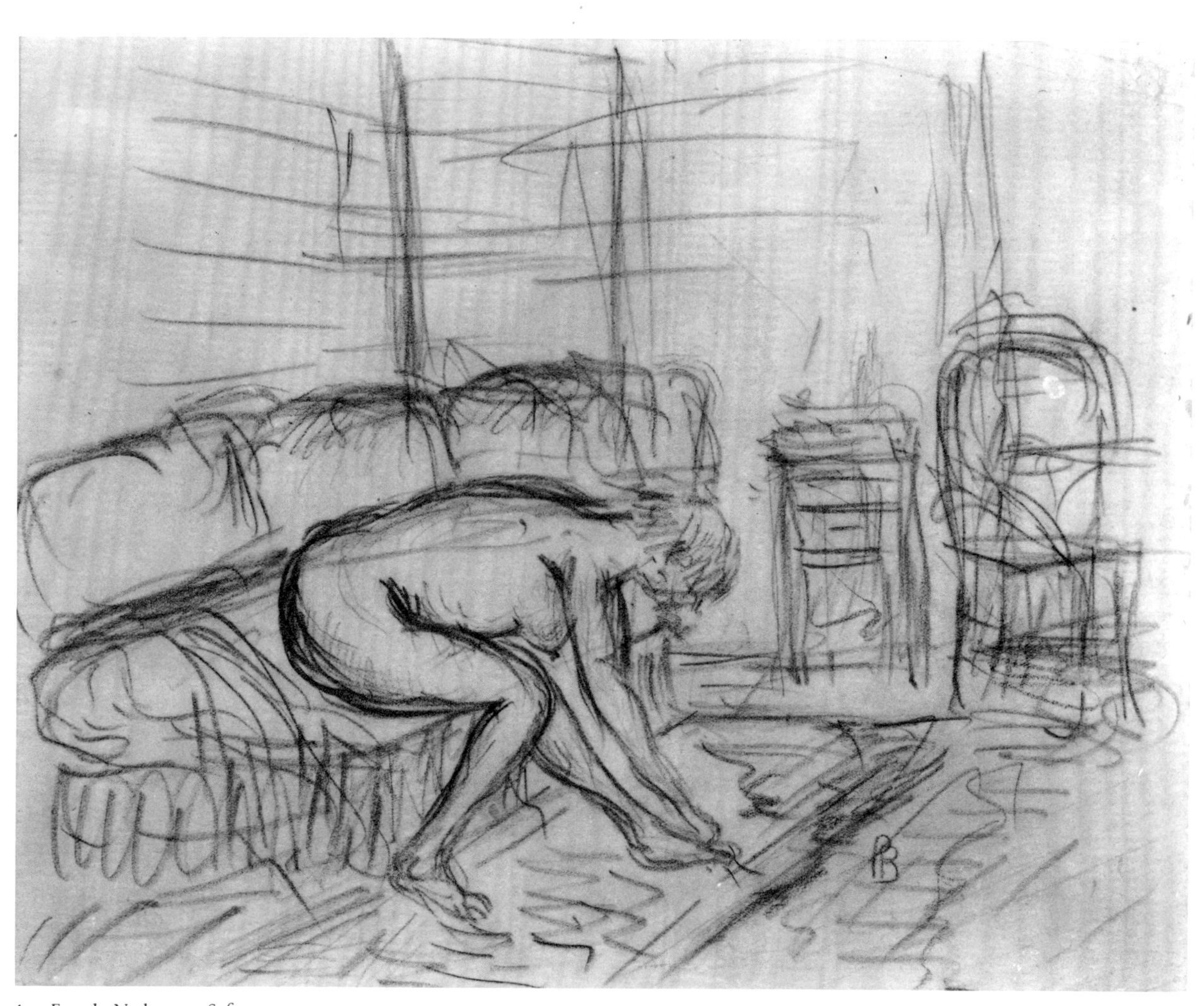

1   *Female Nude on a Sofa*

RODOLPHE BRESDIN
Montrelais 1822–Sèvres 1885

2
Rest on the Flight into Egypt

MB 141
Pen and black ink on transparent paper; laid down; 112 × 148 mm
Signed in pen and black ink: *rodolphe 1860 Bresdin*
Provenance: Acquired 1931
Literature: Rotterdam 1968, cat. no. 8 (ill.); exhib. cat., Cologne/Frankfurt a/M. 1972/73, no. 62.11 (ill.); van Gelder 1976,
vol. I, ill. 113; van Gelder/Sillevis 1978, no. 168 (ill.)

On the left side of this sheet a poorly clad Holy Family rests in the lee of a rocky ledge on the bank of a stream bordered by papyrus plants. Above them two sphinxes' heads are carved out of the rock—the upper sphinx almost completely overgrown, the lower one with a bird sitting atop. Both the papyrus and the sphinxes' heads are allusions to Egypt. In the middle of the sheet sits a small nude angel with large wings. On the right, the donkey's head is visible. The Nile River is depicted in the background.

The Holy Family group in this drawing, dated 1860 by the artist, was used again by Bresdin in an etching of 1871. No print of the first state of this etching is known, but it was transferred by the artist to a lithographic stone in 1873 (see van Gelder/Sillevis 1978, nos. 95, 95a, 95b [ill.]), with the donkey placed closer to the Holy Family, and the scenery in the background changed completely; in atmosphere, it recalls another of Bresdin's etchings of the Holy Family from the same year (van Gelder/Sillevis 1978, no. 94a [ill.]). Both etchings are considered to be among the most beautiful created by Bresdin. Comparison of the Rotterdam drawing to the related etchings from 1871 very clearly demonstrates Bresdin's development during that decade.

J.P.

3
Sheet of Studies

MB 142
Pen and black ink, some pencil, heightened with white on transparent paper; laid down; 275 × 230 mm
Provenance: Acquired 1936
Literature: Rotterdam 1968, cat. no. 9 (ill.); exhib. cat., Cologne/Frankfurt a/M. 1972/73, no. 60.1 (ill.); R. de Montequiou,
Rodolphe Bresdin der Unentwirrbare, ed. P. Hahlbrock, Berlin 1977, ill. 38

A standing woman in a draped garment, wearing a laurel wreath and holding a long spear, is depicted with a lion on the left-hand side of this study sheet. This small group is repeated toward the bottom on the right, but the woman is dressed somewhat differently and has no spear; her right arm rests on a large, open, upright book. Just behind this second group and to the right is what appears to be an oriental warrior. In the middle on the bottom the lion is sketched again, and in the middle on top are two still lifes, which include musical instruments, books, a sword, a bust, and a painter's palette.

This drawing may be considered a preliminary study for an unpublished lithograph from 1883, referred to under the title "La République" (see van Gelder 1976, no. 152 [ill.]). Two drawings in Amsterdam are more closely related to the lithograph, however; they depict the woman in a sitting position (see exhib. cat., Cologne/Frankfurt a/M. 1972/73, nos. 60.2 and 60.3 [ill.]), and in one of these sheets the woman is also accompanied by a lion. The still lifes in the Rotterdam drawing are probably related to the still life depicted at the feet of the woman in the lithograph.

J.P.

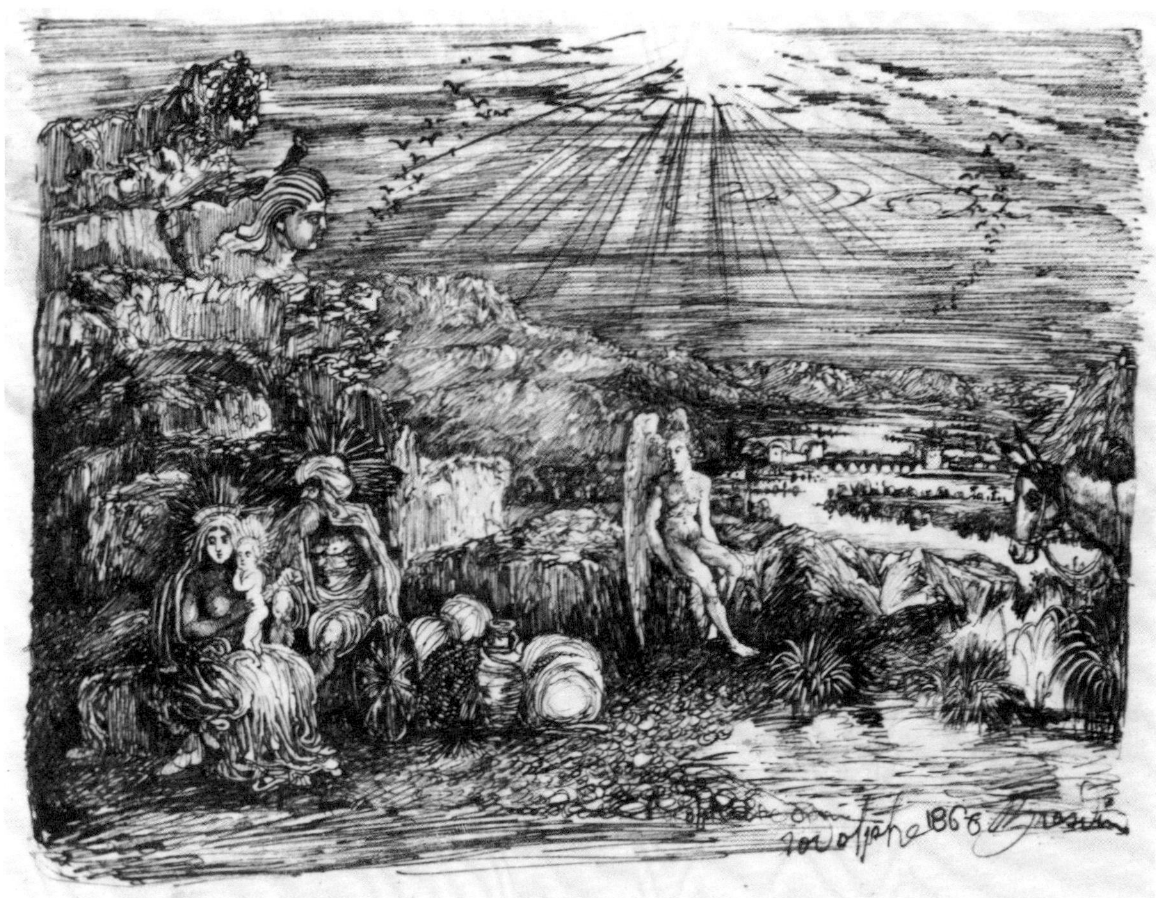

2   *Rest on the Flight into Egypt*

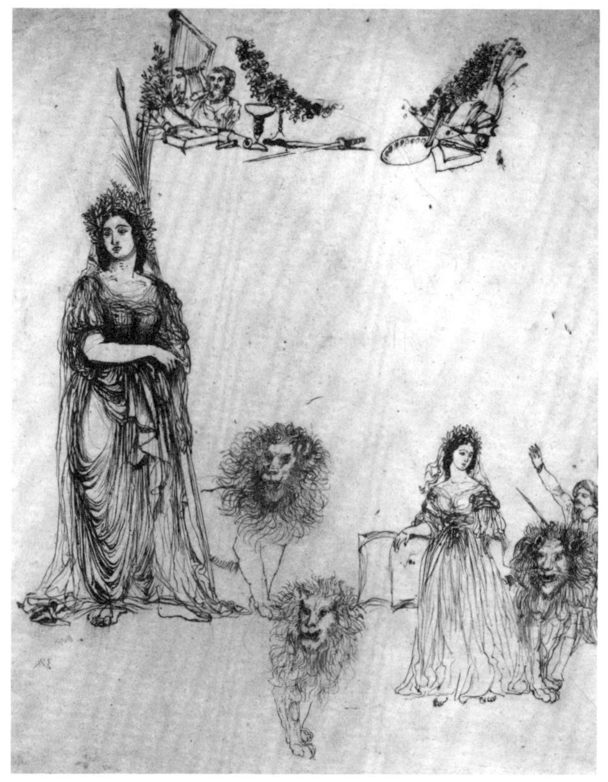

3   *Sheet of Studies*

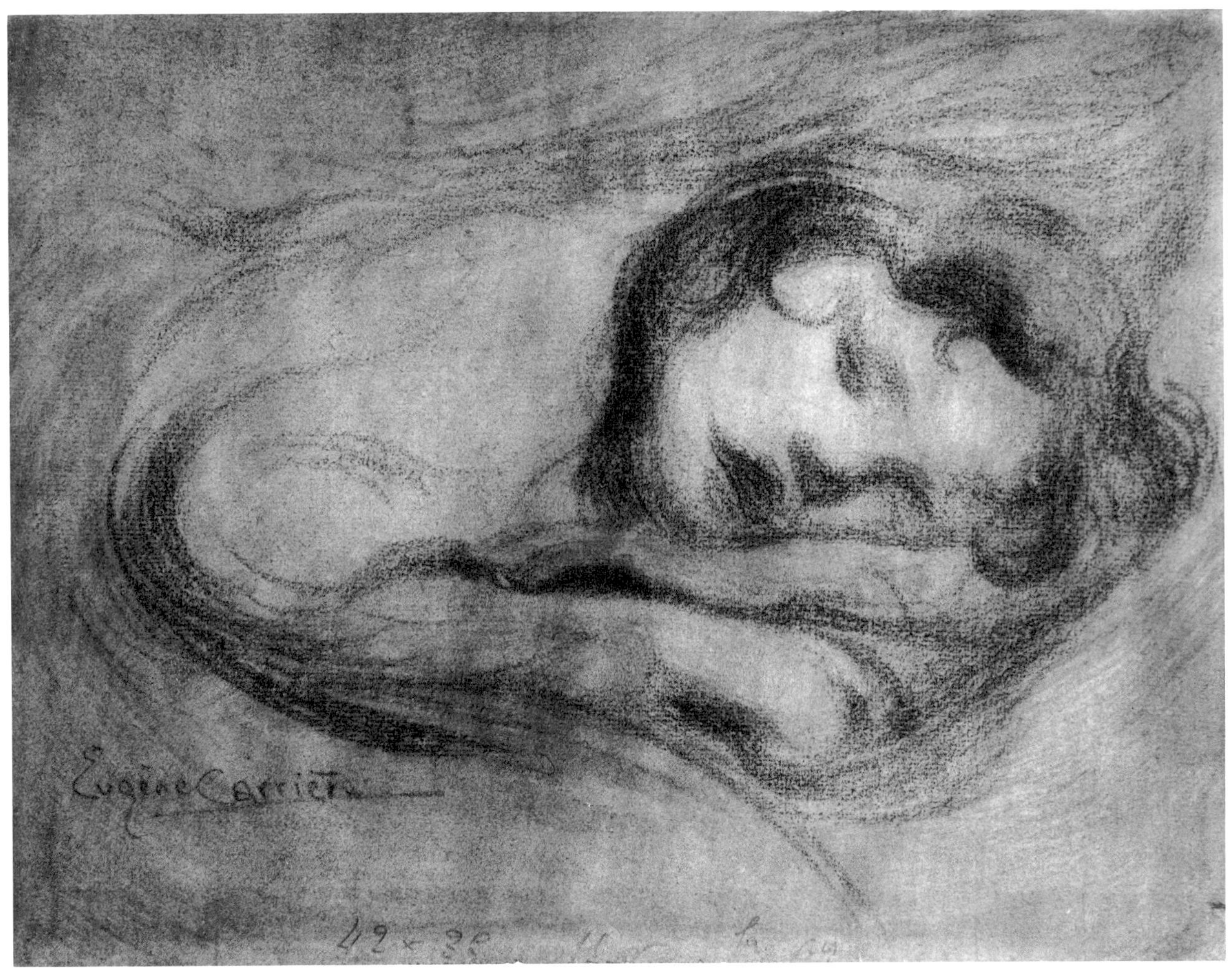

4   *Sleeping Child*

EUGÈNE CARRIÈRE
Gournay-sur-Marne 1849–Paris 1906

4

Sleeping Child

> F II 110
> Black chalk on brown washed paper; 237 × 308 mm
> Signed with black chalk: *Eugène Carrière*
> *Provenance:* F. Koenigs; given by D. G. van Beuningen to the Museum Boymans Foundation, 1940
> *Literature:* Rotterdam 1968, cat. no. 13 (ill.)

The sleeping child in this drawing looks like Marguerite (1882–1964), a daughter of the artist shown in a lithograph of 1901 (see Delteil 1913 [ill.]). It is possible, however, that this drawing is related to one in Strasbourg of a sleeping child, dated around 1897, which is believed to represent Lucie (1889–1959), another of the artist's daughters (see *Eugène Carrière, 1849–1906,* exhib. cat., Château des Rohan, Strasbourg 1964, no. 26 [ill.]). There also appears to be some similarity between the child in the Rotterdam drawing and another child in the lithograph "Le Sommeil" from 1879, a representation of the artist's sleeping son Jean-René (born in 1888) (see Delteil 1913, no. 36 [ill.]).

In addition to Carrière's friends—among them Puvis de Chavannes, Rodin, Verlaine, and Anatole France—the artist's wife and their six children frequently served as his models. They appear time and again in paintings, drawings, and lithographs, which the artist gave such abstract titles as "Maternité" (*Eugène Carrière, 1849–1906,* exhib. cat., Marlborough Fine Art Ltd., London 1970, no. 47 [ill.]).

In the Rotterdam drawing black chalk has been applied in gentle undulating lines and has been blurred in some places; possibly the face has been heightened somewhat with white. It is a good example of the artist's later work, wherein he confines himself to monochromatic tones and seems to abstract lines into arabesques.

J.P.

PAUL CÉZANNE
Aix-en-Provence 1839–1906

5

Portrait of a Man with a Beard

F II 120
Verso: Studies of a flying figure and architectural details
Pencil and black chalk, with some flecks of oil, on paper; 236 × 172 mm
Provenance: F. Koenigs; given by D. G. van Beuningen to the Museum Boymans Foundation, 1940
Literature: Rotterdam 1968, cat. no. 21 (ill.); W. V. Andersen, "Cézanne's Portrait Drawings from the 1860s," *Master Drawings,*
   V (1967), p. 267, ill. 17a; Andersen 1970, no. 226 (ill.), pp. 3, 5; Chappuis 1973, no. 233 (ill.), and verso: no. 206 (ill.);
   exhib. cat., J. Rewald, "Cézanne and Guillaumin," *Etudes d'art français offertes à Charles Sterling,* Paris 1975, ill. 210;
   Tübingen 1978, no. 33 (ill.)

Because of its similarity to a portrait drawing in Basel, this drawing has been considered to be a portrait
of Anthonie Valabrèque, a friend of Cézanne's (see Andersen 1967, ill. 16). It bears some resemblance as
well to a portrait drawing of another friend of the artist, Fortuné Marion, which is also located in Basel
(Andersen 1967, ill. 17b). But Andersen believes—and Chappuis agrees with him—that the Rotterdam
drawing represents a portrait of the painter Armand Guillaumin, with whom Cézanne spent much time
in Paris during the period in which this drawing is dated, around 1866. (Compare the drawing to the
self-portraits of A. Guillaumin in Paris and Amsterdam; and see Chappuis 1973, p. 101, ill. 37; and J.
Rewald, New York 1961, ill. p. 363.)

   Hans R. Hoetink recognized the suspended figure on the verso as a study after the falling figure on
the right side of a painting in Paris by Veronese (see T. Pignatti, *Véronese,* 2 vols., Venezia 1976, no. 25,
ill. 35). Other studies by Cézanne after Veronese occur in some pages from a sketchbook in Basel,
whose dimensions almost exactly match those of the Rotterdam drawing (see Chappuis 1962, nos.
27–29 [ill.]).
J.P.

6

Study After the "Psyche Abandonnée" by Augustin Pajou, and Other Studies

F II 122
Black chalk and pencil on *Michallet* paper; 498 × 322 mm
Provenance: F. Koenigs; given by D. G. van Beuningen to the Museum Boymans Foundation, 1940
Literature: Rotterdam 1968, cat. no. 23 (ill.); Andersen 1970, nos. 15 (ill.), 150; Chappuis 1973, no. 363 (ill.); exhib. cat.,
   Tübingen 1978, no. 52 (ill.); Pignatti 1981, ill. p. 329; Siblík 1984, ill. 7; J. Leymarie, *Dessins de la période impressioniste de
   Manet à Renoir,* ill. p. 84

The three studies on this sheet were executed at different times. It is generally thought that the study
on the left, after the statue *Psyche Abandonnée* by Augustin Pajou (1730–1809) in the Musée du Louvre,
was done first, at some time between 1876 and 1882 (for an illustration of the statue, see Chappuis
1973, ill. 52, p. 124). No other studies by Cézanne after this statue are known, and no direct correlation
exists between the posture of this nude and, for instance, those of the nudes in the landscape paintings
with bathing women, for which Cézanne used model studies from his student years at the Académie
Suisse in Paris as well as studies after works by other artists.

   There is less agreement about the order in which the remaining two studies were drawn. Chappuis
compares the self-portrait at the upper right to a pastel portrait of Cézanne by Auguste Renoir,
estimated to date from 1880 (Rewald 1961, ill. p. 475). It is difficult to determine Cézanne's age in any
of his self-portraits; we know that he was already rather bald when he was thirty-five and looked older
than his age. Andersen compares the self-portrait here with drawings in Chicago and New York

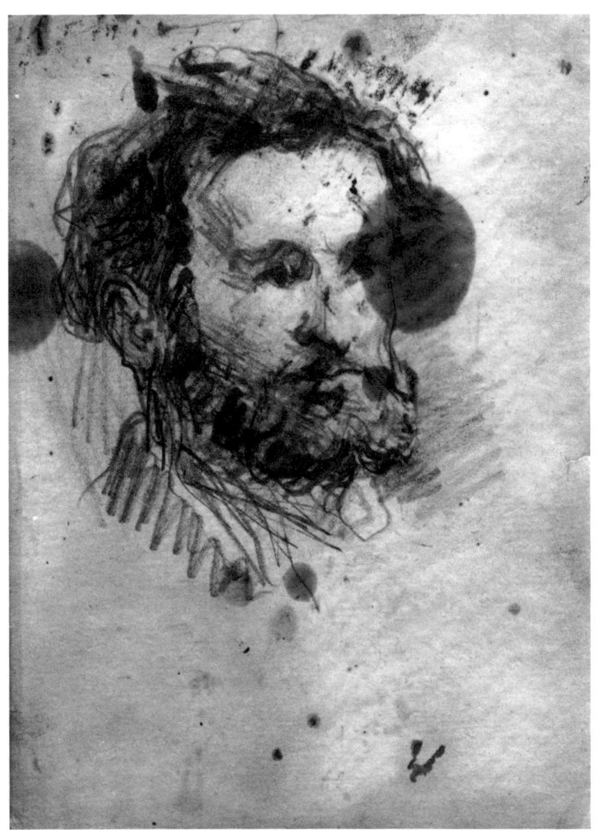

5   *Portrait of a Man with a Beard*

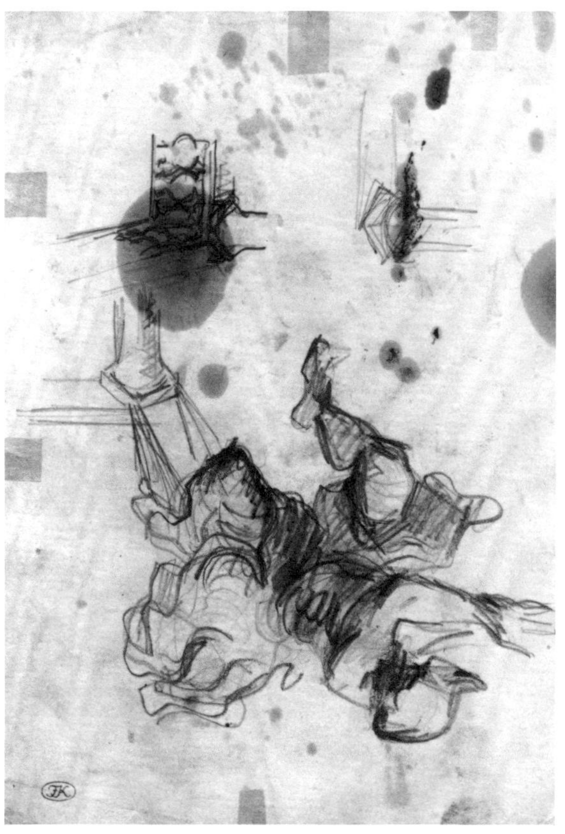

Verso

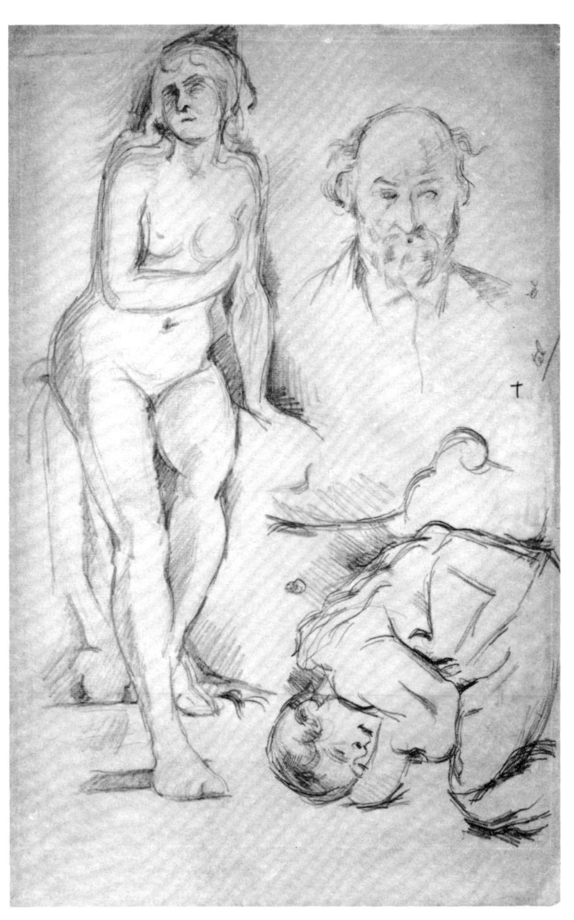

6   *Study After the "Psyche Abandonnée"*
     by Augustin Pajou, and Other Studies

(Andersen 1970, nos. 14, 16 [ill.]) and dates all three to around 1880/82 on the basis of the similarity in draughtsmanship.

The third study probably represents the artist's son Paul while asleep. Andersen sees a similarity between this sketch and a study of the same head, in this case with open eyes, on a study sheet in Basel (Andersen 1970, no. 149 [ill.]). There may also be a second rendering of the sleeping boy's right arm further to the right on the sheet in Rotterdam. Andersen dates the Basel drawing to around 1882/83, the Rotterdam sketch somewhat more broadly, to 1882/84, when the age of the boy represented would correspond to that of Cézanne's son Paul.

J.P.

7

Study After a Statue of a Seated Figure

F II 211
Verso: Pencil studies after an Italian painting and sketches of the annexes of the *Jas de Bouffan*
Pencil and watercolor; 217 × 126 mm
Provenance: F. Koenigs; given by D. G. van Beuningen to the Museum Boymans Foundation, 1940
Literature: Rotterdam 1968, cat. no. 29 (ill.); Chappuis 1973, nos. 625, 626 (ill.), and verso: no. 608 (ill.); exhib. cat.,
    Tübingen 1982, no. 105 (ill.); Rewald 1983, no. 64 (ill.); Siblík 1984, ill. 33

It is not known which statue Cézanne used as the model for this watercolor. The drawing is sometimes thought to represent a seventeenth-century French or Flemish sepulchral monument to a high official. Or it may represent a statue from the Far East exhibited at the Paris World's Fair of 1878 (see *Le Livre des Expositions Universelles 1851–1889,* Paris 1983), although as far as we know, Cézanne did not visit this Fair. Some scholars are of the opinion that the seated man, seen from the front, supports a coat of arms between his knees. We are inclined to think that this section of the drawing shows folds of the man's garment, however, and that the man holds a round box on his lap.

Studies in pencil of the same figure can be seen on pages XIII (verso) and XVI of the so-called Sketchbook Leigh Block in Chicago (Chappuis 1973, nos. 625, 626 [ill.]), thought to date from 1882/86. The Rotterdam watercolor is generally dated somewhat earlier, around 1878/82.

The study of a head on the left side of the verso was drawn after a painting in the Louvre, which was in Cézanne's lifetime considered to be a self-portrait by Raphael (see *Raphael et l'art français,* exhib. cat., Grand Palais, Paris, no. 45 [ill.]); it is now attributed to Bachiacca, Sogliani, or Parmigiannino. On the right side of the verso is a view of *Jas de Bouffan,* an estate outside Aix-en-Provence that was acquired by Cézanne's father in 1859, where the artist often stayed. Cézanne sold the property in 1899 after his mother's death.

J.P.

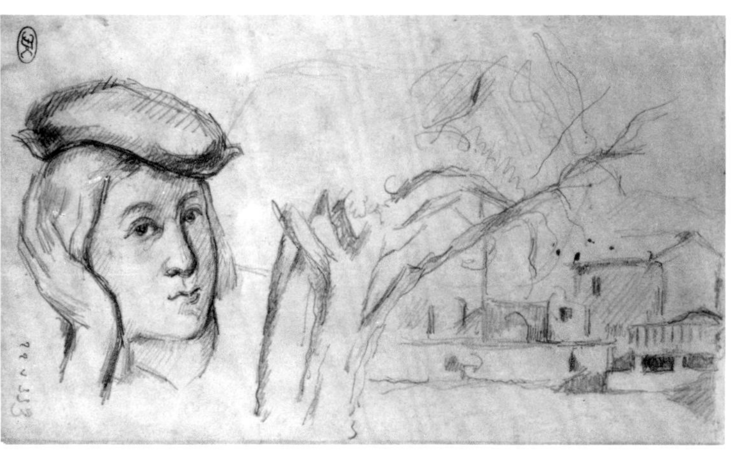

Verso

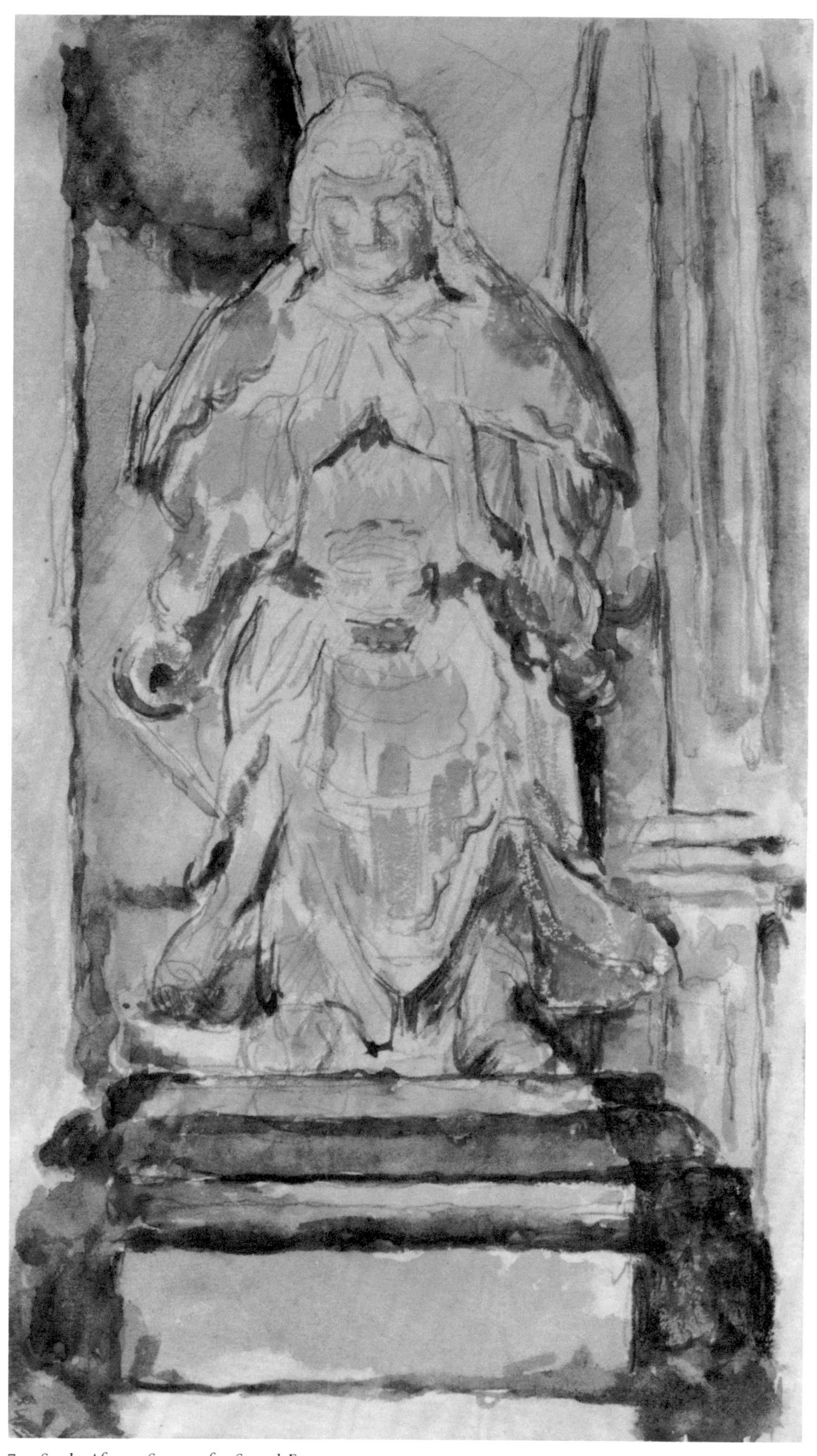

7   *Study After a Statue of a Seated Figure*

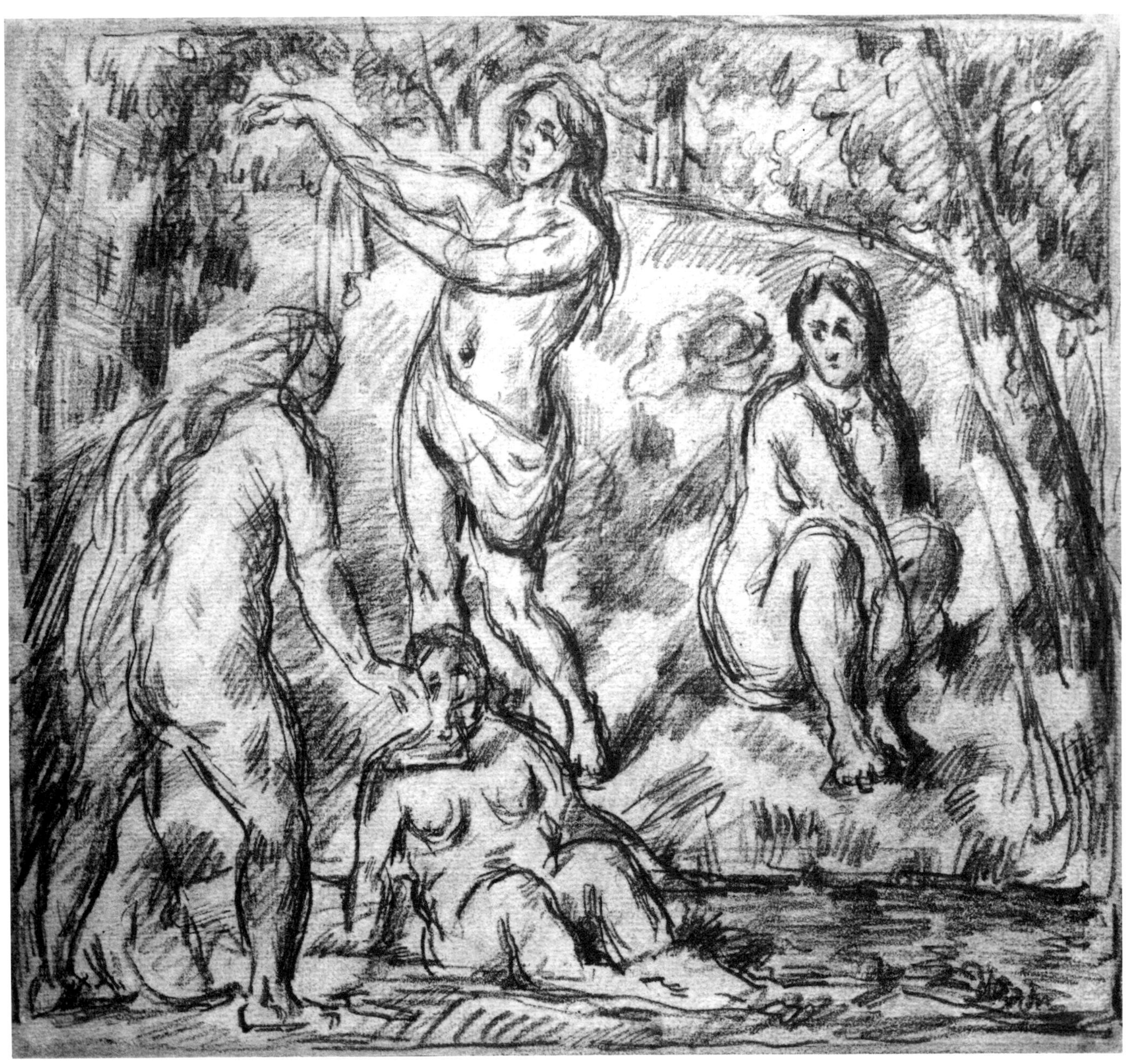

8   *Four Bathing Women*

Four Bathing Women

F II 192
Pencil and black chalk on vergé paper; 203 × 223 mm
Provenance: F. Koenigs; given by D. G. van Beuningen to the Museum Boymans Foundation, 1940
Literature: Rotterdam 1968, cat. no. 27 (ill.); H. Malins, *Drawing Ideas of the Masters,* Oxford 1981, no. 57 (ill.); Chappuis 1973,
   no. 514 (ill.); exhib. cat., Tübingen 1978, no. 137 (ill.); Venturi 1978, ill. p. 29; Siblík 1984, ill. 8

For many years Cézanne occupied himself with the theme of male or female bathers in a landscape, its
apotheosis being the three large compositions with bathing women in London, Philadelphia, and
Merion, Pennsylvania (exhib. cat., Paris 1978, ill. p. 217, 219). In addition to these paintings, Cézanne
created many watercolors and numerous sketches in pencil and black chalk relating to this theme. In
fact, representations of bathing figures are known among the artist's earliest works (Chappuis 1973,
no. 39), and his correspondence with Emile Zola constantly indulges in reminiscences of their joint
excursions along the brooks in the countryside around Aix-en-Provence (see *Paul Cézanne, Correspondance,*
Paris 1937).

From the 1870s on, Cézanne explored this theme in depth. He was probably inspired by the
paintings of nudes in nature by old masters like Giorgione, Titian, Peter Paul Rubens, and Nicolas
Poussin; but also by those of a direct predecessor like Gustave Courbet, or a contemporary artist such as
Edouard Manet. Clearly, Cézanne did not aim to render solely the nude, but rather to combine the nude
figure with nature.

The pencil and black chalk studies for these bathing nudes were not drawn from live models. Rather,
Cézanne referred back to the model drawings from his student days at the Académie Suisse in Paris
(1861) and his copies after sculptures and paintings. According to Chappuis, the figure of the woman
drying off in the background of the Rotterdam drawing shows similarities to the statue from classical
antiquity of Apoxyomenos now in the Vatican (Chappuis 1962, no. 94).

Notable in this drawing is the combination of a traditional compositional structure and an
impressionistic style of drawing, with its sketchy lines and hatched planes. The draughtsmanship is
related to the style of several paintings with dates around 1879/82, such as *Three Bathing Women* in Paris
(exhib. cat., Madrid 1984, no. 22 [ill.]). In addition, there are extant painted versions of the composition
(see Venturi 1936, nos. 384, 547 [ill.]), and one rendition in which a figure has been added in front to
the right (Venturi 1936, no. 383 [ill.]). Apart from these, some sketches of single figures or groups of
figures are known (see Chappuis 1973, nos. 511–513, 515, 517–523, 526–527, 649.1134 [ill.]); one of
these, representing the seated figure on the right, is also in the collection of the Museum Boymans-van
Beuningen in Rotterdam (Chappuis 1973, no. 513 [ill.]).

The Rotterdam drawing of four bathing women immediately gained great renown and was used in
1898 on the invitation to an exhibition of the artist's work in Ambroise Vollard's gallery in Paris; it was
also reproduced on the frontispiece of Vollard's 1914 monograph on Cézanne (see Venturi 1978, ill.
p. 29).

J.P.

9

Landscape with Bare Trees and a House to the Right

F II 26
Verso: Study of a tree
Pencil on smooth paper; 326 × 345 mm
Provenance: F. Koenigs; given by D. G. van Beuningen to the Museum Boymans Foundation, 1940
Literature: Rotterdam 1968, cat. no. 15 (ill.); Chappuis 1973, no. 878 (ill.), and verso: no. 909 (ill.); exhib. cat., Newcastle-
upon-Tyne 1973, no. 45 (ill.); exhib. cat., Tübingen 1978, no. 84 (ill.); Siblík 1984, ill. 25

On the right side of this sheet, the roof of a fairly large house with a dormer is visible, seemingly half hidden behind a wall. Around it a rolling landscape is depicted in pencil lines and hatchings, with several thin bare trees forming vertical accents.

Approximately 1200 black-and-white drawings by Cézanne are known, but they were on the whole considered by the artist as study material for his own use and therefore became known to the public only after his death. Cézanne made many drawings in pencil and black chalk until around 1888; thereafter he concentrated on a combination of lines in pencil or black chalk with watercolor planes, and still later on pure watercolors.

The house in the Rotterdam drawing has not been identified, but the landscape seems to have originated in northern France. Hoetink sees a thematic relationship between this drawing and the Paris painting *Cour d'une Ferme à Anvers* (see Venturi 1936, no. 326 [ill.]), which Venturi dates 1879/82. There could also be a similarity between the trees in the Rotterdam drawing and those in a watercolor formerly in Berlin that Venturi dates around 1883/87 (Venturi 1936, no. 971 [ill.]). Chappuis dates the Rotterdam drawing around 1882/83; the study of a tree on the verso somewhat later, around 1885/87. Adriani dates the front around 1883/85 (exhib. cat., Tübingen 1978, no. 84 [ill.]).

J.P.

10

View of L'Estaque

F II 183
Watercolor and white wash over black chalk on vergé paper; 310 × 475 mm
Provenance: F. Koenigs; given by D. G. van Beuningen to the Museum Boymans Foundation, 1940
Literature: Rotterdam 1968, cat. no. 26 (ill.); exhib. cat., Washington 1971, no. 39 (ill.); exhib. cat., Newcastle-upon-Tyne 1973, no. 42 (ill.); exhib. cat., Tübingen 1982, no. 22 (ill.); Rewald 1983, no. 116 (ill.), ill. p. 26, pp. 4, 112; Siblík 1984, ill. 39; exhib. cat., Madrid 1984, ill. p. 16

In the foreground a view of roofs, chimneys, and a rectangular tower is represented in a rhythmic pattern of color planes in transparent watercolor over a few lines in black chalk. In the background a bay surrounded by hills has been sketched in a few brush strokes. This watercolor is very similar to the lower right corner of the New York painting *La Baie de Marseilles, Vue de l'Estaque,* dated around 1884/86; the watercolor has generally been dated somewhat earlier, around 1878/83 (*Centenaire de l'Impressionisme,* exhib. cat., Grand Palais, Paris 1974, no. 8 [ill.]).

At the outbreak of the Franco-German war of 1870, Cézanne moved to the south and worked in l'Estaque near Marseilles, where he would return many times in later years. The bright sunlight there, which caused changes in colors and shapes, made a great impression on him. From 1876 on, he was enthralled by the motif of roofs silhouetted against the blue skies. In a letter to Camille Pissarro dated 2 July 1876, Cézanne wrote: "There the sunlight is so startling that the objects seem to stick out as silhouettes not only in white or black, but also in blue, red, brown, and violet" (*Paul Cézanne, Correspondance,* Paris 1937, p. 127).

The motif in this drawing can also be seen in some pencil and black chalk drawings that Chappuis dates to approximately 1881/84 (Chappuis 1973, nos. 814–816 [ill.]).

J.P.

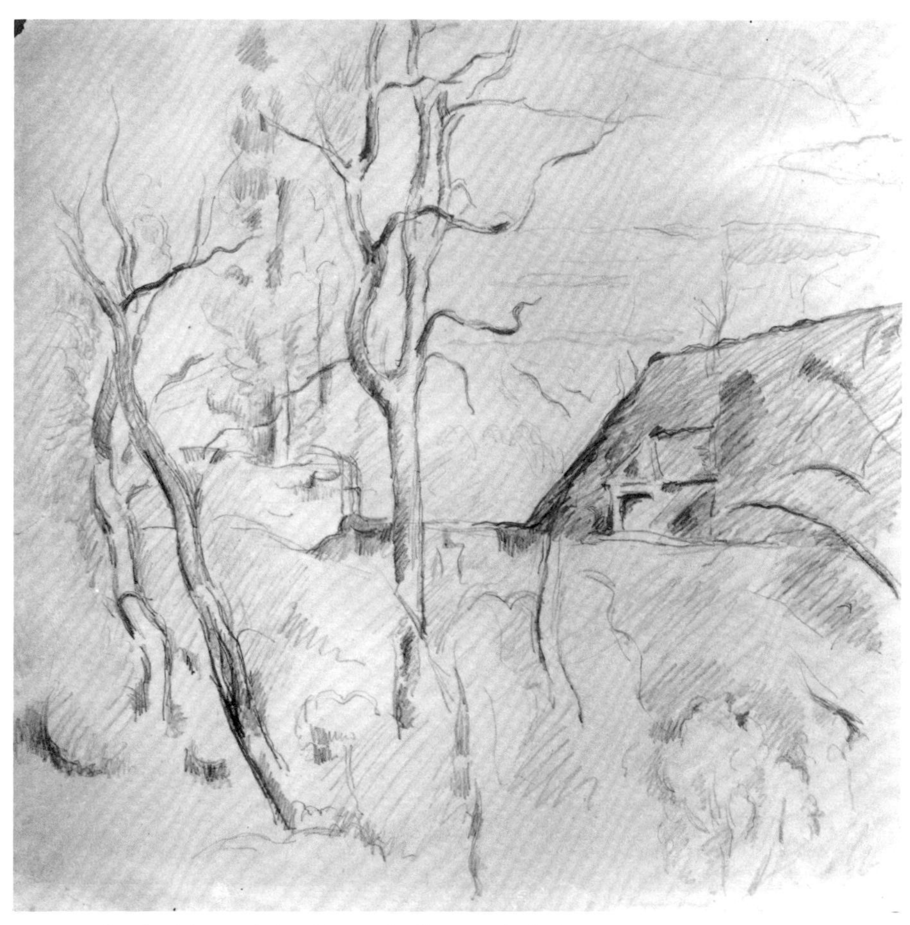

9   Landscape with Bare Trees and a House to the Right

10   View of l'Estaque

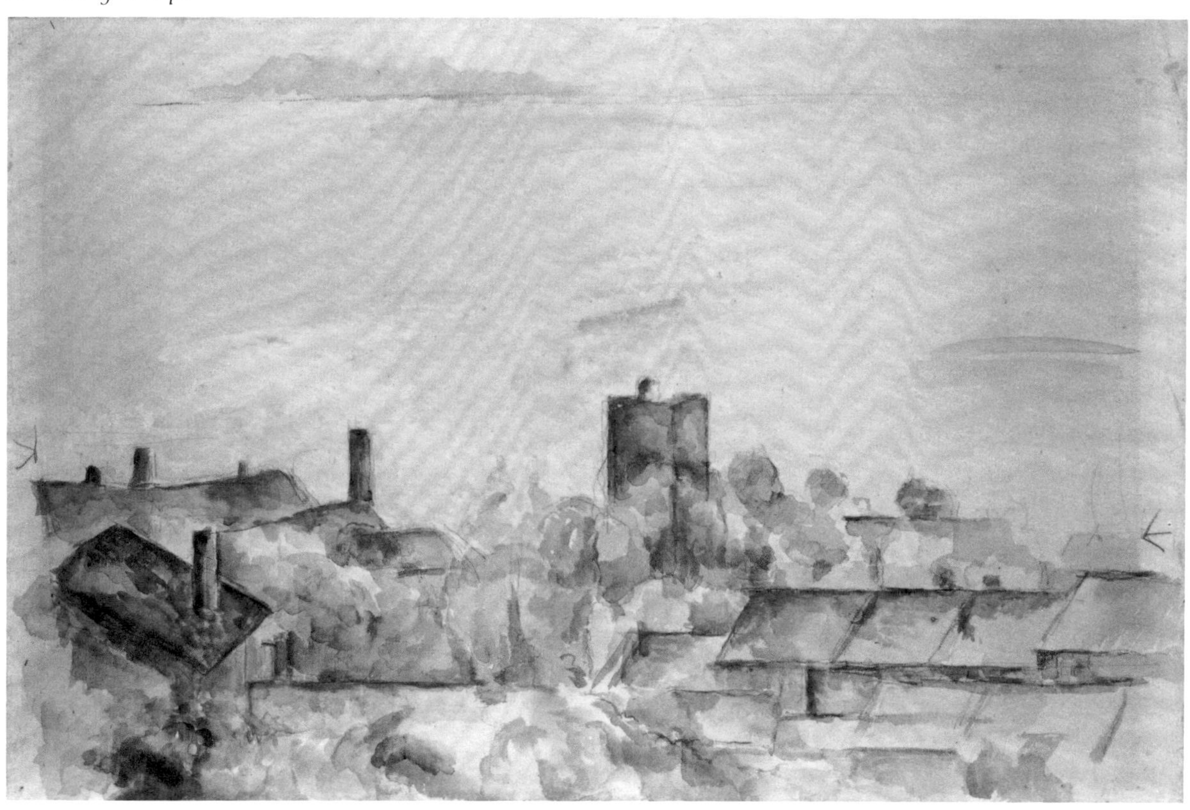

Portrait of Hortense Cézanne-Figuet

F II 220
Pencil on vergé paper; 485 × 322 mm
Provenance: F. Koenigs; given by D. G. van Beuningen to the Museum Boymans Foundation, 1940
Literature: Rotterdam 1968, cat. no. 34 (ill.); Andersen 1970, no. 69 (ill.); exhib. cat., Washington 1971, no. 77 (ill.); Chappuis
1973, no. 1065 (ill.); exhib. cat., Tübingen 1978, no. 59 (ill.); Venturi 1978, ill. p. 74; exhib. cat., Liège 1982, no. 41
(ill.); Siblík 1984, ill. 12; exhib. cat., Madrid 1984, no. 72 (ill.)

Paul Cézanne confined himself in his portraits to people who were close to him; we know of no portraits made on commission. In addition to his son Paul, his wife Hortense was his most frequent model.

Hortense Figuet came from Saligny in the Jura region; she met Cézanne in 1869 in Paris, where she became his model and lover. The liaison, which was kept secret from the artist's father for many years, produced a son, Paul, in 1872 (Rewald, "Cézanne and His Father," *Studies in the History of Art,* National Gallery of Art, Washington, D.C., 1971/72, pp. 38–62). But even after their marriage was contracted in 1886 with the consent of Cézanne's father, they rarely lived together as a family. Mother and son were most often in Paris, while Cézanne lived in Aix-en-Provence. In later years strong ties of trust developed between the artist and his son.

The Rotterdam portrait of Hortense Cézanne-Figuet is generally considered to be one of the strongest of Cézanne's portrait drawings. But opinions differ as to its date; it is estimated between around 1881 and 1891. Because of the fashion consciousness of French ladies like Hortense Cézanne-Figuet in the nineteenth century, Anne Van Buren believes that the Rotterdam drawing cannot have been done after 1888 (A. H. Van Buren, "Madame Cézanne's Fashions and the Dates of Her Portraits," *The Art Quarterly,* XXIX [1966], pp. 115–127).

J.P.

Study After the "Hercules" by Pierre Puget

F II 215
Pencil on vergé paper; 473 × 313 mm
Provenance: F. Koenigs; given by D. G. van Beuningen to the Museum Boymans Foundation, 1940
Literature: Rotterdam 1968, no. 33 (ill.); exhib. cat., Newcastle-upon-Tyne 1973, no. 49 (ill.); Chappuis 1973, no. 999 (ill.);
exhib. cat., Tübingen 1978, no. 174 (ill.); Siblík 1984, ill. 16

We find studies after works by other artists throughout Cézanne's oeuvre: studies after paintings as well as sculptures, including those that could be seen in Paris, for instance in the Musée du Louvre, the Ecole des Beaux-Arts, the Palais du Trocadéro. Approximately a fourth of these drawings consist of copies after statues by the seventeenth-century French sculptor Pierre Puget (Th. Reff, "Puget's Fortunes in France," *Essays in the History of Art Presented to Rudolf Wittkower,* London 1967, pp. 274–284).

Cézanne did a large number of sketches after the *Hercules* by Puget in the Musée du Louvre, a statue that was originally created between 1663 and 1668 for the park of the castle of Sceaux (about the statue, see exhib. cat., Newcastle-upon-Tyne 1973, p. 161, note 49 [ill.]). Adriani argues that Cézanne was compelled to sketch the statue mostly from the side because of its position in the hall of the museum. Reff, on the other hand, is convinced that Cézanne favored this side because the statue had a more dynamic effect when seen from the side than from the front (exhib. cat., Tübingen 1978, p. 59; and Th. Reff, "Cézanne and Hercules," *The Art Bulletin,* XLVIII [1966], pp. 35–44).

Reff also thinks that one of the reasons why Cézanne chose a statue of Hercules as the model for several drawings was that the Hercules figure occupied a special place in poems the artist had written in his youth (Reff, "Cézanne and Hercules"). The fact that Hercules' paraphernalia are not present in

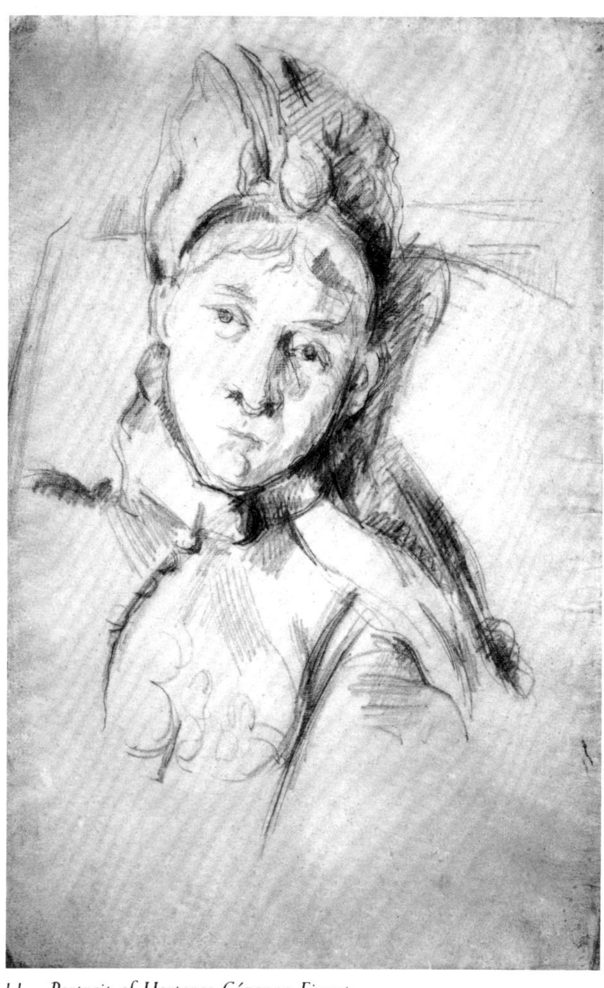

11   Portrait of Hortense Cézanne-Figuet

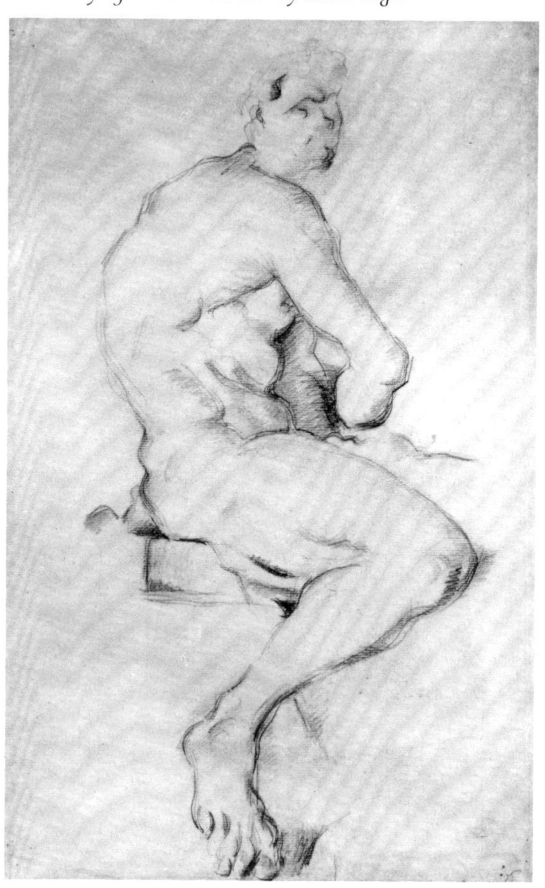

12   Study After the "Hercules" by Pierre Puget

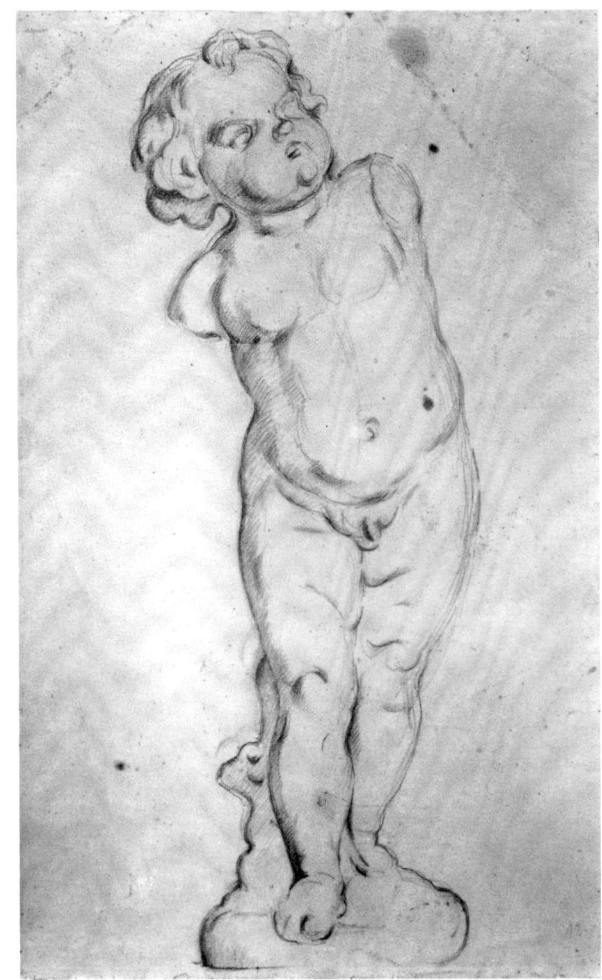

13   Study After a Plaster Cast of a Sculpture of a Putto

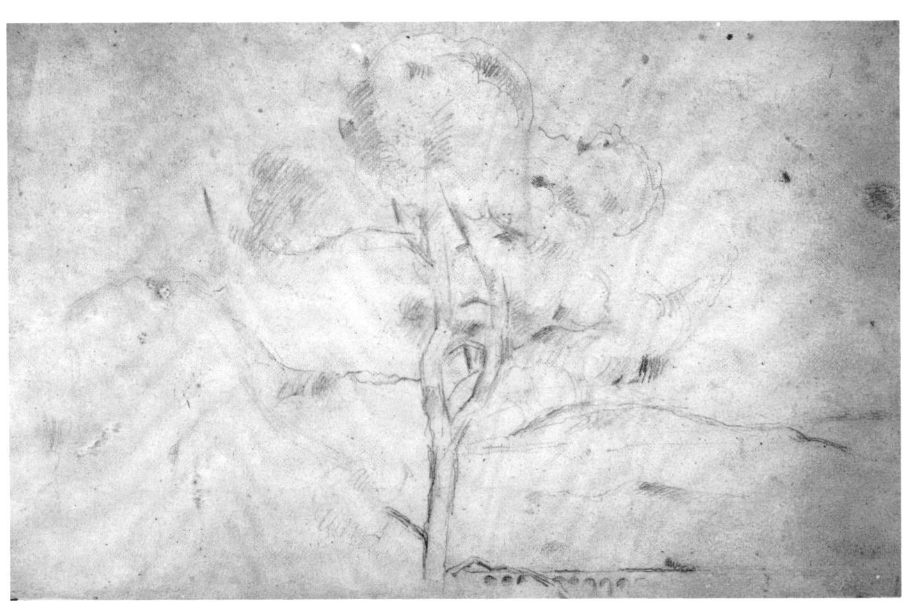

Cézanne's drawings, however, speaks against this view. Chappuis points out the similarity between the Rotterdam drawing and a sketch after the same statue formerly in Budapest (Chappuis 1973, no. 1000 [ill.]). He dates both sheets around 1884/87.

J.P.

13
Study After a Plaster Cast of a Sculpture of a Putto

F II 27
Verso: Study of the Mont St. Victoire, with a tree and an aqueduct
Black chalk and pencil on vergé paper; 482 × 310 mm
Provenance: F. Koenigs; given by D. G. van Beuningen to the Museum Boymans Foundation, 1940
Literature: Rotterdam 1968, cat. no. 16 (ill.); Chappuis 1973, no. 986 (ill.), and verso: no. 896 (ill.); exhib. cat., Newcastle-upon-Tyne 1973, no. 59 (ill.); exhib. cat., Tübingen 1978, no. 178 (ill.)

After the death of Cézanne's mother, the estate *Jas de Bouffan* that the artist's father had purchased in 1859 was sold, and Cézanne settled in Aix-en-Provence, where his housekeeper, Madame Brémont, and his sister Marie took care of him. In 1901 he acquired a piece of property on the Chemin des Lauves north of town where he had a studio built. Among the objects that he used to decorate the studio were two plaster casts, both of which can be seen in a painting in London (Venturi 1978, ill. p. 139) and are even now present in the studio (J. Rewald, "The Last Motifs at Aix," *Cézanne: The Late Work,* ed. W. Rubin, London 1978, ill. p. 103).

The original sculpture from which the plaster cast of the putto in the Rotterdam drawing was made is unknown; it is usually attributed to the seventeenth-century French sculptor Pierre Puget, but also sometimes to François Duquesnoy (1594–1643) and his school (Th. Reff, "Painting and Theory in the Final Decade," *Cézanne: The Late Work,* ed. Rubin, ill. p. 31). Adriani attributes the original sculpture to Nicolas Coustou (1658–1733) (exhib. cat., Tübingen 1978, no. 178 [ill.]). The putto was drawn by Cézanne from all sides (Chappuis 1973, nos. 980 bis, 981–985, 987–990 [ill.]) and can also be seen in some watercolors (Rewald 1983, nos. 556–560 [ill.]). The Rotterdam drawing is usually dated around 1886/95.

The verso shows a scene from Bellevue, where the artist's brother-in-law Maxime Conil had bought a house in 1885, overlooking the Vallée de l'Arc toward the Mont St. Victoire (see Rewald 1983, ill. p. 143, for a photograph of the scenery). A number of drawings, watercolors, and paintings that show views from this point date from the years 1885 to 1887 (see, for instance, Chappuis 1973, nos. 896, 897 [ill.]; Rewald 1983, nos. 239–242 [ill.]; Venturi 1936, nos. 452–455 [ill.]). The Rotterdam drawing is rendered from a perspective somewhat different from the usual; the location of the viaduct corresponds most closely to that in a watercolor in Zürich (Rewald 1983, no. 240 [ill.]), and the location of the tree to that in a watercolor in Vienna (Rewald 1983, no. 239 [ill.]).

J.P.

14

Landscape with Trees and a Small Cottage

F II 149
Pencil and watercolor on vergé paper; 310 × 470 mm
Provenance: F. Koenigs; given by D. G. van Beuningen to the Museum Boymans Foundation, 1940
Literature: Rotterdam 1968, cat. no. 24 (ill.); exhib. cat., Newcastle-upon-Tyne 1973, no. 57 (ill.); exhib. cat., Tübingen 1982, no. 41 (ill.); Rewald 1983, no. 259 (ill.), p. 148; Siblík 1984, ill. 52

A small cottage with a chimney and three windows occupies the center of the sheet. The surrounding landscape is defined in pencil and watercolor laid down in transparent washes. A harmonious balance has been achieved between the vertical lines of the thin tree trunks and the horizontal character of the rolling hillside. The placement of the windows high in the walls identifies the cottage as a Provençal hunting cabin. A similar cabin, but without the high windows, can also be seen in a watercolor in Washington, D.C. (Rewald 1983, no. 258 [ill.]).

This Rotterdam watercolor, dated around 1887/90, is a study for a painting in Merion, Pennsylvania, which Venturi dates around 1890/94. The hunting cabin is represented in the painting at a somewhat greater distance (Venturi 1936, no. 671 [ill.]).

J.P.

15

The Smoker

F II 25
Pencil and some vague washing in gray ink on vergé paper; 500 × 320 mm
Provenance: F. Koenigs; given by D. G. van Beuningen to the Museum Boymans Foundation, 1940
Literature: Rotterdam 1968, cat. no. 36 (ill.); Andersen 1970, no. 254 (ill.); Chappuis 1973, no. 1094 (ill.); exhib. cat., Newcastle-upon-Tyne 1973, no. 68 (ill.); exhib. cat., Tübingen 1978, no. 63 (ill.) Siblík 1984, ill. 21

This pencil study of a man's head belongs to a group of drawings and watercolors that is related to five paintings with card players dating from around 1890 (see Chappuis 1973, nos. 1092–1095 [ill.]; Rewald 1983, nos. 377–380 [ill.]; and Venturi 1936, nos. 556–560 [ill.]). Possibly seventeenth-century or later depictions of scenes with card players led Cézanne to this theme (B. Dorival, *Cézanne,* Paris 1948, ill. XIII, XIV); there is a painting with card players in the Musée Granet in Aix-en-Provence that is from the school of the Le Nain brothers (K. Badt, *Die Kunst Cézannes,* Munich 1956, ill. 17).

Cézanne confined himself in his portraits to people who belonged to his own close circle—friends, his father, but most frequently his wife Hortense and their son Paul. At the time when the compositions with card players were painted, the artist and his family did not live together for the most part; his wife and son were in Paris, Cézanne in Aix-en-Provence. Yet even for the sketches from this period, Cézanne had models who were familiar to him: his housekeeper, the gardener, or in this particular case, a laborer from the estate *Jas de Bouffan* (exhib. cat., Paris 1978, p. 76, no. 5).

The Rotterdam drawing should not be considered a direct study for the figure on the right in three paintings with two card players (two paintings in a Paris collection, one in London) (Venturi 1936, nos. 556–558 [ill.]). But one might consider a watercolor in New York, dating from around 1892/96 (Rewald 1983, no. 380 [ill.]), to be such a direct study indeed. In this watercolor, the man does not smoke a pipe and is sitting at a table. On the other hand, the Rotterdam drawing bears more resemblance to the man on the right in the paintings with two card players than to the same model on the left of two paintings with three card players (in New York and Merion, Pennsylvania) (Venturi 1936, nos. 559–560). A similar study in a Swiss collection, but in watercolor, portrays the man on the left in the paintings with two card players (Rewald 1983, no. 378 [ill.]); this sheet bears a study in pencil of the same man's head on the verso.

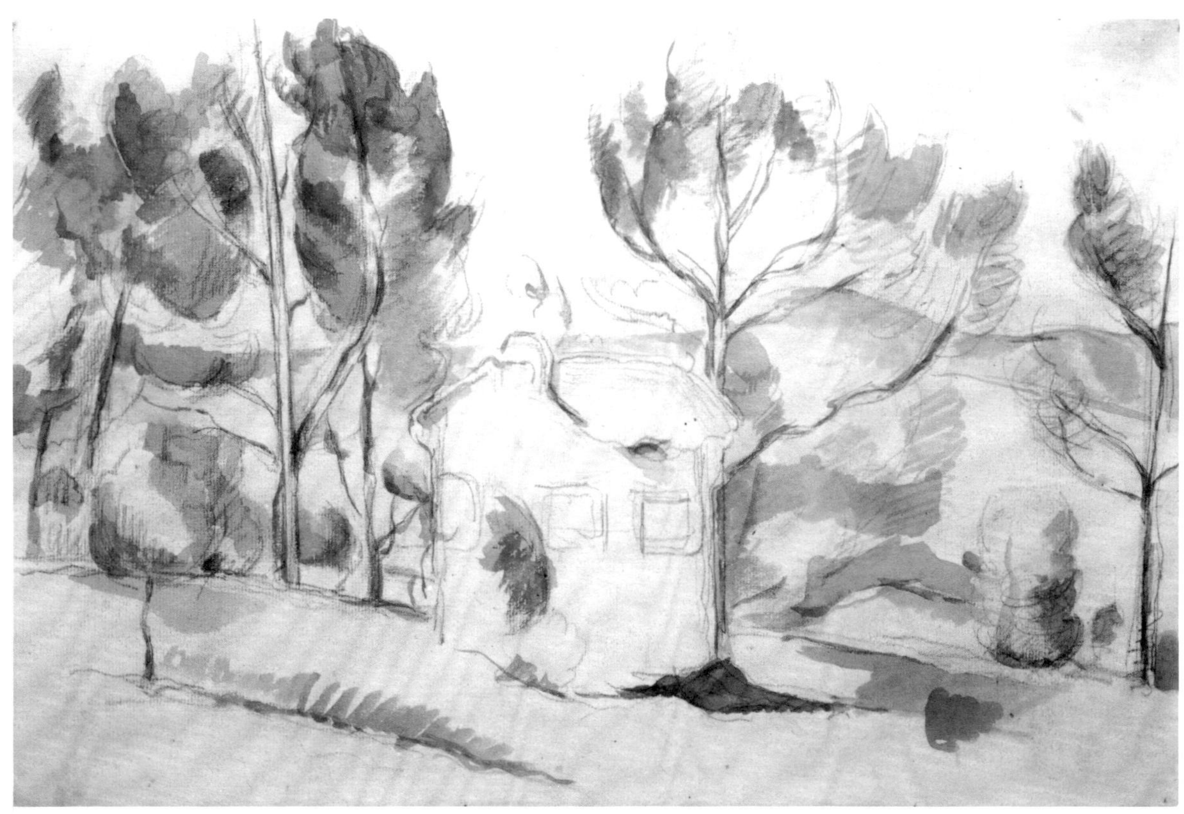

14   Landscape with Trees and a Small Cottage

15   The Smoker

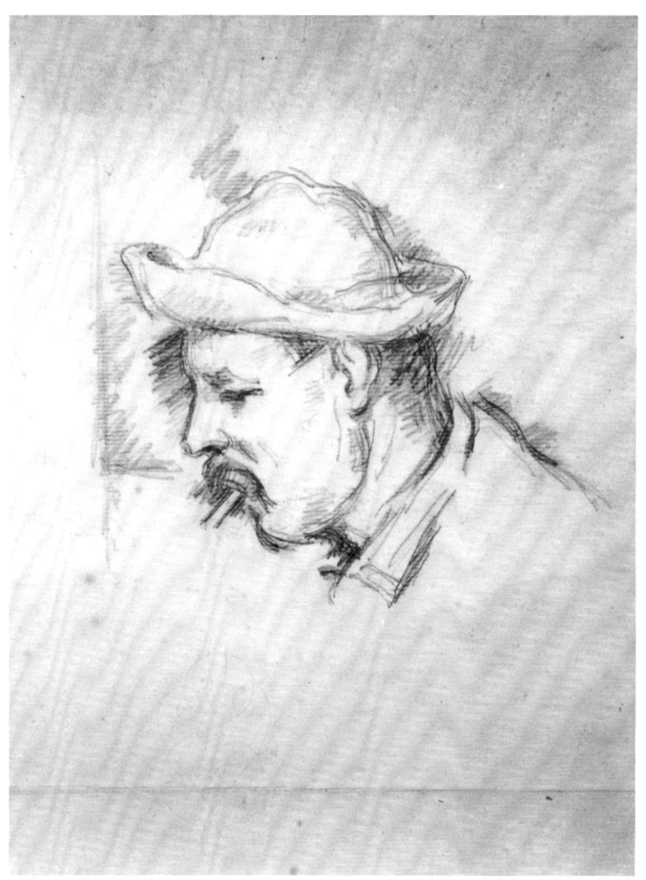

The Rotterdam drawing has been kept folded until now. With the sheet now being shown unfolded in full format, the placement of the drawing on the paper reveals that the artist probably intended to elaborate the study into a full sketch of the man sitting at a table. The paper appears to have been washed very lightly, which causes a luminescent effect in the background that recalls the window in the background of the paintings (Venturi 1936, nos. 556–558 [ill.]). This can also be seen on the watercolor studies (Rewald 1983, nos. 378–380 [ill.]).

The practically identical dimensions of the New York watercolor study of the man on the left (Rewald 1983, no. 378 [ill.]) and the Rotterdam study in pencil of the head of the man on the right, coupled with the fact that the dimensions of both sheets together amount to a paper size that was rather common in the nineteenth century, suggest that the two sheets might originally have been one whole. Therefore the two men may have been represented in the situation shown in the paintings.

J.P.

16
Trees and Buildings

F II 150
Watercolor over black chalk on *Montgolfier Saint Marcel les Annon* paper; 324 × 505 mm
Provenance: F. Koenigs; given by D. G. van Beuningen to the Museum Boymans Foundation, 1940
Literature: Rotterdam 1968, cat. no. 25 (ill.); exhib. cat., Newcastle-upon-Tyne 1973, no. 71 (ill.); exhib. cat., Tübingen 1982, no. 45 (ill.) Siblík 1984, ill. 46

A composition with a clump of trees is created in transparent watercolor planes over a drawing in black chalk, with a few contour lines added in brush strokes. In Cézanne's oeuvre, drawings of this kind should not be considered as chalk or pencil drawings that were later filled in with color; rather, the lines and color planes are equivalent.

Unlike the Impressionists, Cézanne started only late in his career to work in the open air. Around 1880 he developed a great interest in watercolor as an independent medium, perhaps because the watercolor technique made it easier for him to work outdoors. The idea was not to record impressions of the moment, but to create a well-considered composition of lines in pencil and black chalk with brushed-on color planes. Colors and tones were superimposed in such a way that they did not mix and they remained transparent. Stylistic comparison with a watercolor in Switzerland suggests a date around 1890/1900 on the basis of the brushed-in contour lines (Rewald 1983, no. 511 [ill.]).

J.P.

17
View of Roofs and a Landscape with Mountains in the Background

F II 213
Verso: Study of trees
Watercolor on *Berville* paper; 325 × 400 mm
Provenance: F. Koenigs; given by D. G. van Beuningen to the Museum Boymans Foundation, 1940
Literature: Rotterdam 1968, cat. no. 31 (ill.); exhib. cat., Newcastle-upon-Tyne 1973, no. 72 (ill.); exhib. cat., Tübingen 1982, no. 55 (ill.); Rewald 1983, no. 360 (ill.); Siblík 1984, ill. 45

The horizontal character of this landscape, with the geometric planes of the roofs of many houses, is broken by a vertical accent supplied by a towering tree. This watercolor resembles a painting that formerly belonged to Ambroise Vollard's collection (Venturi 1936, no. 482), which Venturi dates around 1885/87. The watercolor sketch, however, is dated by Hoetink around 1895/1900, and by Adriani around 1895, at the beginning of a second period of geometric stylizing in Cézanne's work. Likewise, the

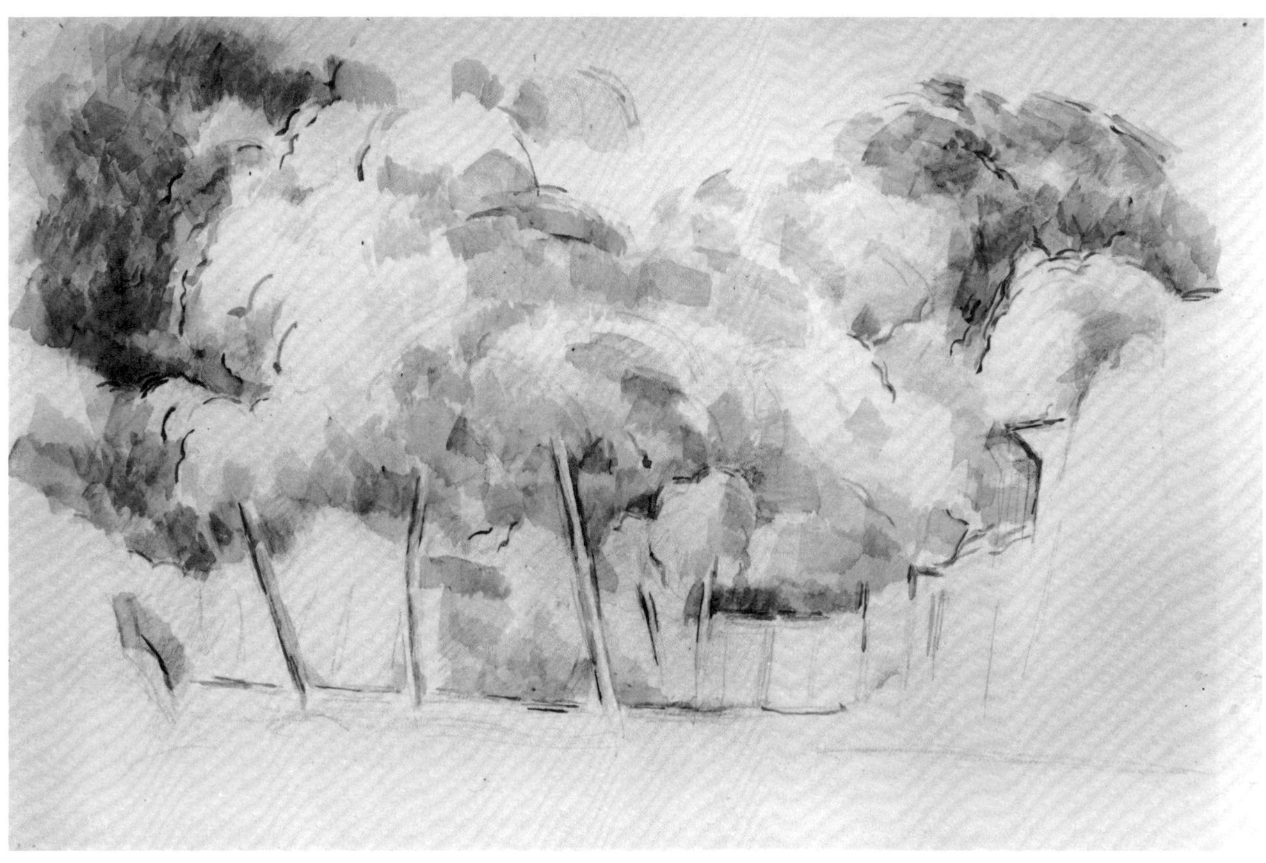

16   *Trees and Buildings*

17   *View of Roofs and a Landscape with Mountains in the Background (see also color plate 1)*

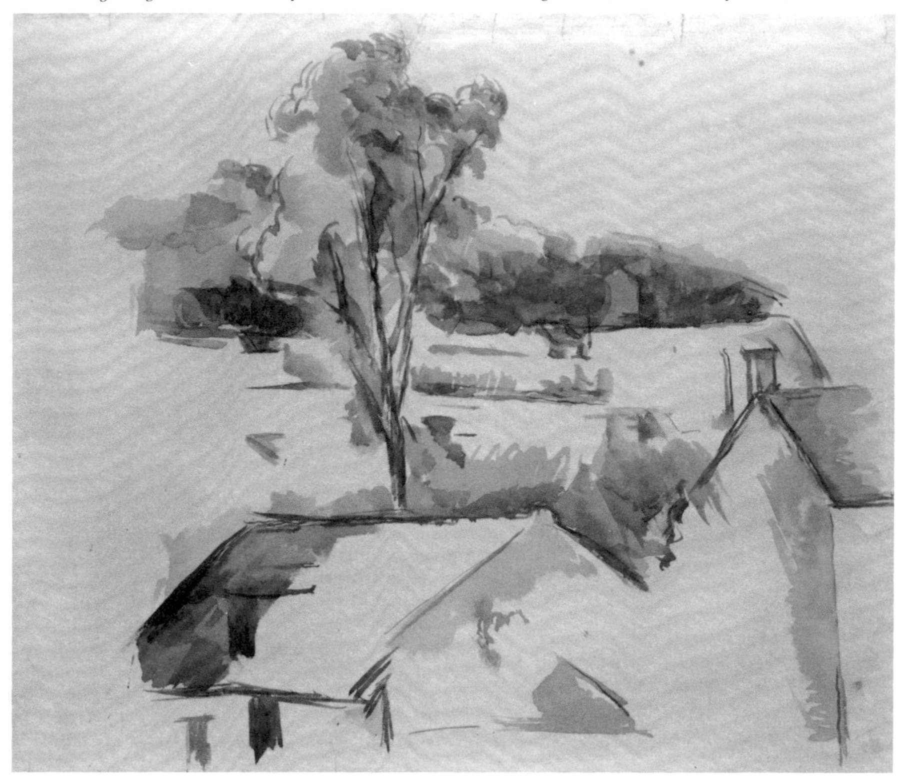

study of trees on the verso (see exhib. cat., Tübingen 1982, ill. p. 272) has been dated around 1900, on the basis of a stylistic comparison with a watercolor in New York (Rewald 1983, no. 507 [ill.]).

It is generally thought that the watercolor originated in northern France, perhaps in 1888, when the artist was working along the banks of the Marne and in the vicinity of Paris (exhib. cat., Newcastle-upon-Tyne 1973, p. 165, note 72).

J.P.

18
"Le Château Noir"

F II 212
Pencil and watercolor; laid down; 360 × 526 mm
Provenance: F. Koenigs; given by D. G. van Beuningen to the Museum Boymans Foundation, 1940
Literature: Rotterdam 1968, cat. no. 30 (ill.); F. Novotny, *Cézanne und das Ende der wissenschaftlichen Perspektive,* Vienna/Munich 1938 (reprint 1970), p. 195, no. 8 (7); H. Hutter, *Die Handzeichnung, Entwicklung, Technik, Eigenart,* Vienna/Munich 1966, p. 106, ill. IX; exhib. cat., Newcastle-upon-Tyne 1973, no. 62 (ill.); Venturi 1978, ill. p. 142; T. Pignatti 1981, p. 330 (ill.); exhib. cat., Tübingen 1982, no. 40 (ill.); Rewald 1983, no. 313 (ill.); Siblík 1984, ill. 60

This drawing depicts the so-called Château Noir, located on the road from Aix-en-Provence to the village of Le Tholonet, as seen from a spot below the terrace. This rendering is a more stylized version of that seen in a painting belonging to a Swiss private collection, which has been dated around 1904 (exhib. cat., Paris 1978, no. 53 [ill.]).

Construction of the "Château Noir" in the orange-brown stone of the region was begun in the second half of the nineteenth century and never finished. It was commissioned by a coal trader, whose profession may have had something to do with the name that was attached in popular speech to the complex of neogothic buildings; or perhaps the name stuck because of the rumor that the proprietor was interested in alchemy.

For many years Cézanne had the use of a small building in the courtyard of the "Château Noir," where he could store painting materials for his work outdoors. And particularly after the 1899 sale of his father's estate, the *Jas de Bouffan,* the artist worked closeby the "castle." The Rotterdam drawing probably must be dated somewhat earlier, however, because of its technique: sketching of the building mass in a few pencil lines, with the surrounding vegetation portrayed in transparent watercolor washes as an equivalent element.

J.P.

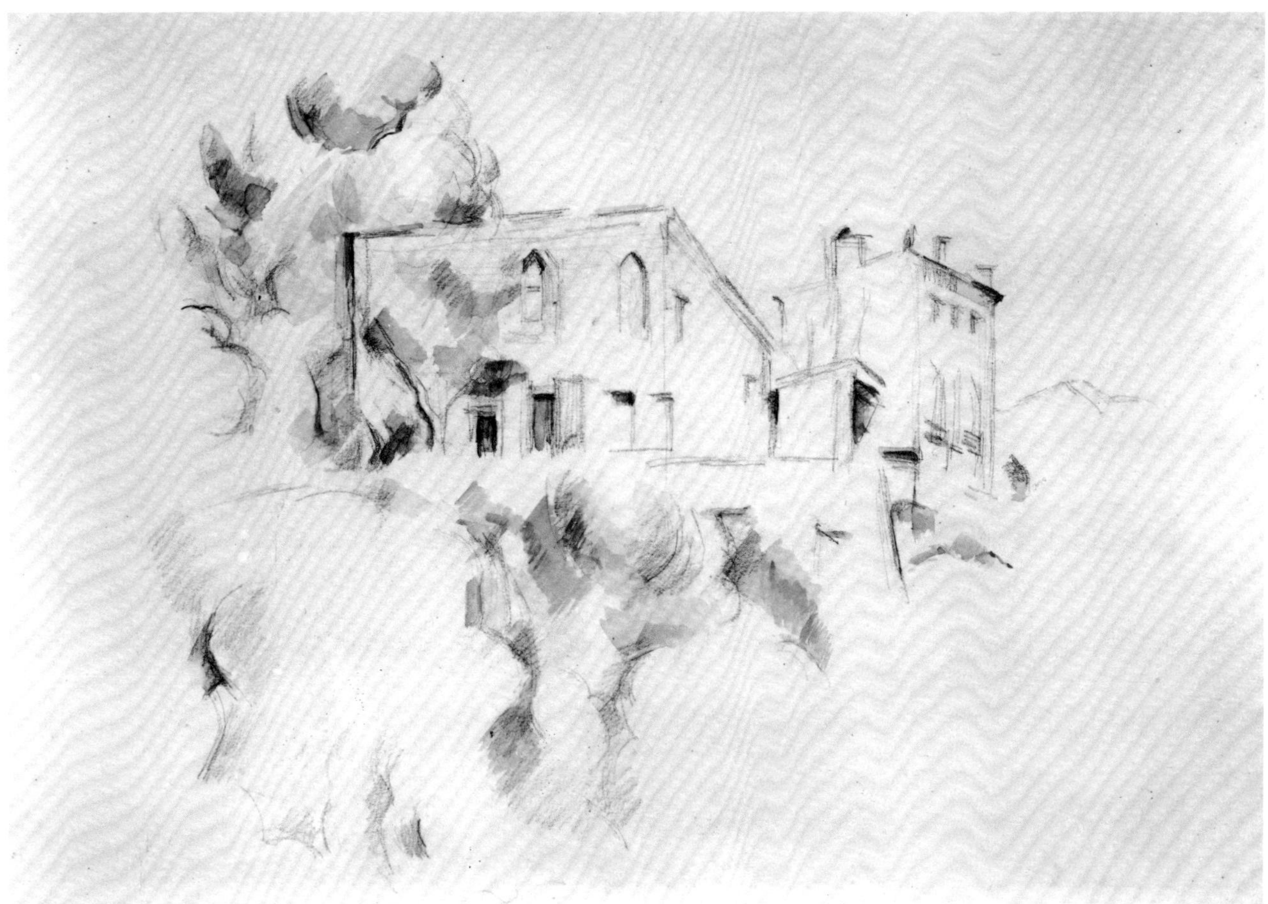

18 *"Le Château Noir"*

CAMILLE COROT
Paris 1796–1875

19
View of the Tiber with Castel St. Angelo, Rome

F II 6
Pen and brown ink on thin, light brown paper; laid down; 134 × 219 mm
Provenance: F. Koenigs; given by D. G. van Beuningen to the Museum Boymans Foundation, 1940
Literature: Rotterdam 1968, cat. no. 37 (ill.)

After a few years of study in Paris, Corot departed in 1825 for Italy, where he stayed until the fall of 1828. In Rome and in the Roman Campagna he painted oil studies after nature and did a large number of drawings of scenery, figures, and city views, all in a precise style of drawing reminiscent of Ingres. He used these drawings as a basis for the paintings he executed in his studio.

An oil sketch and this drawing, both of the Tiber with Castel St. Angelo and the dome of St. Peter's, formed a starting point for two paintings Corot did of the same subject (Robaut nos. 70 bis, 71). The oil sketch, made in Rome during 1826/27 and now in San Francisco (*Corot,* exhib. cat., Wildenstein, New York 1969, ill. no. 8), resembles the Rotterdam drawing in its lack of *staffage.* Back in Paris, Corot created the first version of the two paintings sometime between 1828 and 1835 (*Hommage à Corot,* exhib. cat., Orangerie des Tuileries, Paris 1975, no. 21), and he added trees, figures, and a few small boats to the original composition. He painted the second version of the subject between 1835 and 1840, again adding figures and fishing boats; this painting is now in Williamstown, Massachusetts (*French Paintings of the 19th Century,* Sterling and Francine Clark Art Institute, 1962, no. 15 [ill.]).

In a letter of 1852 that Corot wrote to a certain "Comairas," the artist offered to present an oil sketch, as he had promised a year before. He gave Comairas a choice between two works, which he defined in the letter by means of two quick sketches. One of these was the view of Castel St. Angelo that is now in San Francisco. A week later, however, he wrote Comairas again to say that he had carelessly given him an inaccurate sketch in his previous letter. In the present letter, he said, he had drawn the view of the Tiber accurately. In reality this second sketch represents another study of Castel St. Angelo, a work that is presently in the Louvre (exhib. cat., Paris 1975, no. 10). Apparently Corot was too attached to the San Francisco sketch to be willing to part with it (E. Moreau-Nélaton, *Corot raconté par lui-même,* II, Paris 1924, pp. 163ff.).

Finally in 1874, one year before his death, Corot sketched the view of the Tiber and Castel St. Angelo once more; it is a drawing in black chalk, which he presented to his good friend the Abbé Jouveau (Robaut no. 3037).

A.M.

20
View of the Campagna near Olevano

F II 58
Pen and brown ink on transparent paper; laid down; 105 × 430 mm
Inscribed with pen in brown ink: *Olevano–Près de la Serpentara*
Provenance: F. Koenigs; given by D. G. van Beuningen to the Museum Boymans Foundation, 1940
Literature: Rotterdam 1968, cat. no. 38 (ill.)

During his first stay in Italy, Corot at least three times visited the village of Olevano Romano, southeast of Rome in the Sabine mountains. This drawing describes the expansive landscape around the village, shown to the right of center, with the rocks of the Monte San' Arcangelo on the far right. The inscription indicates that Corot did this drawing at La Serpentara. But in Corot's day, "La Serpentara,"

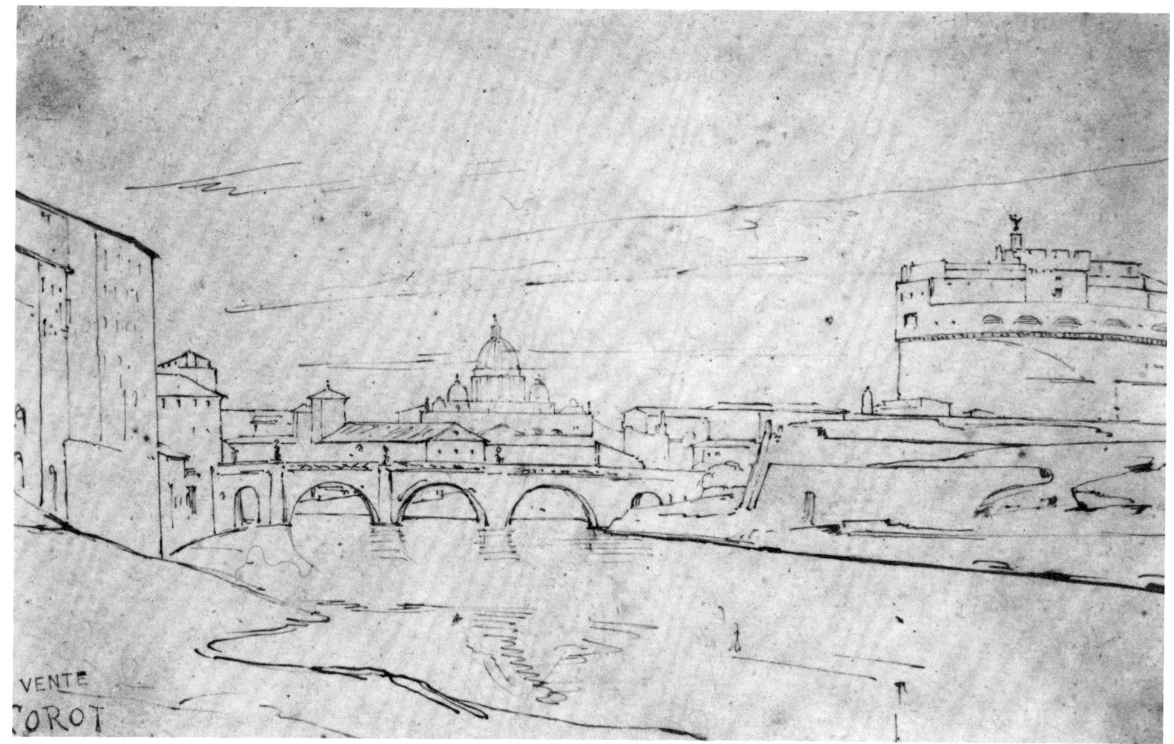

19   *View of the Tiber with Castel St. Angelo, Rome*

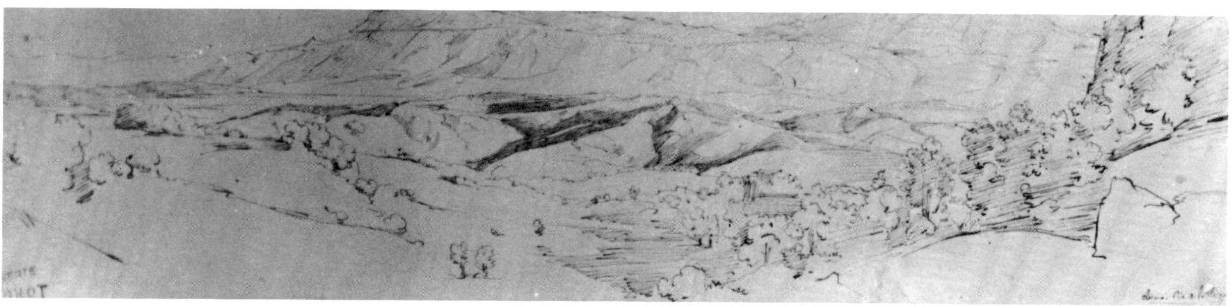

20   *View of the Campagna near Olevano*

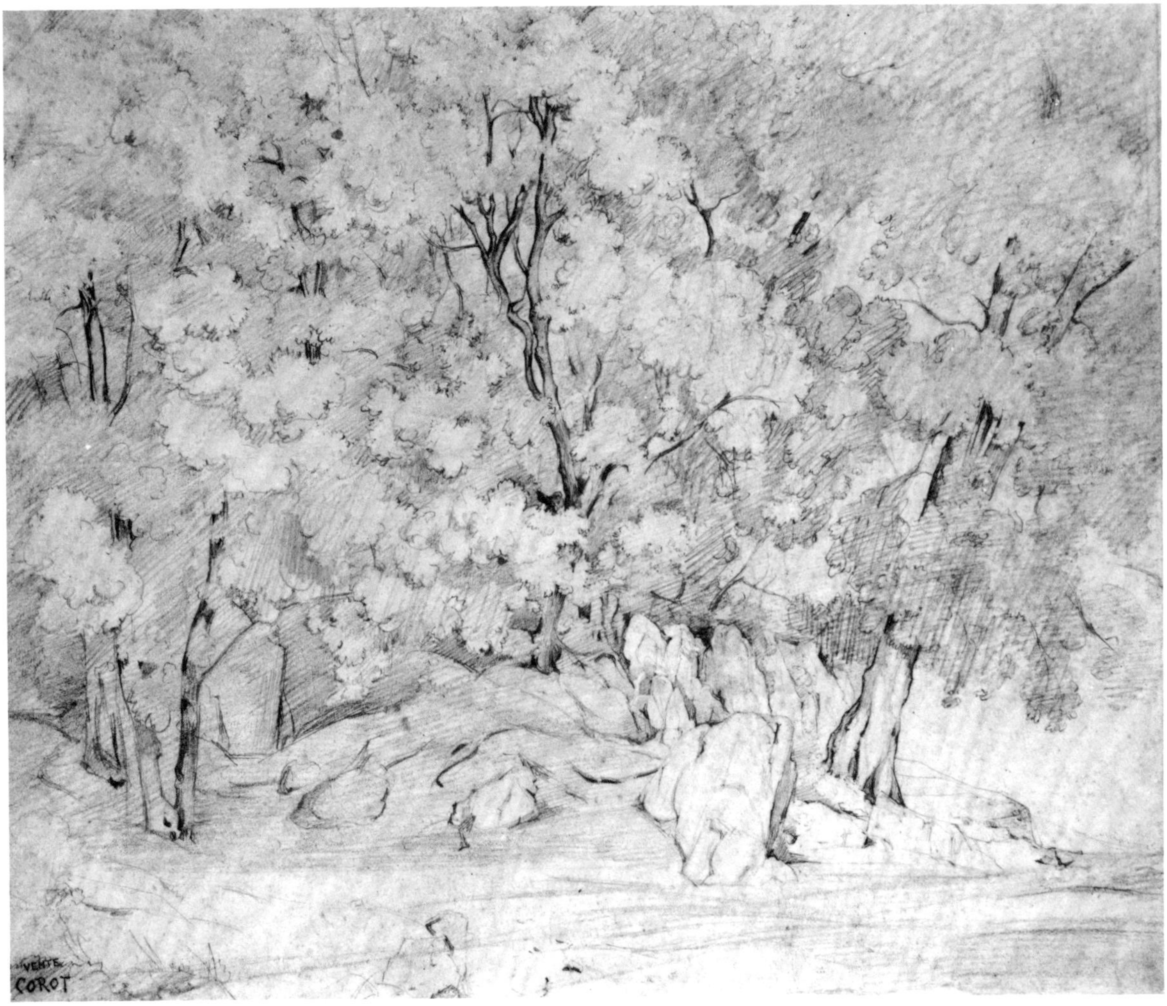

21   *Wooded Landscape with Rocks*

22   *Head and Torso of a Woman, Leaning on Her Right Arm*

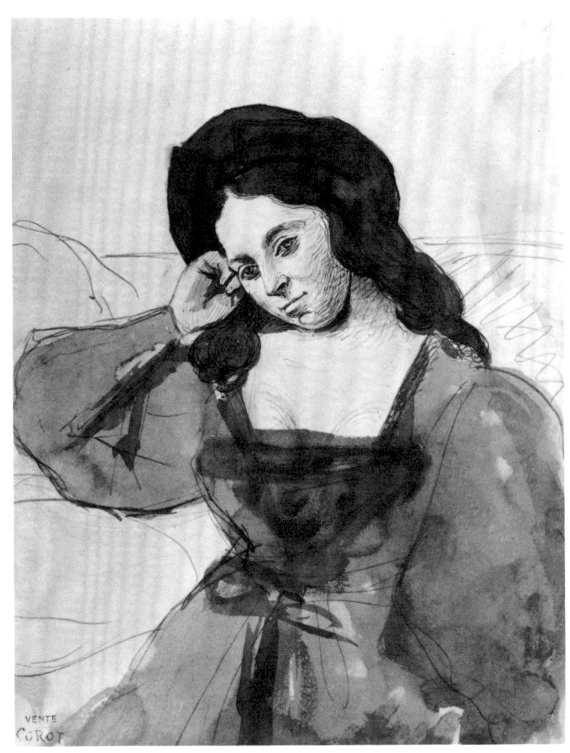

which was originally the name of the winding road between Olevano and Bellegra (formerly "Civitella"), was also the name of the very old oak forest along this road (H. Kühne, P. Merisio, *Latium,* Olten, Freiburg i.B., 1974, pp. 175, 176).

This forest, as well as the village of Olevano and its surroundings, was discovered in 1804 by the German painter Joseph Anton Koch and held a great fascination for French and particularly German artists during the entire nineteenth century (A. Jullien and R. Jullien, "Corot dans les Montagnes de la Sabine," *Gazette des Beaux-Arts,* 1984, pp. 179ff.). Corot also made an oil study after nature from approximately the same location; that study is now in Fort Worth, Texas (Jullien and Jullien, "Corot dans les Montagnes da la Sabine," p. 186, ill. 7a). Both this sketch and the drawing bear the stamp of the Corot auction (this is also true of the drawing described in cat. no. 19), which shows that these works remained in Corot's possession throughout his life.

A.M.

21

Wooded Landscape with Rocks

MB 1976/T16
Pencil; 338 × 413 mm
Provenance: Vitale Bloch bequest, 1976
Literature: Rotterdam 1978, cat. no. 9 (ill.)

This drawing may represent a path through the woods, extending from the right side of the sheet, past a rocky ledge with oak trees, downward to the left. The drawing was at first dated 1825/28 and thus would have been done during Corot's first sojourn in Italy (Robaut no. 2533). But the drawing is stylistically very similar to one that Corot inscribed *Fontainebleau Route d'Orléans,* which is generally dated 1835. During part of that year Corot stayed in the village of Chailly-sur-Bière, to the north of Barbizon in the forest of Fontainebleau.

The composition and the arrangement of the woods and sandstone crags in the Rotterdam drawing show a great similarity to those in two small paintings by Corot that represent the rocks and oaks of the Bas-Bréau, according to Robaut (Robaut nos. 277, 278; sale cat., New York, 12 October 1979, ill. 222). The Bas Bréau is located near Chailly on the road to Fontainebleau. The landscape sketch in Rotterdam may have been drawn on the same spot.

A.M.

22

Head and Torso of a Woman, Leaning on Her Right Arm

F II 103
Pen and brush in gray ink over black chalk; 290 × 229 mm
Provenance: F. Koenigs; given by D. G. van Beuningen to the Museum Boymans Foundation, 1940
Literature: Rotterdam 1968, cat. no. 41 (ill.); Keller 1980, p. 12, text ill. 4

Corot executed this pen and brush portrait of a young woman in the same loose style of drawing seen in the following sheet (cat. no. 23). The identity of the woman who sat for this portrait is not known, but the draughtsmanship suggests a date between 1865 and 1870. In this same period Corot created a small number of paintings representing women in more or less exotic garb, and in poses comparable to that of the young woman in this drawing. Some of these paintings were given the title "Bohémienne rêveuse" by Robaut (Robaut nos. 1422, 1424). The costume and the flowing hair of the woman in the Rotterdam drawing might suggest that this drawing also represents a "Bohémienne."

A.M.

Landscape with Trees on the Water

F II 159
Pen and brown ink on vergé paper; laid down; 292 × 449 mm
Signed with pen and brown ink: *Corot*
Provenance: F. Koenigs; given by D. G. van Beuningen to the Museum Boymans Foundation, 1940
Literature: Rotterdam 1968, cat. no. 42 (ill.); exhib. cat., Bremen 1977/78, no. 29, ill. no. 37

Toward the far right in this drawing a woman is gathering wood near some pollard willows on the bank of a lake. To the left, in the distance, a small boat is being rowed across the lake. At the far side of the lake the roofs of some houses can be barely discerned.

In all probability, this drawing shows a view of one of the two lakes or ponds near Ville-d'Avray, to the southeast of Paris near the Parc de St. Cloud. Corot's parents had owned an estate near Ville-d'Avray since 1817, and the artist often stayed there. This house and its surroundings appear regularly in Corot's work.

The sketch must have been executed in the years around 1870, and it differs considerably in its draughtsmanship from the three landscape drawings described in previous entries (cat. nos. 19, 20, and 21). Whereas the earlier sheets are characterized by precise line and great attention to detail, this drawing gives an impression of the atmosphere of the countryside by means of loose, sketchy lines. The composition of the drawing is clearly related to a number of Corot's paintings from the same time (Robaut nos. 1488, 1505, 2062).

A.M.

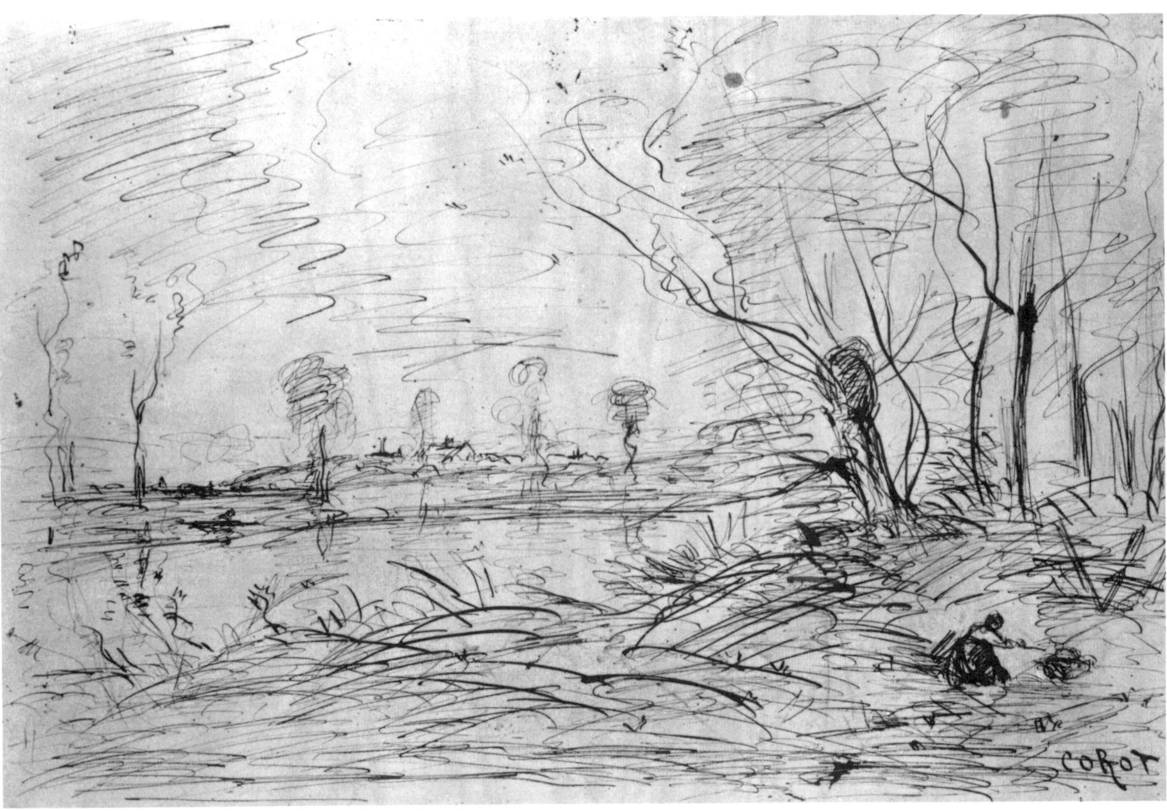

23   *Landscape with Trees on the Water*

GUSTAVE COURBET
Ornans 1819–La Tour de Peilz, Vevey 1877

24
Portrait of a Man, Three-Quarters to the Right

F II 14
Charcoal on yellowish paper; 156 × 112 mm
Signed with black chalk: *G. Courbet*
Provenance: F. Koenigs; given by D. G. van Beuningen to the Museum Boymans Foundation, 1940
Literature: Rotterdam 1968, cat. no. 45 (ill.); P. ten Doesschate-Chu, "Courbet's Last Drawing?" *Master Drawings,* XII, 1974,
   p. 391; Fernier 1978, II, dessins, no. 64 (ill.); Keller 1980, text ill. 12, p. 31; *Dessins Destins,* exhib. cat., Musée natale
   Gustave Courbet, Ornans 1982, no. 43 (ill.)

This portrait is believed to represent Amand Gautier, a painter and graphic artist whom Courbet had met at the Brasserie Andler in Paris. Both were later involved with the Paris Commune and became members of the Fédération des Artistes in April 1871 (Weisberg 1980, p. 291 and cat. no. 34 [ill.]). Gautier was the only artist whose work was hung in Courbet's studio (T. J. Clark, *Image of the People: Gustave Courbet and the 1848 Revolution,* London 1973, p. 39).

   The man in the Rotterdam drawing resembles the man in Courbet's painted *Portrait of Amand Gautier* in Lille from 1867 (Fernier 1969, ill. 72). But the subject in the painting seems younger and fuller in the face, suggesting that Courbet made this drawing of Gautier while both were imprisoned after the bloody demise of the Paris Commune in 1871 (for Courbet's involvement with the Commune, see exhib. cat., Baden Baden/Zürich 1984, pp. 329–330). Courbet also made a self-portrait during this imprisonment. He eventually took refuge in Switzerland in 1873 (exhib. cat., Hamburg 1978, ill. e and f, p. 53), but until this time, Gautier faithfully visited Courbet in prison (Weisberg 1980, p. 291).
J.P.

25
A Clearing in a Forest

F II 187
Black, blue, green, reddish brown, and white chalk on gray paper; 190 × 305 mm
Signed with black chalk: *G. Courbet*
Provenance: F. Koenigs; given by D. G. van Beuningen to the Museum Boymans Foundation, 1940
Literature: Rotterdam 1968, cat. no. 46 (ill.); exhib. cat., Bremen 1977, no. 432; Fernier 1978, II, dessins, no. 11 (ill.); exhib.
   cat., Hamburg 1978, no. 320 (ill.)

A forest is depicted on this sheet with a large tree in the right front and a clearing in the middle distance. Color has been subtly applied to the black chalk in some areas: green to the foliage, reddish brown to the tree trunks. The blue chalk in the center foreground may represent water or the reflection of light from the clearing.

   Knowledge of Gustave Courbet's production as a draughtsman was very limited until a few years ago; only thirty drawings and three sketchbooks were known. Then in 1984 these numbers were augmented dramatically by the publication of over 200 travel sketches (exhib. cat., Baden Baden/Zürich 1984). These drawings have not enabled us to identify the exact location represented in the Rotterdam drawing. The scenery is reminiscent of the German countryside near Frankfurt am Main, where the artist spent some time in 1858 (exhib. cat., Baden Baden/Zürich 1984, pp. 327–328), but similar landscapes appear throughout Courbet's oeuvre. Compare the paintings *La Forêt en Automne* from 1841 in Paris, *Cerf et Biche sous Bois* from 1859 in London, and *Etude de Châtaigniers* from 1875, in an auction in London in 1959 (Fernier 1978, nos. 19, 243, 995 [ill.]). Indeed, the drawing might represent an idealized landscape rather than an actual forest.
J.P.

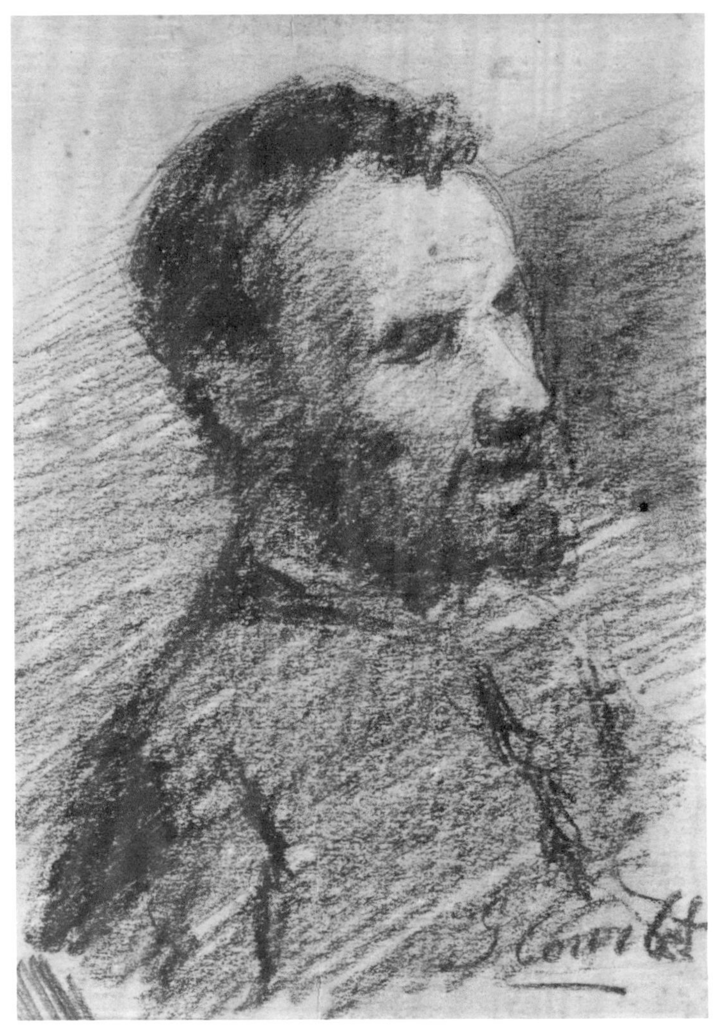

24   *Portrait of a Man, Three-Quarters to the Right*

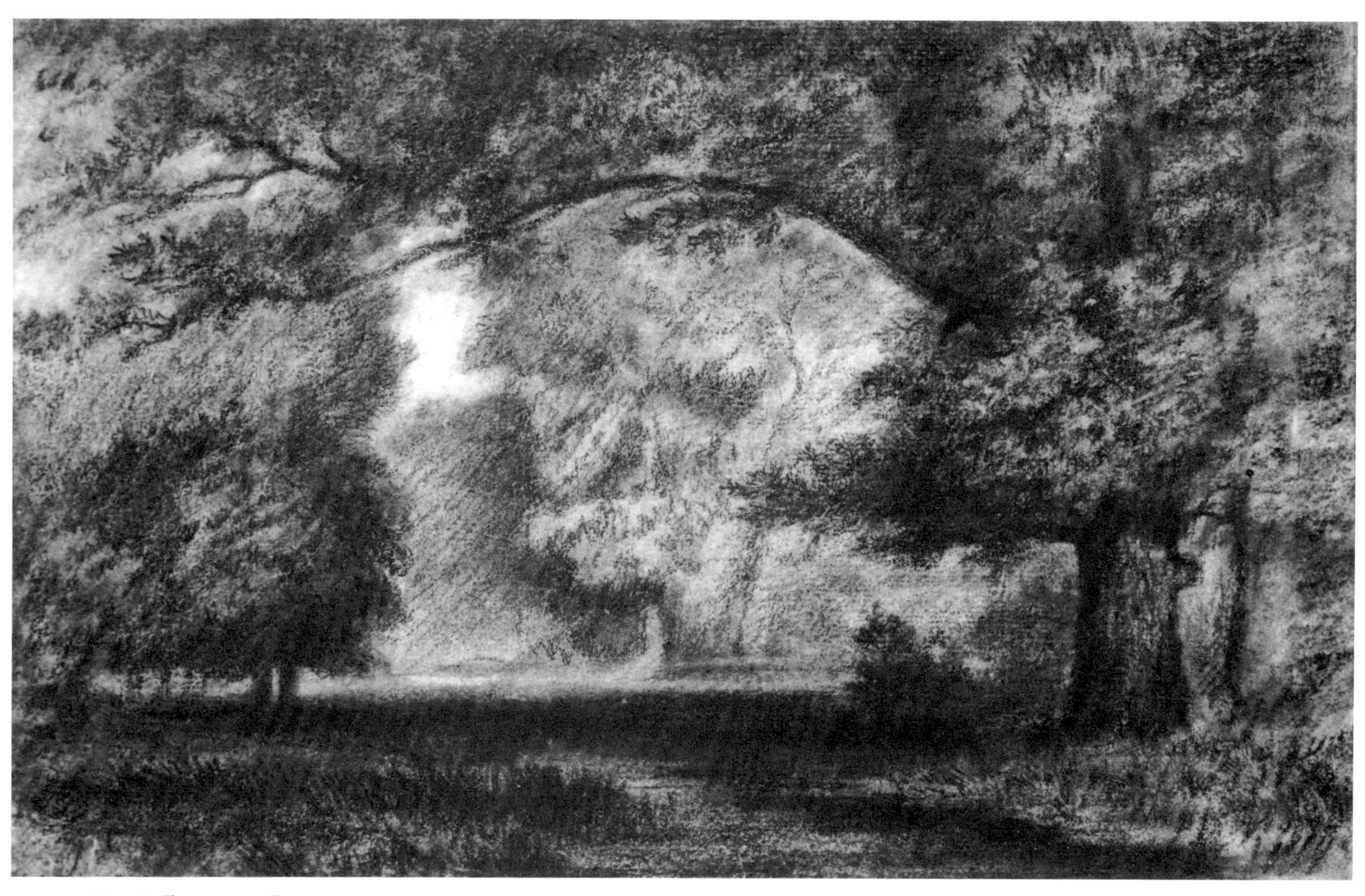

25   *A Clearing in a Forest*

CHARLES DAUBIGNY
Paris 1817–1878

26
Landscape with a Flock of Sheep

F II 94
Red chalk on thin, cream-colored paper; laid down; 183 × 283 mm
Signed with black chalk: *Daubigny*
Provenance: F. Koenigs; given by D. G. van Beuningen to the Museum Boymans Foundation, 1940
Literature: Rotterdam 1968, cat. no. 47 (ill.)

A flock of sheep is shown grazing in the foreground of this drawing, while a dog stands guard on a low rise in the background. Several bare trees and bushes are sketched to the left.

This sheet is probably a preparatory study for the etching *Le Guet du Chien,* which is dated around 1857 (Delteil 1921, no. 90 [ill.]). The image is reversed in the etching, but with a few watch dogs added, with slight differences in the composition of the flock, and with no shrubbery in the background.

Daubigny first worked as a graphic artist, illustrating song collections (Delteil 1921, nos. 26–42 [ill.]). His earliest prints reveal an idealized treatment of his subjects, but when he began to do more painting, his style became more naturalistic. In the Rotterdam drawing the lines in the sky probably indicate rain; possibly the hatchings in the sky of the print also represent severe weather. See also the etching *L'Ondée,* which is dated around 1831 (Delteil 1921, no. 85 [ill.]).

J.P.

27
Landscape with a River

F II 185
Black chalk and pastel on gray paper; laid down; 330 × 490 mm
Signed with black chalk: *Daubigny*
Provenance: F. Koenigs; given by D. G. van Beuningen to the Museum Boymans Foundation, 1940
Literature: Rotterdam 1968, cat. no. 48 (ill.); exhib. cat., Bremen 1977, no. 43, ill. 71

Just off-center in this drawing a small boat with two figures floats along the irregular bank of a river. A tree on the bank to the left and the row of trees in the background are reflected on the smooth surface of the water.

In 1857 Daubigny purchased a boat that he turned into a studio and named "Le Botin"; he made trips along several rivers in France in this boat, particularly the Oise, and he settled in Auvers-sur-Oise in 1865 (for a photograph of "Le Botin," see M. Fidell-Beaufort and J. Bailly-Herzburg, *Daubigny,* Paris 1975, ill. p. 56). In 1862 Daubigny published a series of etchings called *Le Voyage en Bâteau,* in which he depicted events aboard "Le Botin" (Delteil 1921, nos. 99–115 [ill.]).

The landscape in the Rotterdam drawing is related to that in paintings that originated along the banks of the Oise (Hellebranth 1976, nos. 221–435 [ill.]). Compare, for instance, the paintings *Sur l'Oise* from 1865 in Lisbon and *Les Bords de l'Oise, Ile de Vaux,* from 1875 at Obbach (Hellebranth 1976, nos. 267, 286, and 237 [ill.]). Because Daubigny's views along the Oise were created over many years, however, it is difficult to assign a date to the Rotterdam drawing.

J.P.

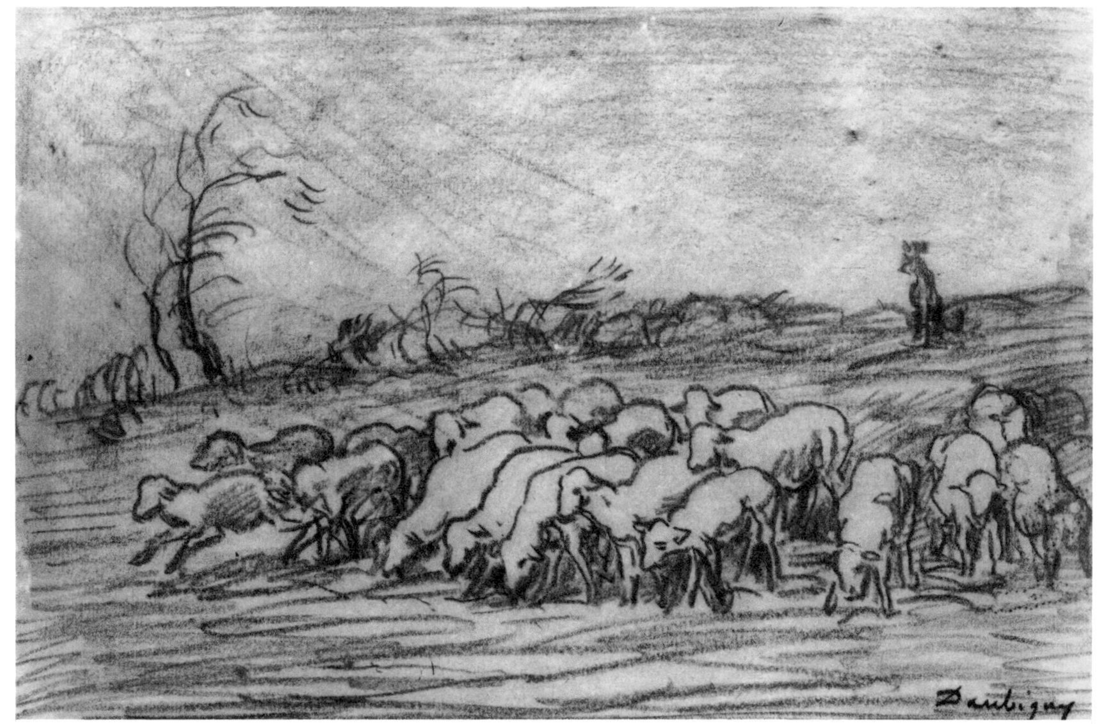

26   *Landscape with a Flock of Sheep*

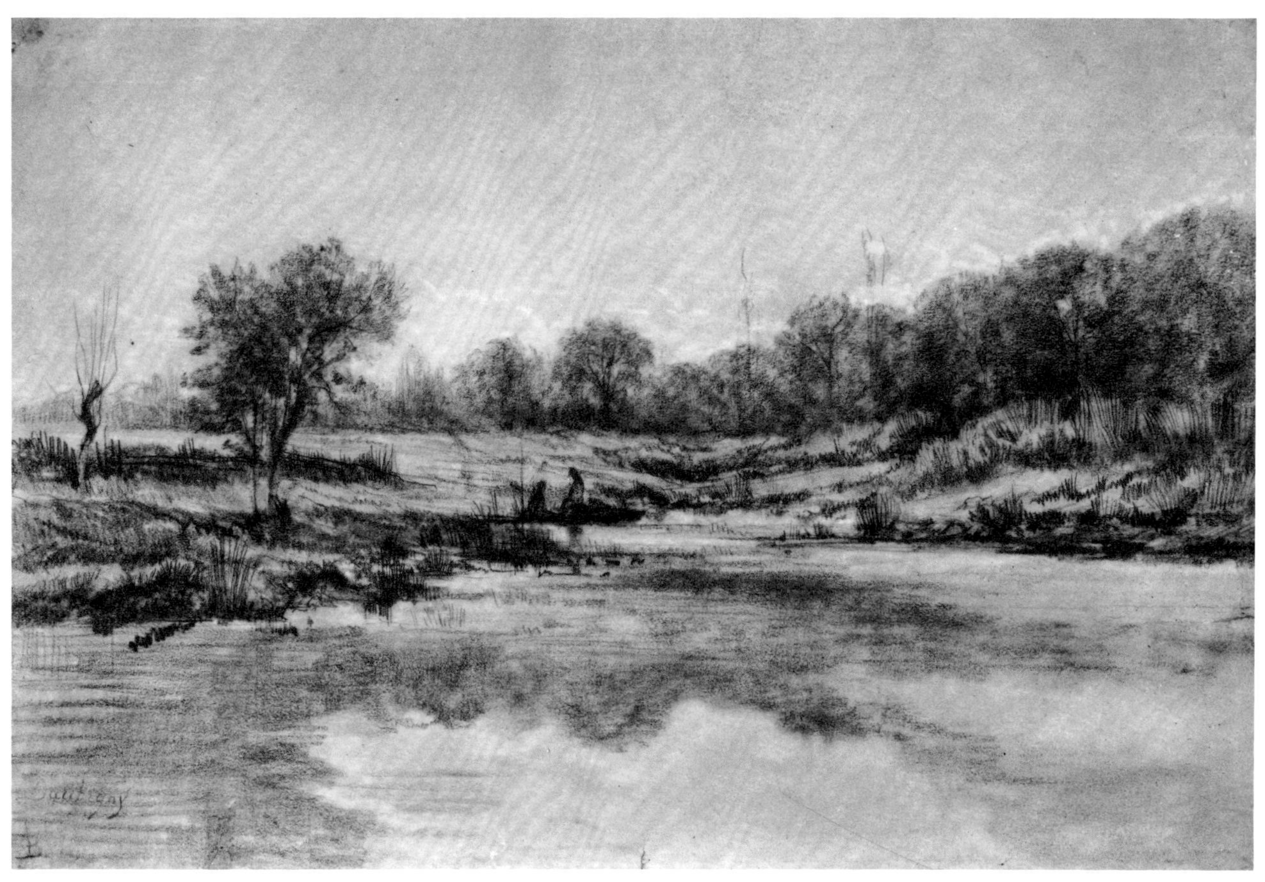

27   *Landscape with a River*

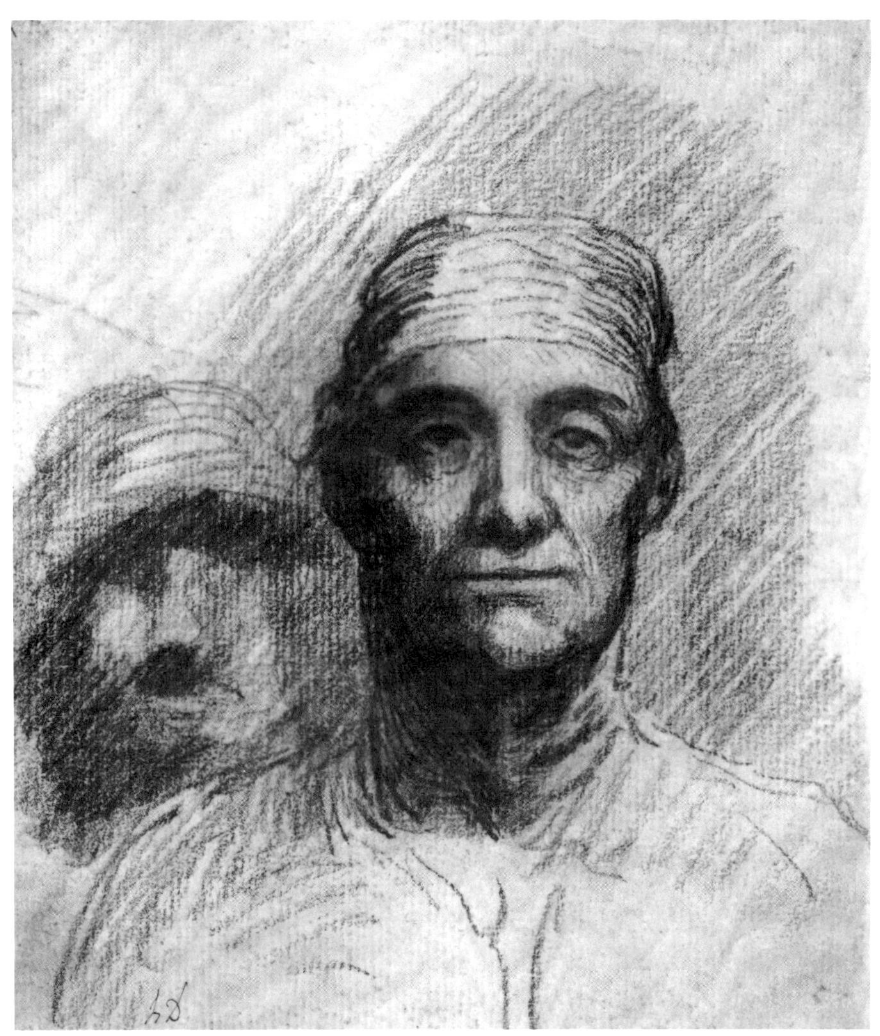

28   Studies of the Heads of Two Men

Verso

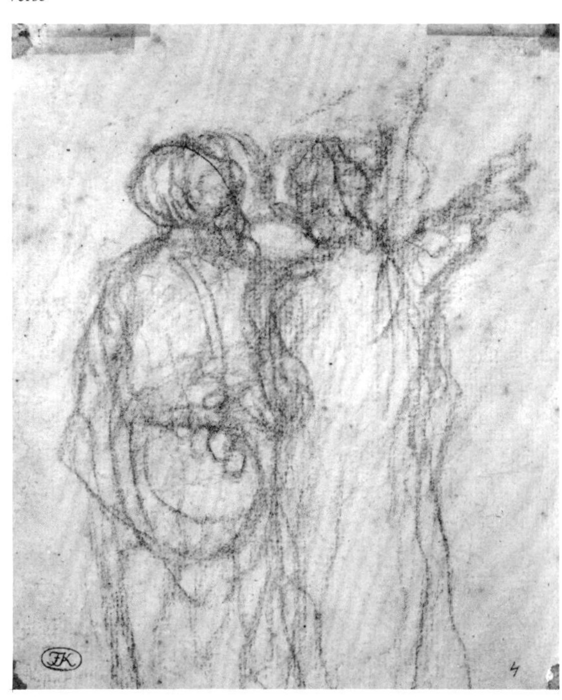

HONORÉ DAUMIER
Marseilles 1808–Valmondois 1879

28
Studies of the Heads of Two Men

> F II 172
> Black chalk on vergé paper; 167 × 150 mm
> Verso in charcoal: Two standing figures
> Signed with pen and black ink: *hD*
> *Provenance:* F. Koenigs; given D. G. van Beuningen to the Museum Boymans Foundation, 1940
> *Literature:* Rotterdam 1968, cat. no. 65 (ill.); Maison 1968, II, no. 120, pl. 21 (recto), no. 179, pl. 37 (verso)

This drawing is notable in Daumier's oeuvre because especially in the head on the right the aspects of a caricature are completely lacking. Indeed, this man is represented so realistically that it could be a portrait drawn from life. The man's features resemble those of the central judge in a Chicago watercolor (H. Joachim, *The Helen Regenstein Collection of European Drawings,* The Art Institute of Chicago, Chicago 1974, no. 68 [ill.]); perhaps Daumier used this study in black chalk as a preparatory sketch for the watercolor. According to Bruce Laughton, this drawing must have been executed around 1848 or earlier (letter, October 1985).

A.M.

29
The Collector

> F II 31
> Black chalk, pen and black ink, charcoal, brown coal, and some gray ink wash on vergé paper; 542 × 418 mm
>   (image: 465 × 340 mm)
> Signed and inscribed with pen in black ink: *h. Daumier à Cléophas*
> *Provenance:* F. Koenigs; given by D. G. van Beuningen to the Museum Boymans Foundation, 1940
> *Literature:* Rotterdam 1968, cat. no. 51 (ill.); Maison 1968, II, no. 369, pl. 117; *Dessins français du Metropolitan Museum of Art, New York,* exhib. cat., Musée du Louvre, Paris 1973/74, under no. 20 (ill.)

A collector is shown here sitting in an armchair, absorbed in viewing a small copy of the famous classical statue of the Venus de Milo in the Louvre that stands on the table to his side. A portfolio with prints or drawings leans against his chair. On the wall behind him the indistinct outlines of several paintings are visible.

    This drawing is the preparatory sketch for the highly finished watercolor in the Metropolitan Museum, New York. The watercolor was in all probability meant to be sold (Maison 1968, II, no. 370, pl. 118), but Daumier presented the Rotterdam drawing to his friend Vincent-Alfred Baron, nicknamed "Cléophas," who was a painter, sculptor, and actor. J. Adhémar maintains that the New York watercolor could be dated 1865 and that Baron may have been the model for the collector (J. Adhémar, *Daumier: Zeichnungen und Aquarelle,* Basel 1954, no. 92). But Baron was only forty-five years old in 1865, and the seated figure seems to be considerably older in both the drawing and the watercolor. Daumier made several detail studies for the total composition: of the seated man, for instance (Maison 1968, II, nos. 113, 114, pl. 20), and of the Venus de Milo (Maison 1968, II, no. 806, pl. 313).

A.M.

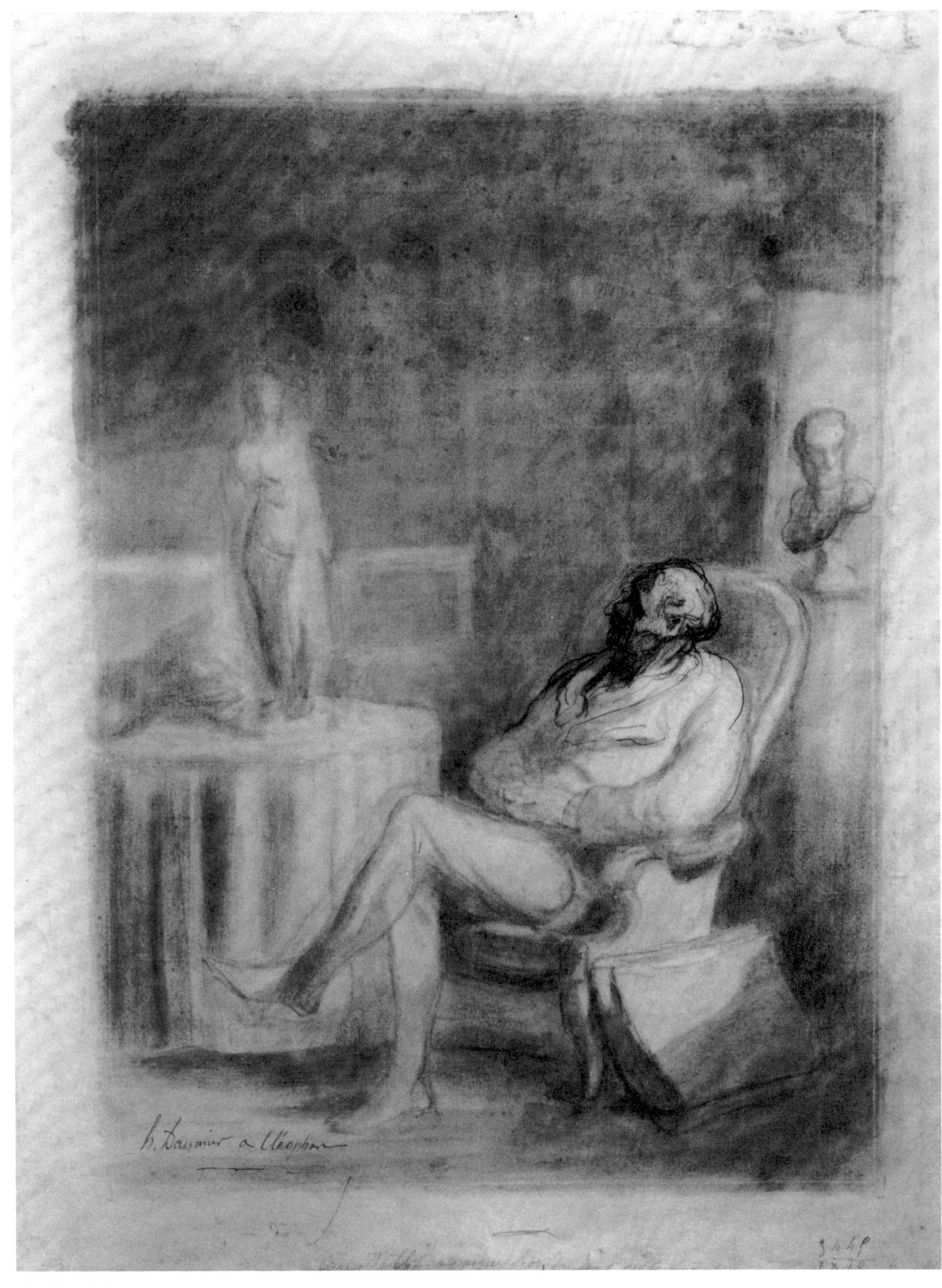

29 *The Collector*

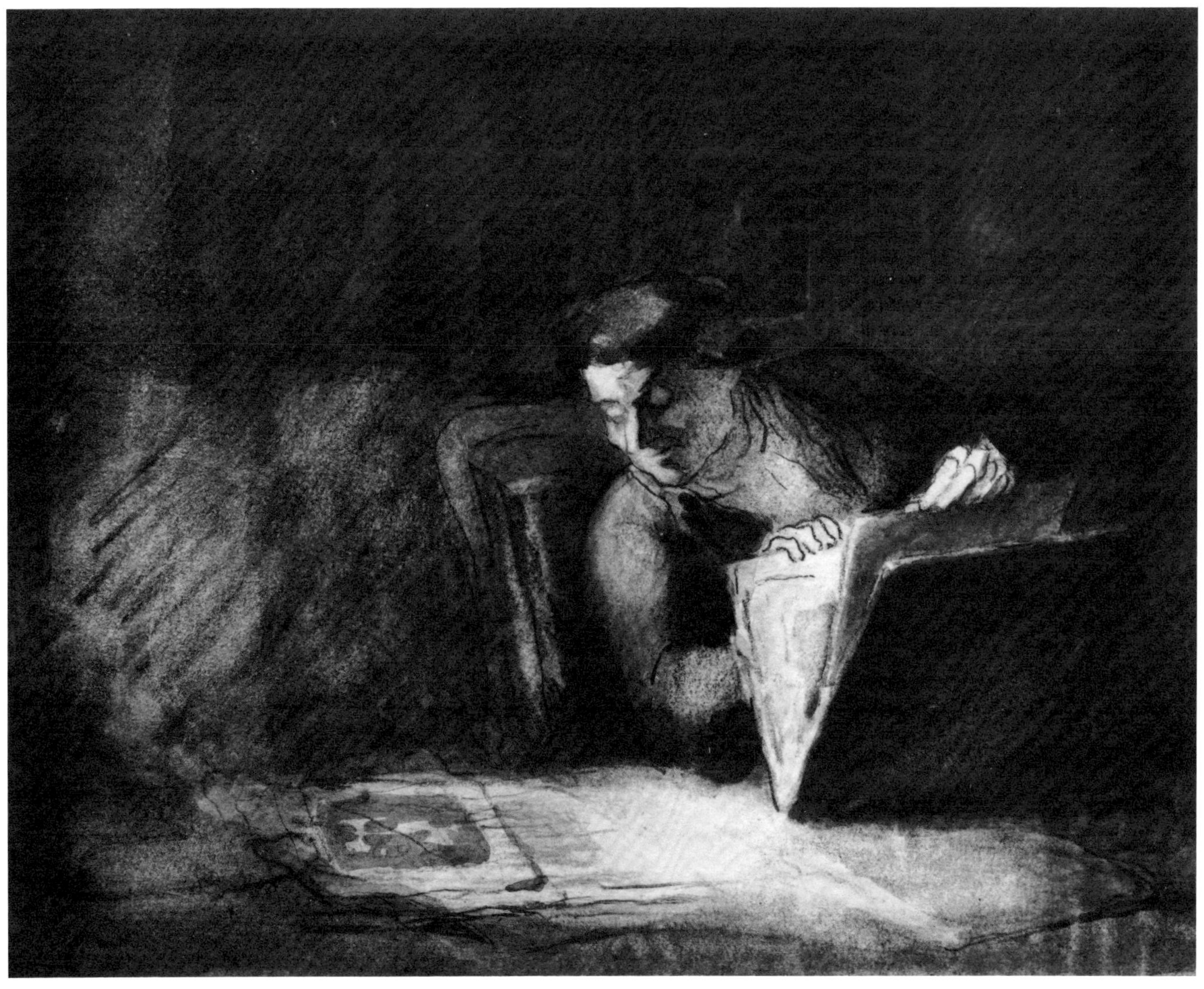

30   The Print Collector

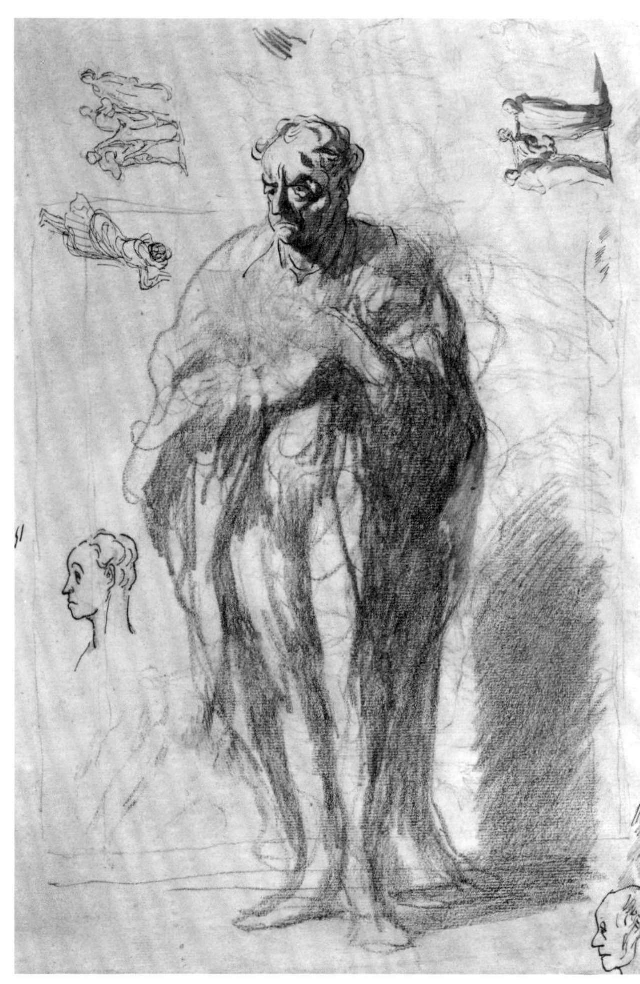

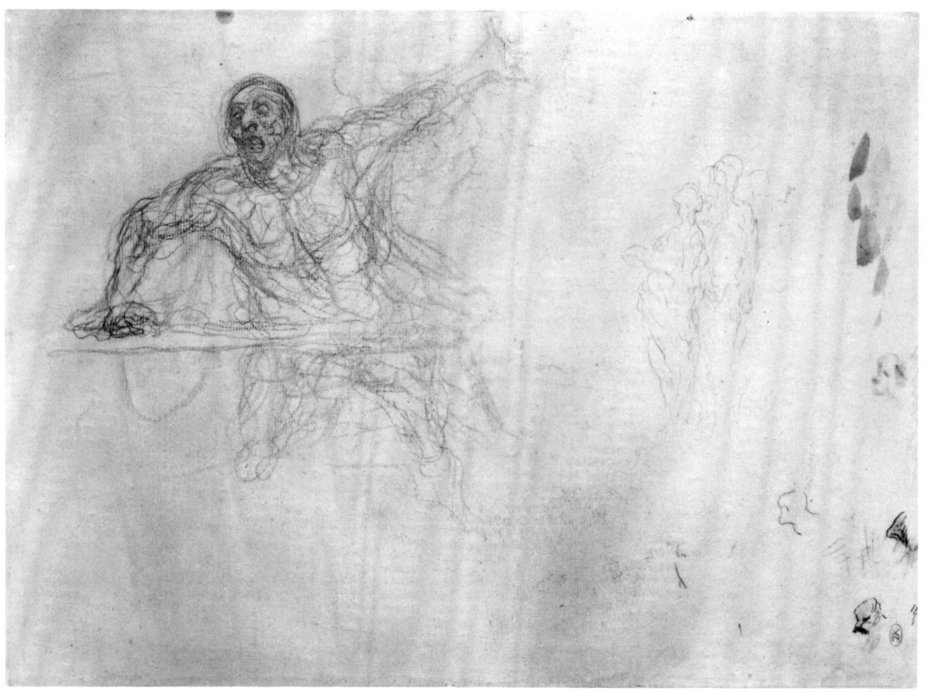

Verso

F II 12
Black chalk, pen, and watercolor; laid down; 189 × 237 mm
Signed with black chalk: *h.D*
Provenance: F. Koenigs; given by D. G. van Beuningen to the Museum Boymans Foundation, 1940
Literature: Rotterdam 1968, cat. no. 49 (ill.); Maison 1968, II, no. 374, pl. 120

In this drawing a man is seated at a table in a fairly dark room with some paintings on the wall behind him. In front of him is an open portfolio with prints on a stand, whose right support is only barely discernible. The man takes a sheet from the portfolio, while beside him on the table lie more separate sheets and a book.

The same scene is represented in a watercolor in Winterthur, except that an older man is represented in full face to the left of the man with the portfolio. This second man leans forward on the table and attentively examines the prints put in front of him (Maison 1968, II, no. 376, pl. 121). In the Rotterdam drawing this second figure has been erased by the artist, but in looking carefully, one can still make out the contours of the figure, particularly on the right side. After erasing this figure, Daumier enlarged the back of the chair with a few brush strokes.

A third sheet is also related to this scene; it is a so-called semi-tracing (location unknown, Maison 1968, II, no. 375, pl. 120), in which the man with the portfolio has been traced from the same figure in the Rotterdam drawing; the man beside him was drawn by the artist in black chalk in a completely different attitude, namely, in profile.

The theme of *amateurs d'estampes* or *amateurs de tableaux* (connoisseurs of prints or paintings) often occurs in Daumier's oeuvre, both in his drawings and in his paintings (Maison 1968, I, pls. 88–97).
A.M.

31
Henry Monnier, Acting, and Other Studies

F II 61
Verso: Study of a bawler
Black chalk, pen and black ink, some gray wash on vergé paper; 420 × 303 mm
Provenance: F. Koenigs; given by D. G. van Beuningen to the Museum Boymans Foundation, 1940
Literature: Rotterdam 1968, cat. no. 56 (ill.); Maison 1968, II, no. 448, pl. 153 (recto), no. 509, pl. 175 (verso); M. Sérullaz
    and A. Sérullaz, *l'Ottocento francese,* Milan 1970, no. 14 (ill.); Paula Hayes Harper, *Daumier's Clowns,* New York and London
    1981, p. 166, ill. 54 (verso)

Daumier drew the monumental figure of actor Henry Monnier over another composition—whose frame was defined by a line in black chalk—after rotating the sheet a quarter-turn. Monnier, a friend of Daumier's, was very well known not only as an actor but also as a lithographer, a creator of caricature drawings, and a writer (Champfleury, *Henry Monnier: Sa Vie, Son Oeuvre,* Paris 1889).

According to Adhémar, Monnier is represented here in the role of Joseph Prudhomme, a middle class fellow, the type of the bourgeois displaying self-importance, created by Monnier himself (Adhémar, *Daumier: Zeichnungen und Aquarelle,* Basel 1954, no. 28 [ill.]). From the 1830s to the 1860s Prudhomme appeared in several so-called *Scènes Populaires* written by Monnier in which the bourgeoisie was ridiculed. It is doubtful, to say the least, whether Monnier is indeed represented here in the role of Prudhomme; Monnier's own drawings of Prudhomme from 1860 show a type quite different from the dramatic figure in the Rotterdam drawing (Champfleury, *Henry Monnier,* p. 127 [ill.]; and exhib. cat., *French Drawings: Post Neo-Classicism,* P. Colnaghi and D. Colnaghi, London 1975, nos. 124, 125 [ill.]).

Daumier drew a few other small studies on the Rotterdam sheet, which possibly date from around 1860; among these are, on top to the right, two physicians with a skeleton, an illustration of La

Fontaine's fable entitled *Les Médecins*. This fable tells how two physicians at a patient's bedside cannot agree about the treatment, whereupon the patient dies. One doctor says he was right because the man is dead, while the other contends that if only they had believed him, the patient would still be alive (*Fables de La Fontaine,* ed. D. Jouaust, Paris, V, 12).

The street-bawler on the verso is a preparatory study for the same figure in the painting *Hercule de foire* (wrestler at the fair) in the Phillips Collection, Washington, D.C. (Maison 1968, I, no. 189, ill. 139).
A.M.

32
A Pleading Lawyer

F II 13
Verso: Study of two women
Black chalk, pen and ink, and watercolor; 204 × 227 mm
Signed with black chalk: *h.D.*
Provenance: F. Koenigs; given by D. G. van Beuningen to the Museum Boymans Foundation, 1940
Literature: Rotterdam 1968, cat. no. 50 (ill.); Maison 1968, II, no. 661, pl. 252 (recto), no. 215, pl. 46 (verso); Passeron 1979, p. 238, ill. 176

With one hand on the table in front of him, the lawyer in this drawing makes a sweeping and dramatic gesture backward, presumably toward his client. On the table are his papers and his cap. This same lawyer appears in the same pose in three other drawings by Daumier (Maison 1968, II, nos. 662, 663, 664), but the four representations differ in details. For instance, in the drawing in the Phillips Collection, Washington, D.C., the lawyer's client is defined clearly, whereas in the Rotterdam drawing he is sketched only vaguely in black chalk (Maison 1968, II, no. 664).

Laughton believes that the verso of the exhibited drawing is a compositional try-out for the design of the oil painting *Nymphs Pursued by Satyrs* (Maison 1968, I, no. 32) in the Museum of Fine Arts, Montreal (Laughton, letter, October 1985). Daumier exhibited this painting at the Salon in the winter of 1850/51. The rubbed and stained character of the verso of the Rotterdam drawing suggests that the sheet must have been lying around in Daumier's studio for years before he used it again to sketch the lawyer on what is now deemed the recto.
A.M.

33
A Pleading Lawyer Addressing a Witness

F II 170
Black chalk, pen and gray ink, gray wash on vergé paper; 182 × 277
Signed with pen in black ink: *h.D.*
Provenance: F. Koenigs; given by D. G. van Beuningen to the Museum Boymans Foundation, 1940
Literature: Rotterdam 1968, cat. no. 63 (ill.); Maison 1968, II, no. 647, pl. 244; *Honoré Daumier,* exhib. cat., Villa Schneider, Ingelheim am Rhein 1971, no. 46, ill. 6; Passeron 1979, p. 235, ill. 173

Among Daumier's many drawings and watercolors of pleading lawyers, this is one of the most forceful. The lawyer, in concluding his plea, presents the decisive argument with a piercing and accusative gesture. Accordingly, the traditional title of this drawing is *L'Argument décisif.* There is a drawing with the same subject in a private collection in Paris (Maison 1968, II, no. 646, pl. 244).
A.M.

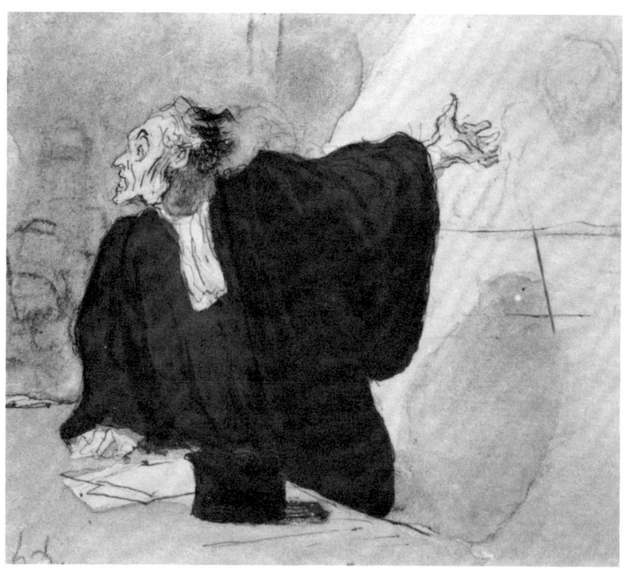

32   *A Pleading Lawyer (see also color plate 2)*

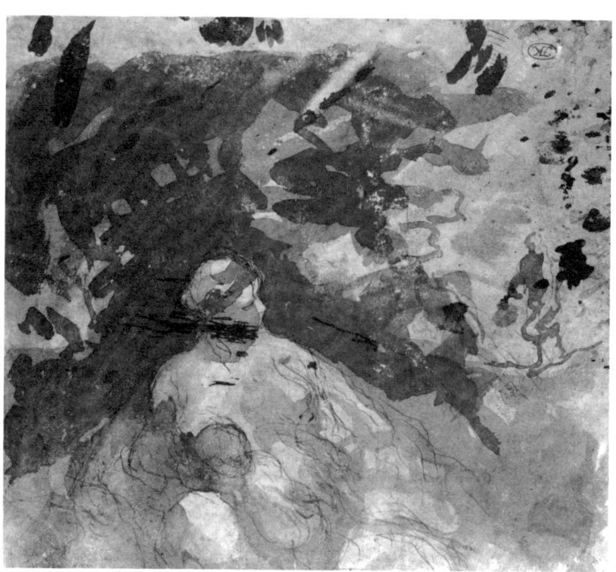

Verso

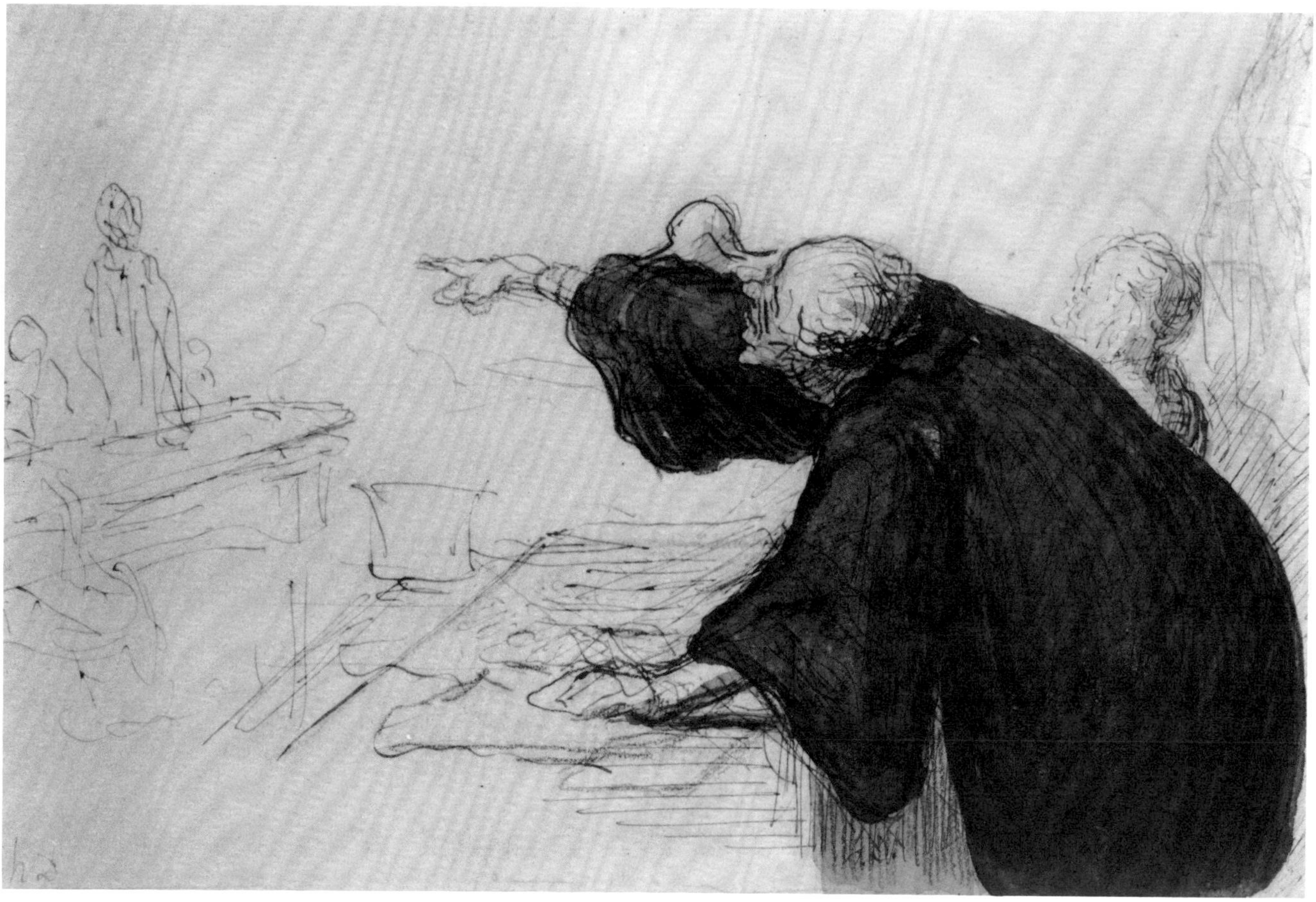

33   *A Pleading Lawyer Addressing a Witness*

F II 70
Black chalk, pen and brush with gray and black ink on vergé paper; 207 × 139 mm
Signed with pen and black ink: *hD.*
Provenance: F. Koenigs; given by D. G. van Beuningen to the Museum Boymans Foundation, 1940
Literature: Rotterdam 1968, cat. no. 57 (ill.); Maison 1968, II, no. 567, pl. 203

Daumier's bitter and sarcastic criticism of the social and political structures of his day, expressed in thousands of lithographs—which on several occasions brought him into conflict with the authorities —is also evident in his paintings and drawings. The judicial power was a principal target for Daumier's mockery: judges, lawyers, attorneys-general, as well as, of course, the witnesses and the accused.

No fewer than 130 drawings and watercolors and eighteen paintings on this subject exist (Maison 1968, II, nos. 557–687, I, pls. 108–119). From 1845 until the end of 1848, there appeared in the satirical periodical *Le Charivari* (French for "disorder") a series of thirty-nine lithographs by Daumier, entitled "Gens de Justice," in which he mocked all aspects of the judicial profession (Delteil 1923, nos. 1337–1377). Daumier also devoted himself to this theme during the 1860s, as evidenced by several lithographs published in *Le Charivari, Le Journal Amusant,* and *Le Petit Journal au Rire* (Delteil 1928, nos. 3278, 3284, 3288, and 3408–3410). In our opinion, the drawings discussed in this and in the two preceding entries (cat. nos. 32–34) also belong to those years, for the style of drawing is more closely related to that of the last-mentioned lithographs than to, for instance, that of the series from 1845/48.
A.M.

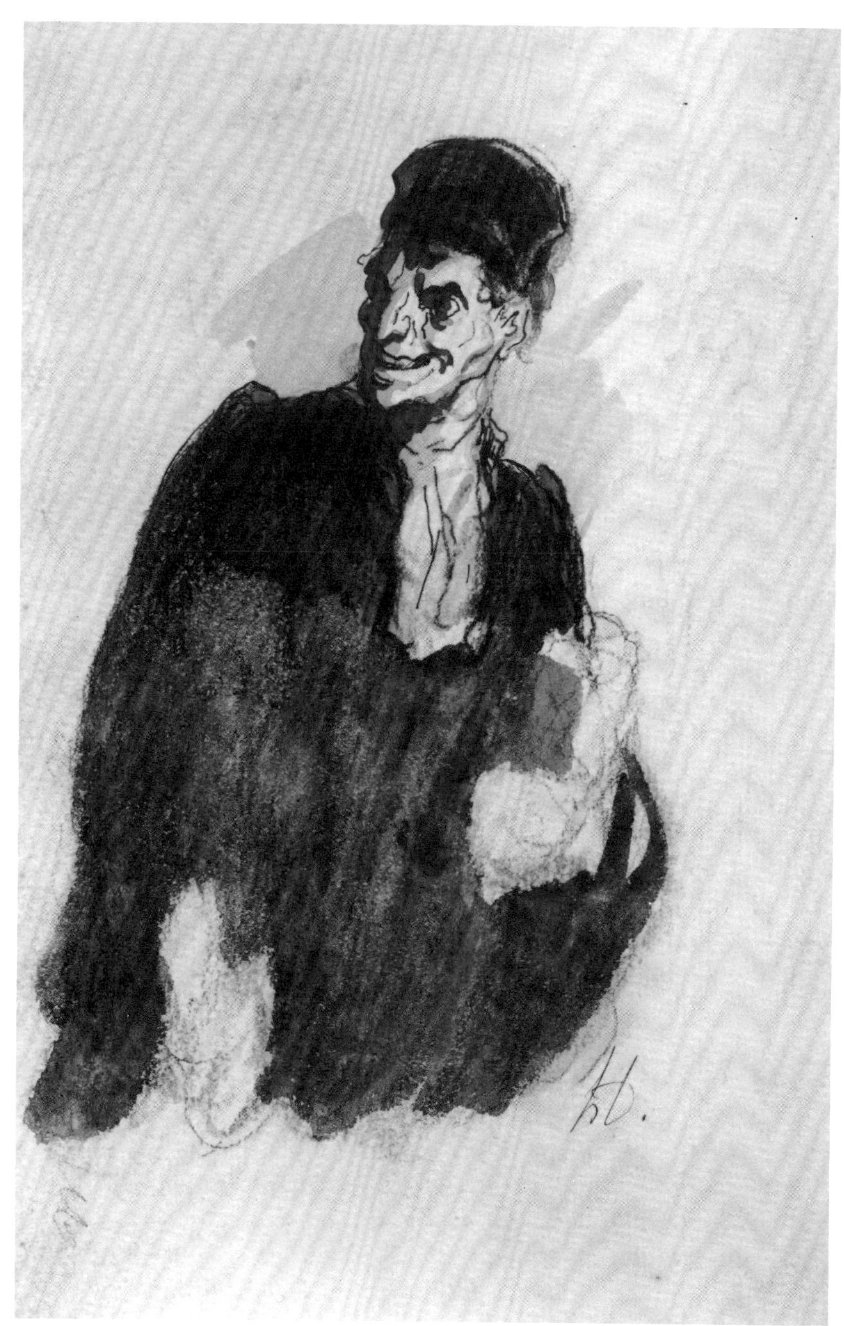

34 A Lawyer

EDGAR DEGAS
Paris 1834–1917

35
Standing Horse, to the Right

F II 125
Black chalk on vergé paper; 242 × 301 mm
Provenance: F. Koenigs; given by D. G. van Beuningen to the Museum Boymans Foundation, 1940
Literature: Rotterdam 1968, no. 78 (ill.); Adriani 1984, no. 142 (ill.); Guillaud 1984, no. 21 bis, ill. 105

The horse in this drawing, which stands facing to the right, occupies almost the full width of the sheet, and the hooves of its right front and right hind legs touch the bottom edge of the paper. Originally the horse was drawn somewhat more to the right; traces of this are still visible at the head, the neck, and the legs. The horse is drawn in fairly robust contour lines, shaded with hatchings applied in a regular manner. The verso contains a chalk study of the same horse in light sketchy lines (Rotterdam 1968, cat. no. 78, verso [ill.]).

A great similarity exists between the horse in this drawing and a bronze horse that was poured after Degas's death by A. A. Hébrard using a wax model (J. Rewald, *E. Degas: Works in Sculpture,* New York 1944, no. III, ill. 37). The last of a series of twenty-two casts of this bronze is in the Museum Boymans-van Beuningen on extended loan (D. Hannema, *Beschrijvende catalogus van de schilderijen uit de kunstverzameling Stichting Willem van der Vorm,* Rotterdam 1962, no. 18).

The drawing and the wax model for the bronze are dated early, because the horse is standing still; in later work Degas shows more interest in the horse's movements.

The drawing also bears strong resemblance to another drawing of a horse that was sold in an auction in London in 1977 (auction cat., Sotheby's, London, 7 December 1977, no. 105 [ill.]).

J.P.

36
Rider on Horseback

F II 124
Black chalk on thin, white paper; 302 × 223 mm
Provenance: F. Koenigs; given by D. G. van Beuningen to the Museum Boymans Foundation, 1940
Literature: Rotterdam 1968, cat. no. 77 (ill.); Adriani 1984, no. 49 (ill.)

The horse in this drawing, which faces toward the right, is represented in greater detail than the rider. Usually the drawing is dated around 1861/63, again on the basis of the horse's stationary pose (see cat. no. 35). In later years Degas became more interested in showing horses in motion, influenced in part by the movement photographs by Eadweard Muybridge (*Eadweard Muybridge,* exhib. cat., Württembergischer Kunstverein, Stuttgart 1976). Around 1860 Degas began to draw countless studies of horses, with and without rider, to familiarize himself with the movements and attitudes of the subject.

A rider dressed in the manner shown here is called a "gentleman rider" in English as well as in French. Other studies by Degas of this kind of rider exist, but the identity of the man represented here is problematic (Brettell/McCullagh 1984, nos. 19, 20 [ill.]; and Rotterdam 1978, cat. no. 12 [ill.]). It is sometimes thought that Edouard Manet was the model for the rider, possibly because this drawing was sold in the fourth auction of Degas's studio together with a portrait drawing of Manet (Paris, 2 July 1919). But a comparison of the two subjects, both now in the Museum Boymans-van Beuningen, does not confirm this supposition (Rotterdam 1968, cat. no. 76 [ill.]).

J.P.

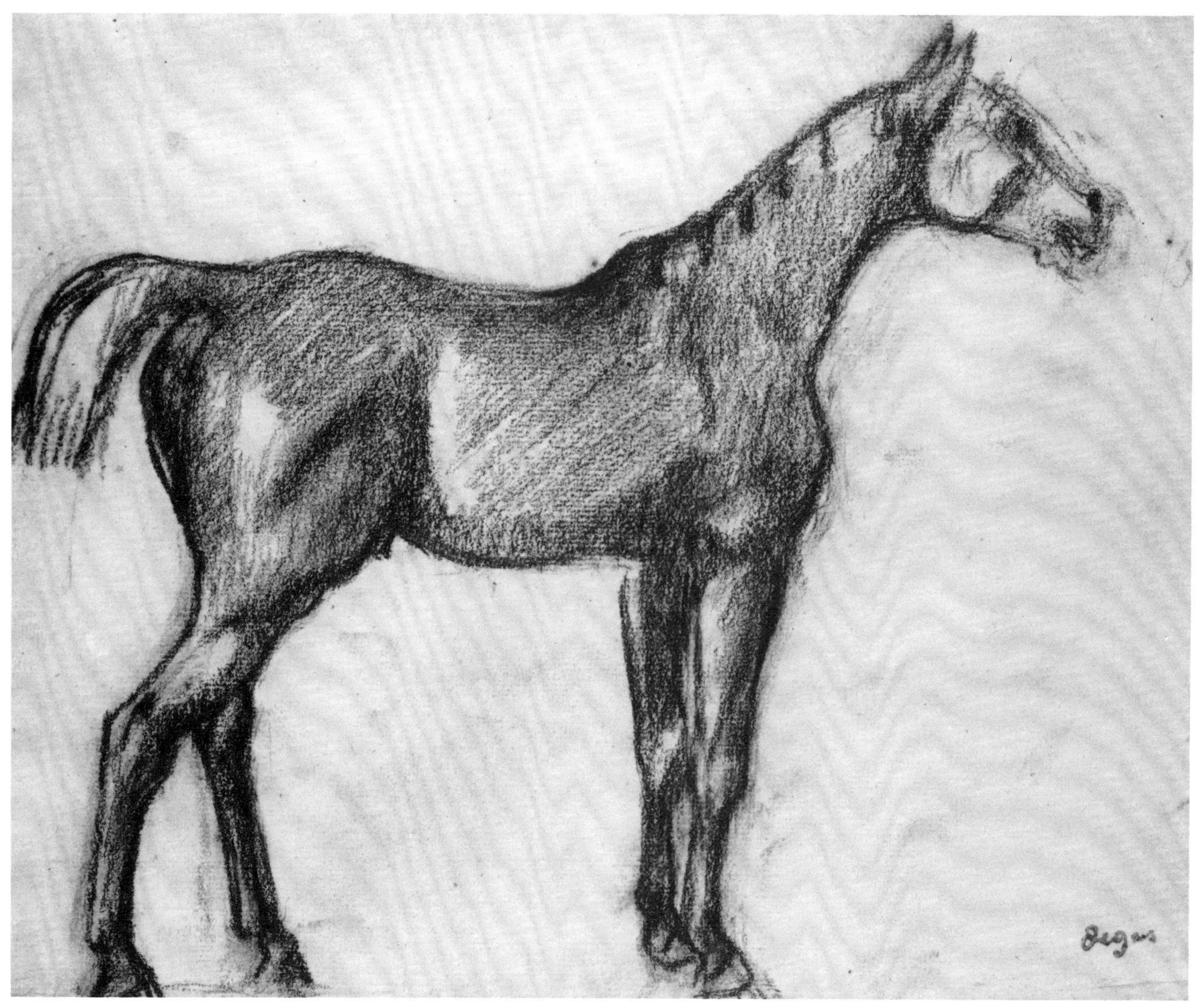

35   Standing Horse, to the Right

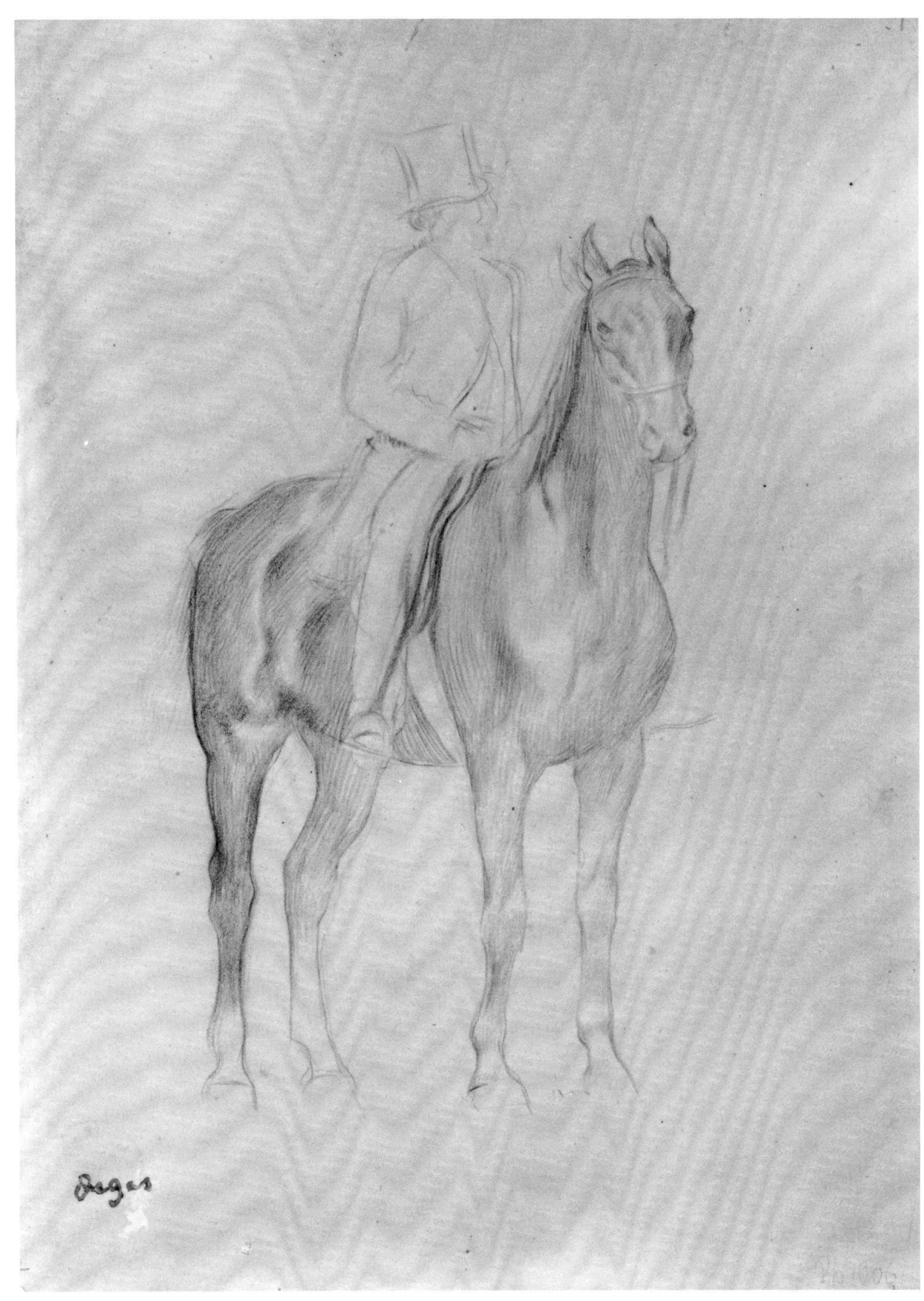

36   *Rider on Horseback*

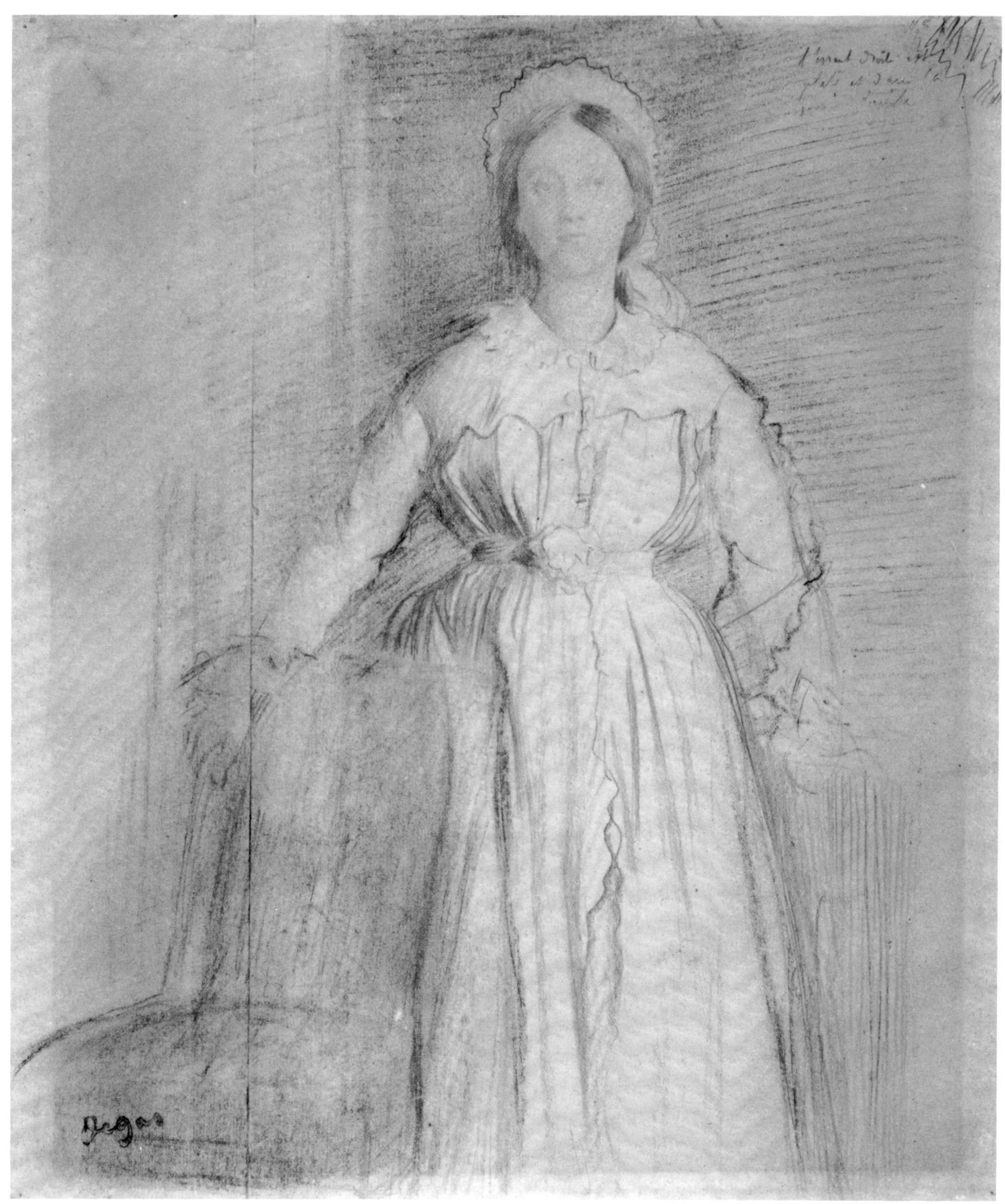

37   *Portrait of Marguerite De Gas*

37
Portrait of Marguerite De Gas

MB 1976/T19
Pencil and black chalk on yellowed paper; 263 × 227 mm (two pieces of paper)
Inscribed with pencil: *l'épaule droite est plate et dans la jaune teinte*
Provenance: Vitale Bloch bequest, 1976
Literature: Rotterdam 1978, cat. no. 11 (ill.); Guillaud 1984, no. 7 bis, ill. 54; Adriani 1984, no. 45 (ill.)

A young woman wearing a lace cap and a simple dress with a lace collar is shown from the front to below the knees. She stands before a cabinet or a mantle on her right, resting her left hand on it; her right hand rests on the back of a chair, which is placed in front of her to the left.

This drawing is a study for an oil portrait now in Paris of Degas's sister Marguerite, on which he worked from 1858 to 1860 (Lemoisne 1946/48, no. 60 [ill.]). Laure-Marguerite De Gas (1842–1895) was eight years younger than Degas; she was a singer and married architect Henri Fèvre, with whom she went to live in Buenos Aires. Several studies for the portrait are known (Lemoisne 1946/48, no. 61 [ill.]; and auction cat., Sotheby Parke Bernet, New York, 23 October 1980, no. 309 [ill.]), but the Rotterdam drawing is most like a study now in Chicago, where the face is left blank (exhib. cat., Chicago 1984, no. 7 [ill.]).

Marguerite De Gas's pose in the Paris painting and in the Chicago and Rotterdam studies is very similar to that of Rosa Adelaide, duchess of Morbilli, in the watercolor portrait painted by Degas in 1857, now in New York (exhib. cat., Chicago 1984, ill. 7.2). Both portraits also recall Ingres's portrait of Madame d'Haussonville and the studies for this portrait (Naef, III, p. 327f. [ill.]).

J.P.

38
Giovanna and Giulia Bellelli

F II 166
Pencil and charcoal on thin, white paper; laid down; 294 × 228 mm
Provenance: F. Koenigs; given by D. G. van Beuningen to the Museum Boymans Foundation, 1940
Literature: Rotterdam 1968, cat. no. 86 (ill.); Finsen 1983, no. G (ill.); Adriani 1984, no. 70 (ill.); Guillaud 1984, no. 9, ill. 60

This three-quarter-length portrait shows two simply dressed girls standing together but facing in different directions. The girl on the left is turned slightly to the left with her hands clasped together in front of her. The girl on the right is represented in profile to the right.

The drawing is a fairly detailed study for a double portrait now in Los Angeles of Giovanna and Giulia Bellelli (Finsen 1983, no. A [ill.]), daughters of Gennaro Bellelli (1812–1864) and Laure De Gas (1814–1897), an aunt of the artist. The girls were born in 1849 and 1851, respectively. Degas visited the family in Florence and Naples between 1856 and 1860, and he worked on a Bellelli family portrait from 1858 until 1862 (Finsen 1983, no. 1 [ill.]). The double portrait in Los Angeles must have been painted later, considering the girls' ages, but probably before their father's death in 1864, for they are not in mourning.

Degas did not travel to Italy between 1860 and 1864, but he probably worked from daguerrotypes, as the Rotterdam drawing strongly suggests. In addition to this drawing, several other studies for the painting in Los Angeles are known (Finsen 1983, nos. B, C, D, E, F [ill.]). The painted double portrait was probably exhibited at the Salon of 1867 (Adriani 1984, p. 42).

J.P.

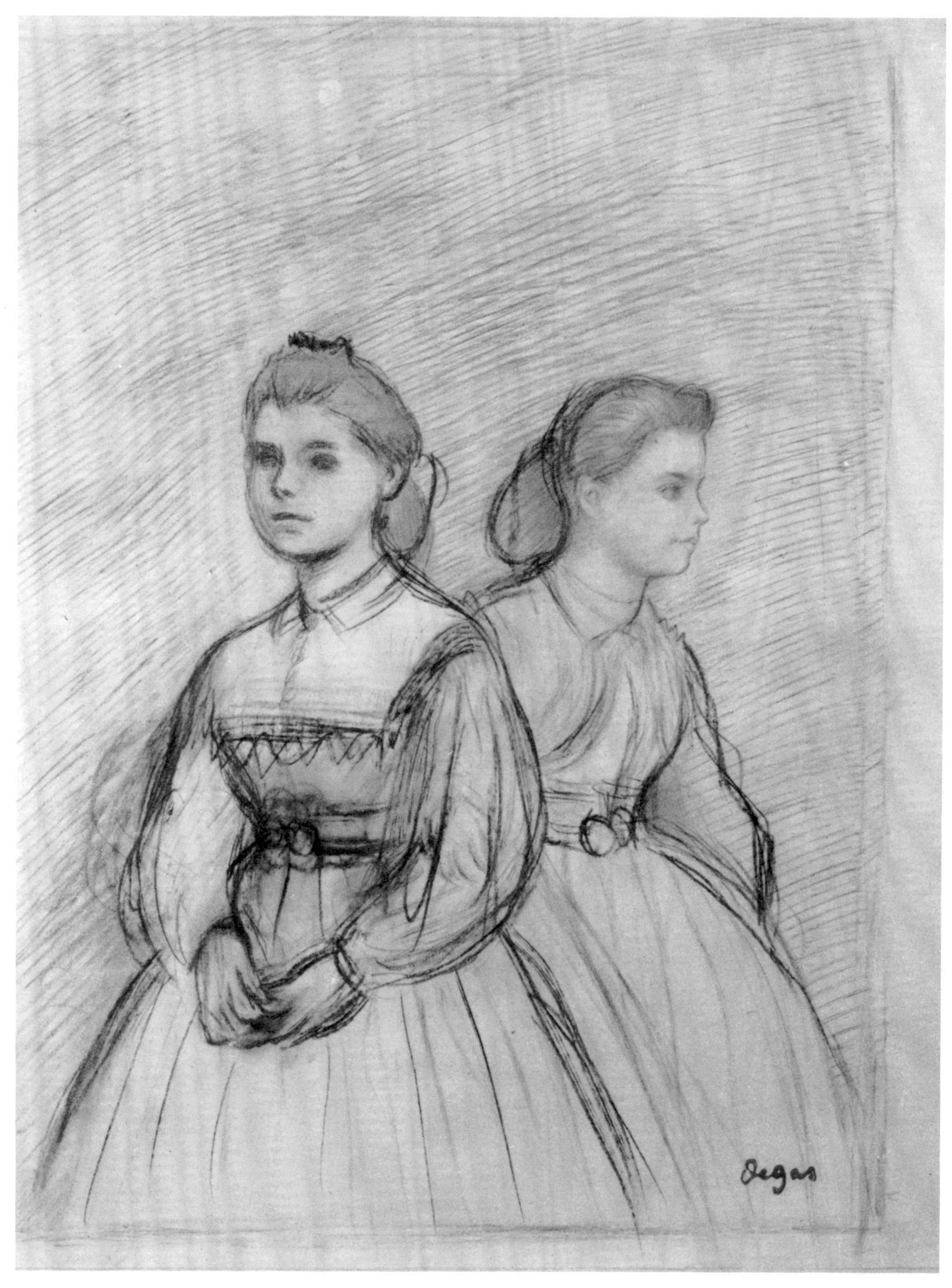

38   *Giovanna and Guilia Bellelli*

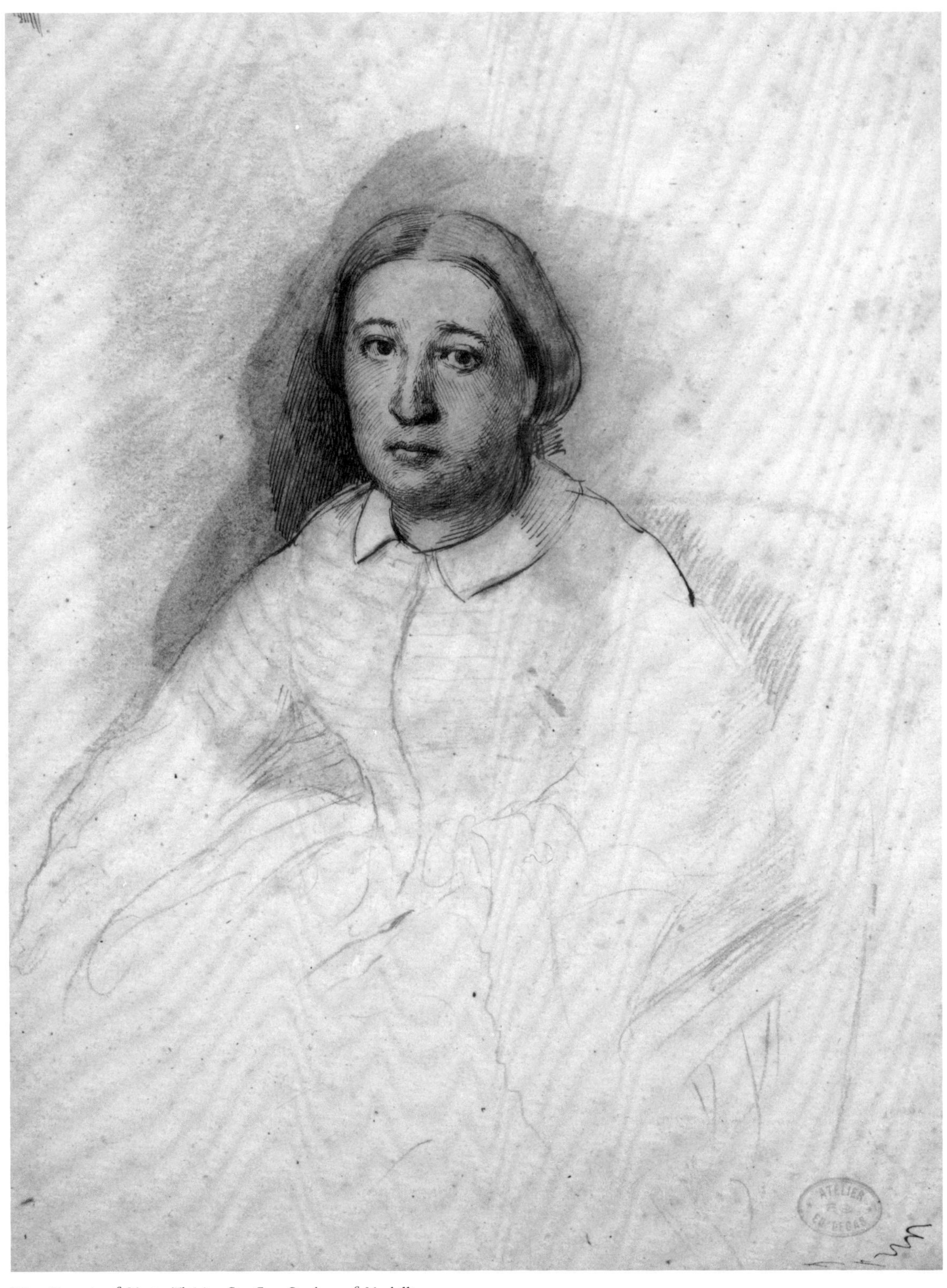

39   *Portrait of Marie-Thérèse De Gas, Duchess of Morbilli*

39
Portrait of Marie-Thérèse De Gas, Duchess of Morbilli

F II 226
Red chalk, pen and black ink, charcoal; 310 × 240 mm
Provenance: F. Koenigs; given by D. G. van Beuningen to the Museum Boymans Foundation, 1940
Literature: Rotterdam 1968, cat. no. 92 (ill.); Adriani 1984, no. 53 (ill.); Guillaud 1984, no. 15 (ill. 94)

This is a portrait of Marie-Thérèse De Gas (1840–1897), the oldest sister of the artist, who married her cousin Edmondo, duke of Morbilli, in 1863 and went to live in Naples. Degas drew many portraits of her, with as well as without her husband (see Lemoisne 1946/48, nos. 131, 132, and 164 [ill.]). She is shown here in a simple dress, seated in an armchair and turned somewhat to her left.

The Rotterdam sheet, drawn in a style reminiscent of Ingres, is very similar to a portrait drawing of Marie-Thérèse now in Boston, which was sold at the auction of the collection of René De Gas in 1927 together with a portrait of Edmondo, likewise now in Boston (*Drawings by Degas,* exhib. cat., The St. Louis Art Museum, St. Louis 1967, no. 4 [ill.]; *Van Clouet tot Matisse,* exhib. cat., Museum Boymans-van Beuningen, Rotterdam 1958, no. 162 [ill.]). The Boston drawing is usually dated 1855, but Marie-Thérèse seems older in the Rotterdam drawing, which can probably be dated around 1865/67. A clear water wash, applied around her head, has blurred the red chalk, black ink, and charcoal of the drawing.
J.P.

40
Female Dancer with a Fan

F II 222
Black chalk, heightened with white on blue-gray paper; 480 × 315 mm
Provenance: F. Koenigs; given by D. G. van Beuningen to the Museum Boymans Foundation, 1940
Literature: Rotterdam 1968, cat. no. 91 (ill.); B. Chaet, *The Art of Drawing,* New York 1978, ill. 206; exhib. cat., Edinburgh
    1979, no. 19 (ill.); Adriani 1984, no. 109 (ill.); Guillaud 1984, no. 29 (ill.)

Degas has drawn a full-length frontal view of a dancer at rest. She wears a knee-length ballet costume and holds an open fan in her right hand. The artist has provided a vertical line near the middle of the sheet as a point of reference, and also a base line on which he has placed the tip of the dancer's right shoe.

Just as Degas recorded the various aspects of horseback riding, so he made numerous studies of the attitudes of ballet dancers. When Mrs. Louisine Havemeyer, a collector and friend of Mary Cassatt's, asked him why he painted so many dancers, Degas answered: "Because, Madame, it is only there that I can rediscover the movements of the Greeks" (exhib. cat., Edinburgh 1979, p. 18).

This sheet should be considered apart from the main body of drawings of dancers by Degas, however. The woman seems older than the dancers in other drawings by Degas. And the same model is shown in a drawing in Paris (exhib. cat., Edinburgh 1979, no.18 [ill.]), which according to the inscription, Degas presented to his friend Théodore Duret (1838–1927), an art critic and art historian. Both sheets are dated around 1876/80.

We know of no painting in which this model is represented, although a dancer with a fan appears in a similar pose in the painting *La Leçon de Danse,* now in Williamstown, Massachusetts, and dated around 1880 (Shackelford 1984, no. 32 [ill.]).
J.P.

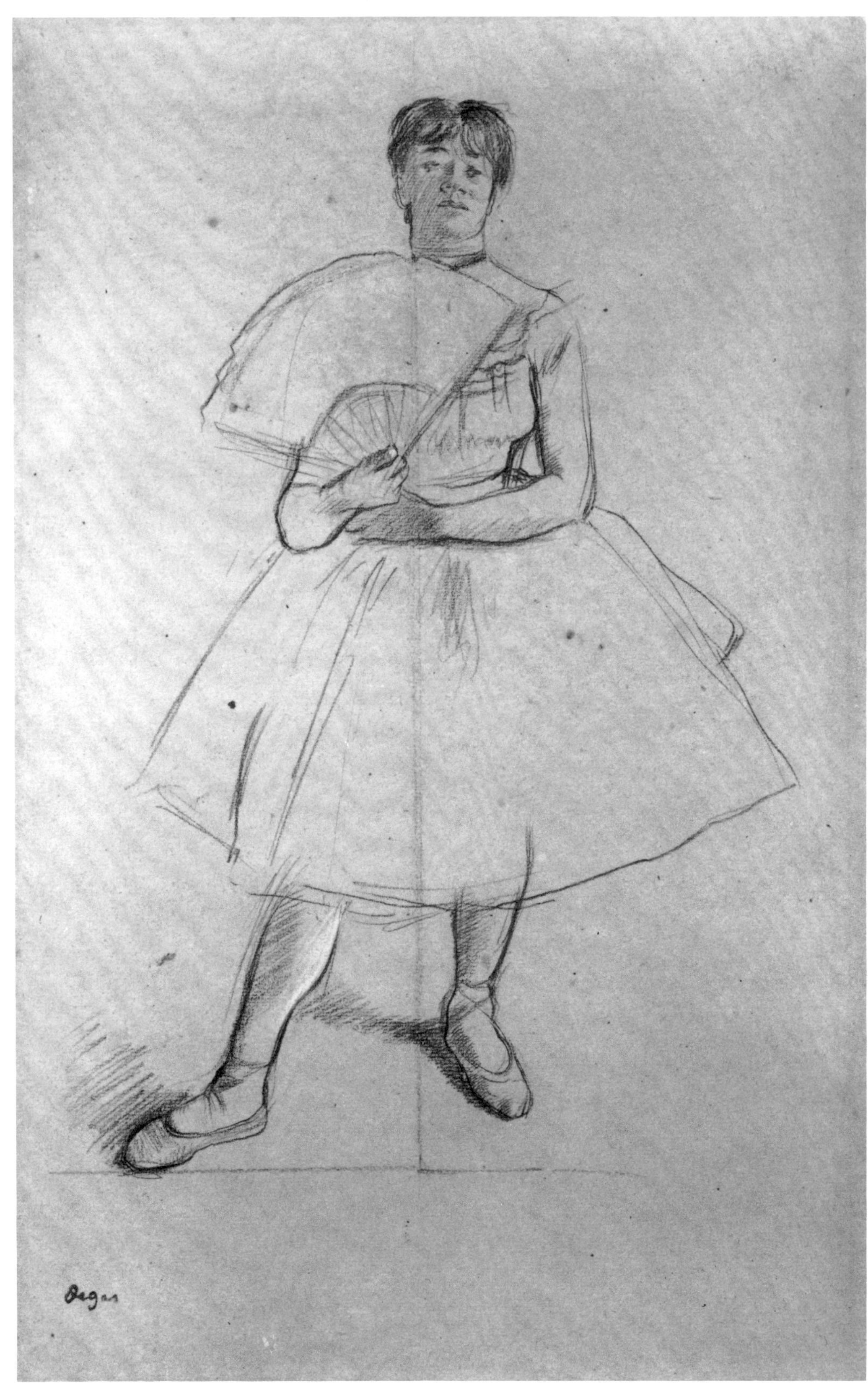

40   *Female Dancer with a Fan*

MB 1976/T17
Black chalk on blue paper; 311 × 243 mm
Provenance: Vitale Bloch bequest, 1976
Literature: Rotterdam 1978, cat. no. 13 (ill.); Adriani 1984, no. 170 (ill.)

A female dancer is shown from behind and turned to the left, with a large bow around her waist. She is bending over to adjust her left shoe, which she rests on a string bass lying on the floor.

In his many studies of ballet dancers Degas preferred to depict the "petits rats" of the opera ballet rather than the stars. This term, "petits rats," was first used in 1830, probably with reference to the way the ballerinas lived within the opera house (L. D. Muehlig, "Degas as an Observer of the Ballet," exhib. cat., Northampton, Mass., 1979, pp. 6–14). The dancer in this drawing reappears on the left of a dance studio shown in a frieze-shaped painting whose present whereabouts are not known. She also resembles the dancer in a drawing in Basel (*Sammlung Richard Doetsch-Benzinger,* exhib. cat., Kunstmuseum, Basel 1956, no. 3 [ill.]). Both drawings are in fact preparatory for the painting, which is usually dated 1880/87 (Lemoisne 1946/48, no. 900 [ill.]).

Two paintings with similar subjects and dimensions, and with a string bass on the left, are known in New York and in Upperville, Virginia (Shackelford 1984, no. 30, ill. p. 90; *The New Painting: Impressionism, 1874–1886,* exhib. cat., National Gallery of Art, Washington, D.C., Los Angeles 1986, no. 93 [ill.]). Another study of the two dancers in the middle of the painting in Upperville is on extended loan in the Museum Boymans-van Beuningen (Shackelford 1984, no. 26 [ill.]).

J.P.

41   Female Dancer (see also color plate 3)

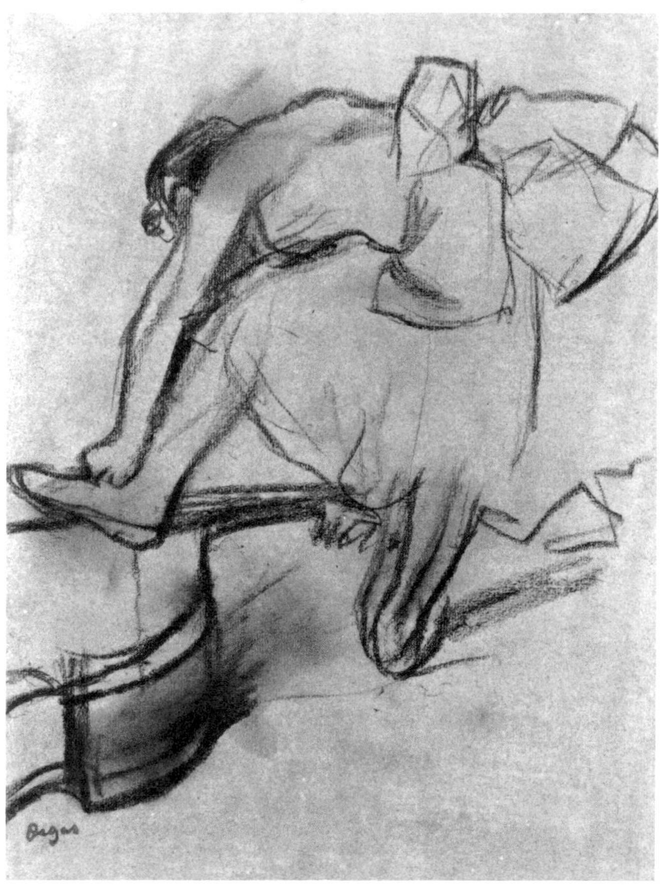

EUGÈNE DELACROIX
Charenton-St. Maurice 1798–Paris 1863

42
Portrait of a Young Woman

F II 223
Watercolor; 190 × 135 mm
Provenance: F. Koenigs; given by D. G. van Beuningen to the Museum Boymans Foundation, 1940
Literature: Rotterdam 1968, cat. no. 118 (ill.); Sérullaz 1981, p. 41 (ill.)

The young woman represented in this watercolor is traditionally identified as Caroline Guillemardet, who later became baroness de Conflans; she was the sister of Delacroix's good friend Felix Guillemardet. Attempts to identify the subject as Marie-Elise Blavot, another friend of Delacroix's, are not convincing (M. Sérullaz, *Mémorial de l'exposition Eugène Delacroix,* Paris 1963, no. 67).

This watercolor by Delacroix shows a clear similarity in technique and use of color to watercolors by English artists from the 1820s, particularly those by John Constable. Delacroix met Constable in London in 1825, when he lived there from May until the end of August. Constable presented Delacroix with a partially used sketchbook, containing drawings and watercolors from 1824, which is now in the Louvre in Paris and to which Delacroix himself also contributed drawings (G. Reynolds, *The Later Paintings and Drawings of John Constable,* London 1984, I, pp. 105ff.). The Rotterdam watercolor was probably painted in 1825 or shortly thereafter.

A.M.

43
Portrait of Mme Pierret

F II 90
Pencil; 250 × 218 mm
Dated with pencil: *13 avril vendredi saint/1827*
Provenance: F. Koenigs; given by D. G. van Beuningen to the Museum Boymans Foundation, 1940
Literature: Rotterdam 1968, cat. no. 108 (ill.); L. Johnson, "Some Historical Sketches by Delacroix," *The Burlington Magazine* 115 (1973), p. 672; Sérullaz 1981, p. 57 (ill.); L. Johnson, *The Paintings of Delacroix, 1816–1831,* Oxford 1981, under cat. no. 127

The subject of this portrait is Marguerite Jeanne Aimée Heydinger, who in 1820 married Jean Baptiste Pierret, a friend of Delacroix's from his youth. She is dressed in a white spencer with wide upper sleeves, ornamented with fluted pleats (A. Moreau, *E. Delacroix,* Paris 1873, p. 232).

The Pierrets were among Delacroix's most intimate and trusted friends. The artist lived with them in Paris from 1825 until 1827 and drew this portrait on Good Friday, 13 April 1827. The friendship between the artist and Mme Pierret continued even after Jean Baptiste's death in 1854 (Johnson 1981, p. 44).

Delacroix made other portraits of the Pierret family as well, among them a drawing—also in the Museum Boymans-van Beuningen—of Marguerite's sister-in-law Victoire Pierret. Because the latter portrait is comparable in size and technique to the portrait of Marguerite, it can be considered a companion piece. The artist marked the drawing of Victoire Pierret with a "1" in pencil on the back, and the exhibited drawing with a "2." Both drawings remained in possession of the Pierret family and their descendants until Franz Koenig acquired them in the 1920s.

A.M.

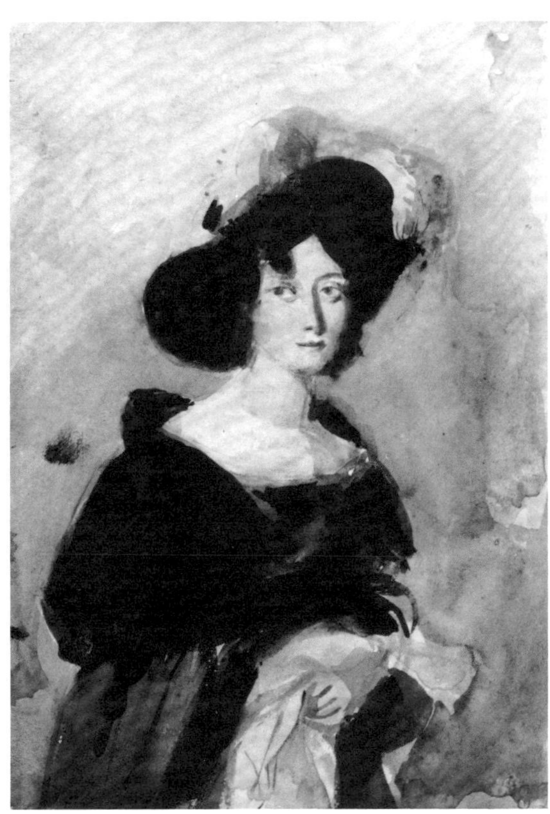

42 Portrait of a Young Woman

43 Portrait of Mme Pierret

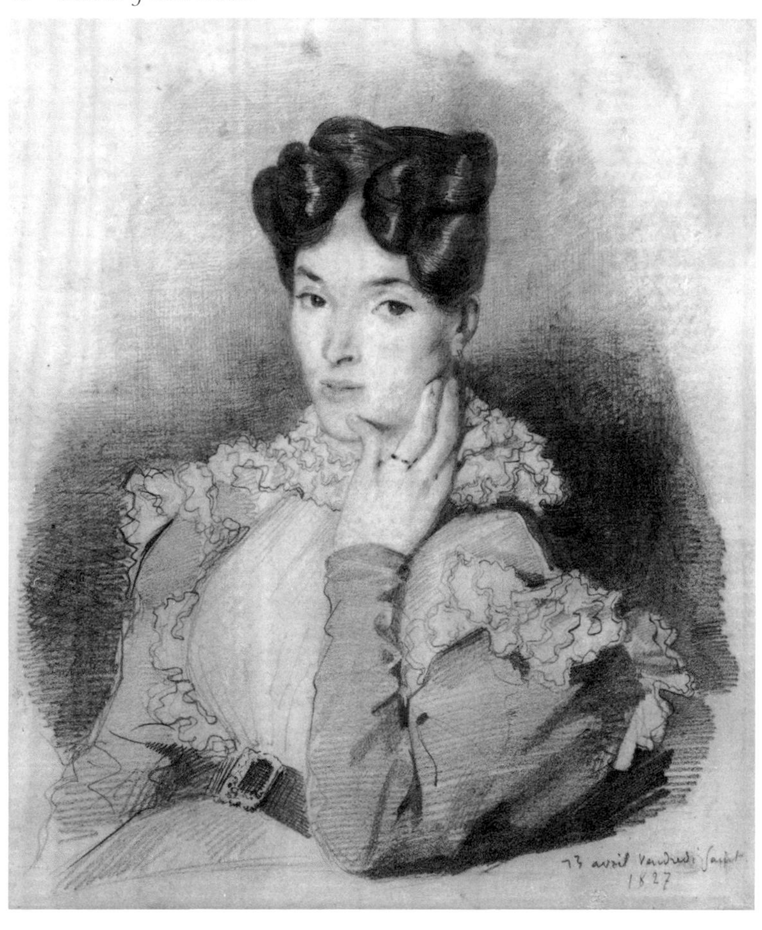

44
"Erlkönig"

F II 162
Brush and brown ink over pencil; 198 × 310 mm
Provenance: F. Koenigs; given by D. G. van Beuningen to the Museum Boymans Foundation, 1940
Literature: Rotterdam 1968, cat. no. 111 (ill.)

The first two verses of Goethe's famous ballad "Erlkönig" from 1782 were the inspiration for this drawing:

> Who rides so late through night and wind?
> It is the father with his child;
> He has the boy cradled in his arm
> He holds him firmly, he keeps him warm
>
> "My son, why do you hide your face as if afraid?"
> "Don't you see the Erl King, father?
> The Erl King with crown and train?"
> "My son, it is a wisp of fog."
> (*Goethes Werke,* ed. K. Heinemann, Leipzig, Vienna, I, 1900, p. 105)

During his stay of several months in London during 1825, Delacroix saw an English adaptation of Goethe's *Faust* in Drury Lane Theatre, which, as he wrote his friend Pierret in Paris, made a deep impression on him (J. O. Kehrli, *Die Lithographien zu Goethes "Faust" von Eugène Delacroix,* Bern 1949, p. 8). Indeed, this performance led Delacroix to create a number of illustrations for a French edition of *Faust,* an idea he had been considering for some years (Kehrli, *Lithographien,* p. 9). This French translation of *Faust* was published in 1828 and contained seventeen lithographs by Delacroix. Some twenty studies for the illustrations of *Faust* have been preserved (Ph. Hofer, *Some Drawings and Lithographs for Goethe's "Faust" by Eugène Delacroix,* Cambridge, Mass., 1964).

Although Robaut dates this sheet to 1835, the style of drawing suggests that it was done during the latter half of the 1820s when Delacroix was working on the illustrations for *Faust* (Robaut 1885, p. 164, no. 619). A second indication that the drawing was created considerably earlier than 1835 is the watermark in the paper: a double crowned eagle surrounded by the words *Dieu protège la France* ("may God protect France") and the year 1811.
A.M.

45
Dancing Moroccan

F II 82
Pen and brown ink; 190 × 154 mm
Provenance: F. Koenigs; given by D. G. van Beuningen to the Museum Boymans Foundation, 1940
Literature: Rotterdam 1968, cat. no. 101 (ill.)

In this drawing a Moroccan in a white costume dances with his arms outstretched. A sense of exhuberance is conveyed by the bold arabesque that defines his garment. The artist has suggested the dark skin of the head, arms, and legs with fine hatchings, using the upper right corner of the sheet to practice his pen strokes.

From January until July 1832 Delacroix traveled in Morocco and Algeria with Charles Count de Mornay. King Louis-Philippe had sent the count as a diplomatic envoy to the sultan of Morocco, Abd-er-Rahman, in order to persuade the latter to lessen his support of the Algerian rebels (R. Huyghe, *Delacroix,* London 1964, p. 300). Delacroix had been invited along as a painter-historiographer. The artist recorded his impressions of these north African countries in at least eight sketchbooks, which contain drawings and watercolors of scenery, architecture, animals, and people. Three of these sketchbooks have

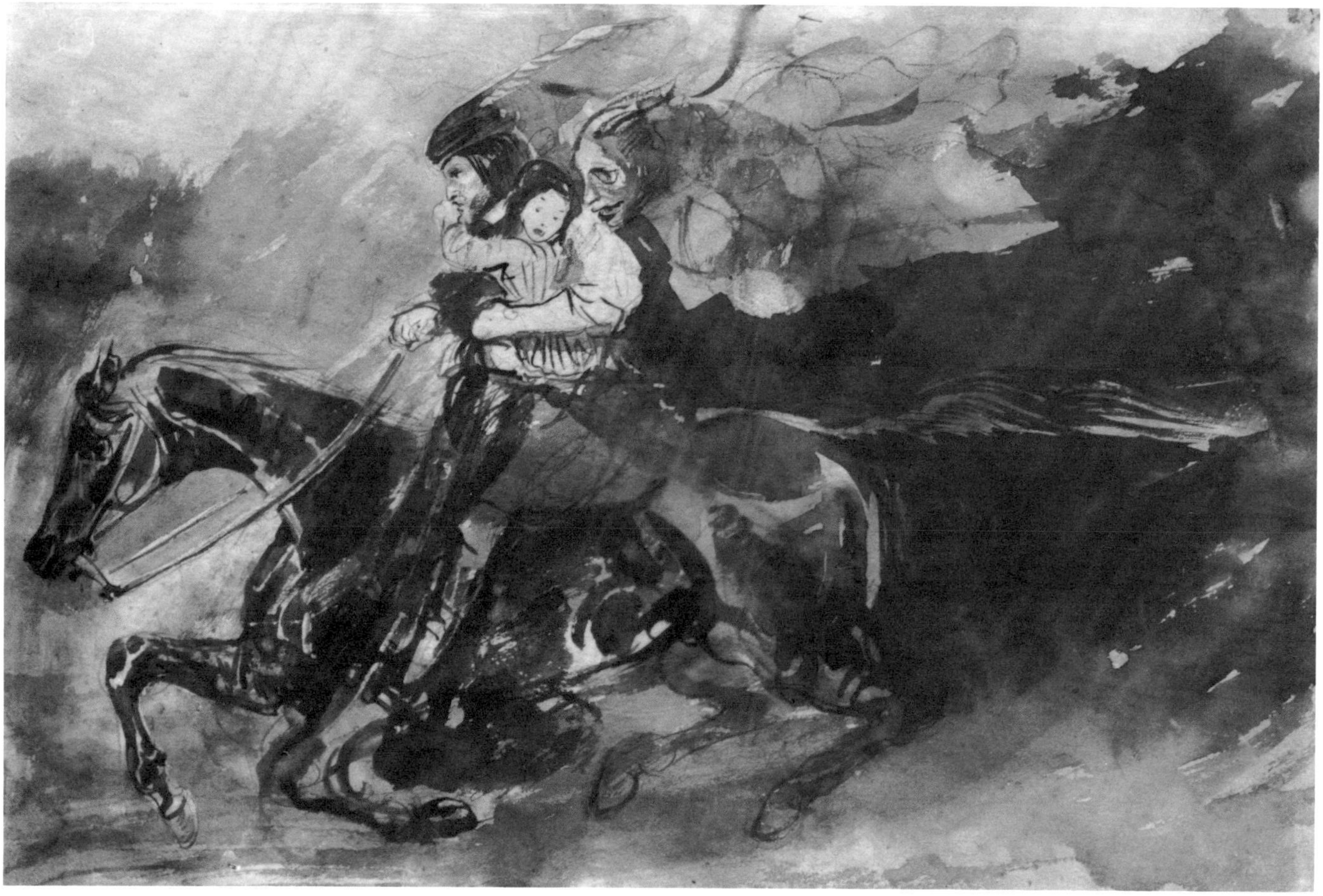

44 "Erlkönig"

45 Dancing Moroccan (see also color plate 4)

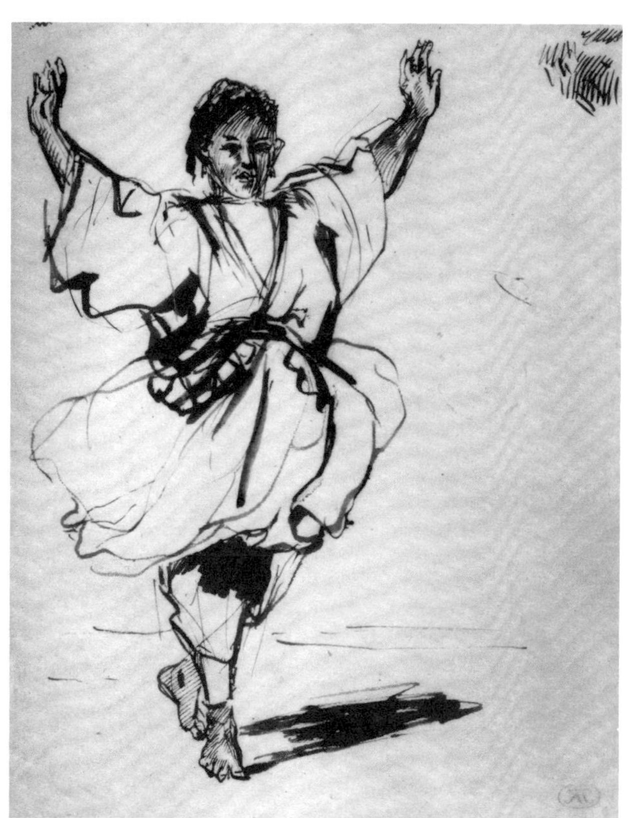

been preserved in their entirety—two at the Louvre in Paris and one at the Musée Condé in Chantilly. The sheets of the other five have been dispersed over time. It is very probable that Delacroix made this drawing during his journey through Morocco.

A.M.

46
Landscape with Fishermen's Cottages

F II 204
Watercolor, gouache, and pencil on white cardboard; 166 × 276 mm
Provenance: F. Koenigs; given by D. G. van Beuningen to the Museum Boymans Foundation, 1940
Literature: Rotterdam 1968, cat. no. 117 (ill.)

Two stone cottages with thatched roofs are shown near a small river, adjacent to three huts and a haystack. Three fishing boats have been pulled out of the water onto the riverbank. On the right two other small buildings have been sketched in pencil.

This watercolor very probably represents the scenery around Valmont, east of Fécamp in Normandy (*Les dessins français dans les collections hollandaises,* exhib. cat., Paris 1964, no. 155), where Delacroix's uncle Alexandre Bataille—and after him, Delacroix's two cousins—owned and lived in the old Benedictine abbey. From 1829 to 1849, Delacroix used to spend a few weeks at Valmont every year in the fall. The drawing exhibited here must have been sketched during one of Delacroix's visits to Valmont, although the exact year cannot be determined.

To suggest greater three-dimensionality, the artist scored the still wet paint with the tip of his brush handle.

A.M.

47
View of the Pyrenees

F II 86
Black chalk, pencil, and watercolor on vergé paper; 187 × 225 mm
Inscribed on the verso with pencil: *Dans les pyrenees/vers 1876*
Provenance: F. Koenigs; given by D. G. van Beuningen to the Museum Boymans Foundation, 1940
Literature: Rotterdam 1968, cat. no. 104 (ill.)

On the advice of his physician, Delacroix spent a few weeks during July–August 1845 in Eaux-Bonnes, a health resort, to seek a cure for his laryngitis. Eaux-Bonnes is situated south of Pau in the Pyrenees near the Spanish border. According to the annotation on the verso, no doubt in Delacroix's own handwriting, the artist painted this watercolor in the mountains around Eaux-Bonnes, *"vers 1876"* meaning at an elevation of nearly 1876 meters.

The letters that Delacroix wrote from Eaux-Bonnes to his friends in Paris indicate that he was completely overwhelmed by the scenery. But he asserted, "il n'y a jamais de papier assez grand pour donner l'idée de ces masses et les détails sont si nombreux qu'il n'est pas de patience qui puisse en triompher" (A. Joubin, *Correspondance générale de Eugène Delacroix,* II, Paris 1936, p. 229). Moreover, he lacked time for serious work because of the many glasses of water he had to drink daily, and the long walks he had to take in order to stimulate their effect (Joubin, p. 229). Probably this quick sketch in pencil was made during one of those walks, and the watercolor added later.

A.M.

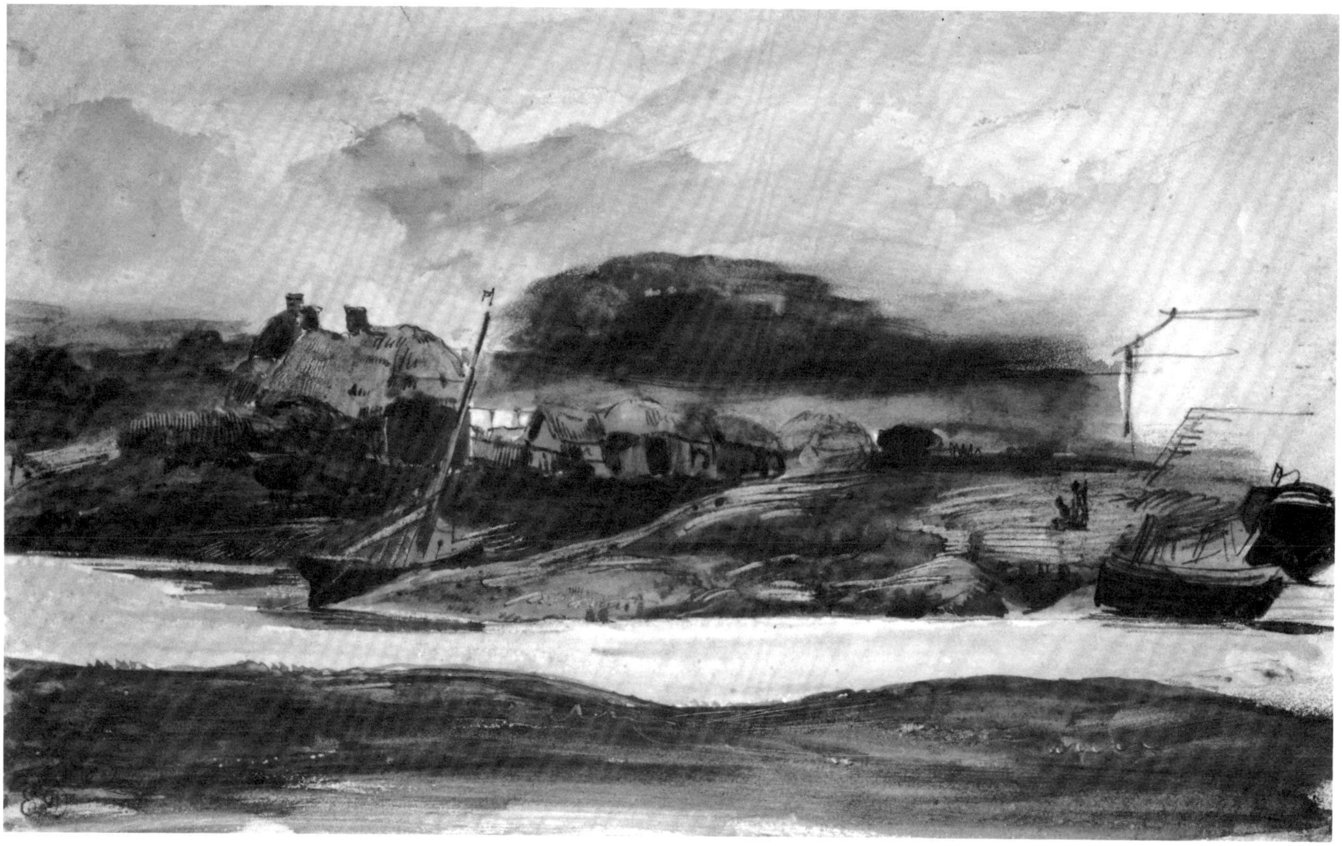

46   *Landscape with Fishermen's Cottages*

47   *View of the Pyrenees*

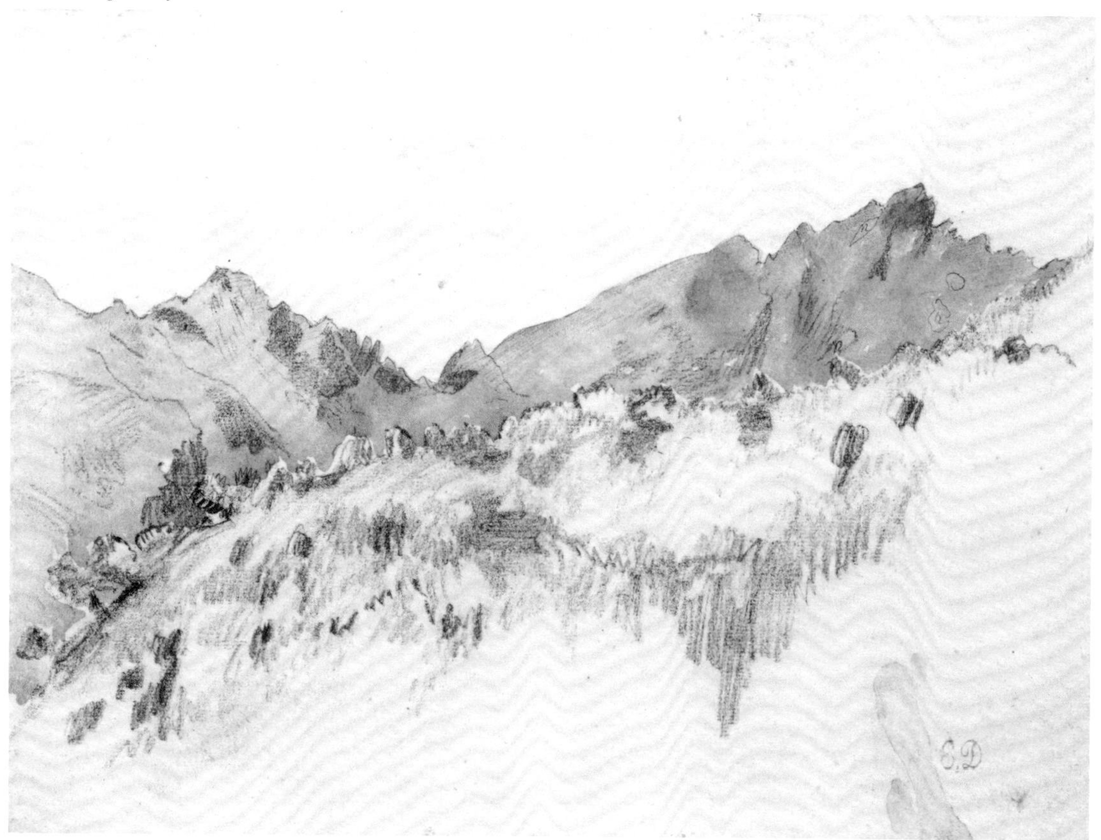

MB 144
Pen and brown ink, brown wash over pencil; laid down; 192 × 242 mm
Signed and dated with pen and brown ink: *Augerville 17 oct. 57./Eug Delacroix*
Provenance: Gift from P. Cassirer, 1928
Literature: Rotterdam 1968, cat. no. 94 (ill.)

Pierre-Antoine Berryer, Delacroix's second cousin and a famous lawyer in his time, owned an estate in Augerville-les-Rivières, 60 kilometers south of Paris. Delacroix liked to go there and was a frequent guest. In particular, he spent two weeks in Augerville during October 1857. An entry in his diary on Tuesday, 6 October, mentions that he was leaving Paris for Augerville.

Among Berryer's other regular guests at Augerville was the famous Parisian cellist Alexandre Batta. On 16 October, Delacroix wrote in his diary that Batta had played a simple piece for cello and organ both before and after dinner, which Delacroix had enjoyed very much (*Journal d'Eugène Delacroix*, III, Paris 1895, pp. 292ff.). The next day he made this drawing, presumably for Batta, since the sheet belonged to the latter's estate (Robaut 1885, no. 1325).

The almost human features of the lion's head reflect Delacroix's interest in certain nineteenth-century theories about physiognomy, which claimed to deduce people's inner characteristics from their personal appearance; the external similarities between men and animals also played a role in these theories (Eve Twose Kliman, "Delacroix's Lions and Tigers: A Link Between Man and Nature," *The Art Bulletin* 64 [1982], pp. 446ff.).

A drawing of the same subject, dated 1835 by Robaut (1885, no. 624), belongs to the collection of the Walters Art Gallery, Baltimore (*The Journal of the Walters Art Gallery*, I, 1938, ill. p. 112). Delacroix painted a tiger playing with a turtle in 1858 (*Eugène Delacroix*, exhib. cat., Kunsthaus, Zürich 1939, no. 368, ill. XX).

A.M.

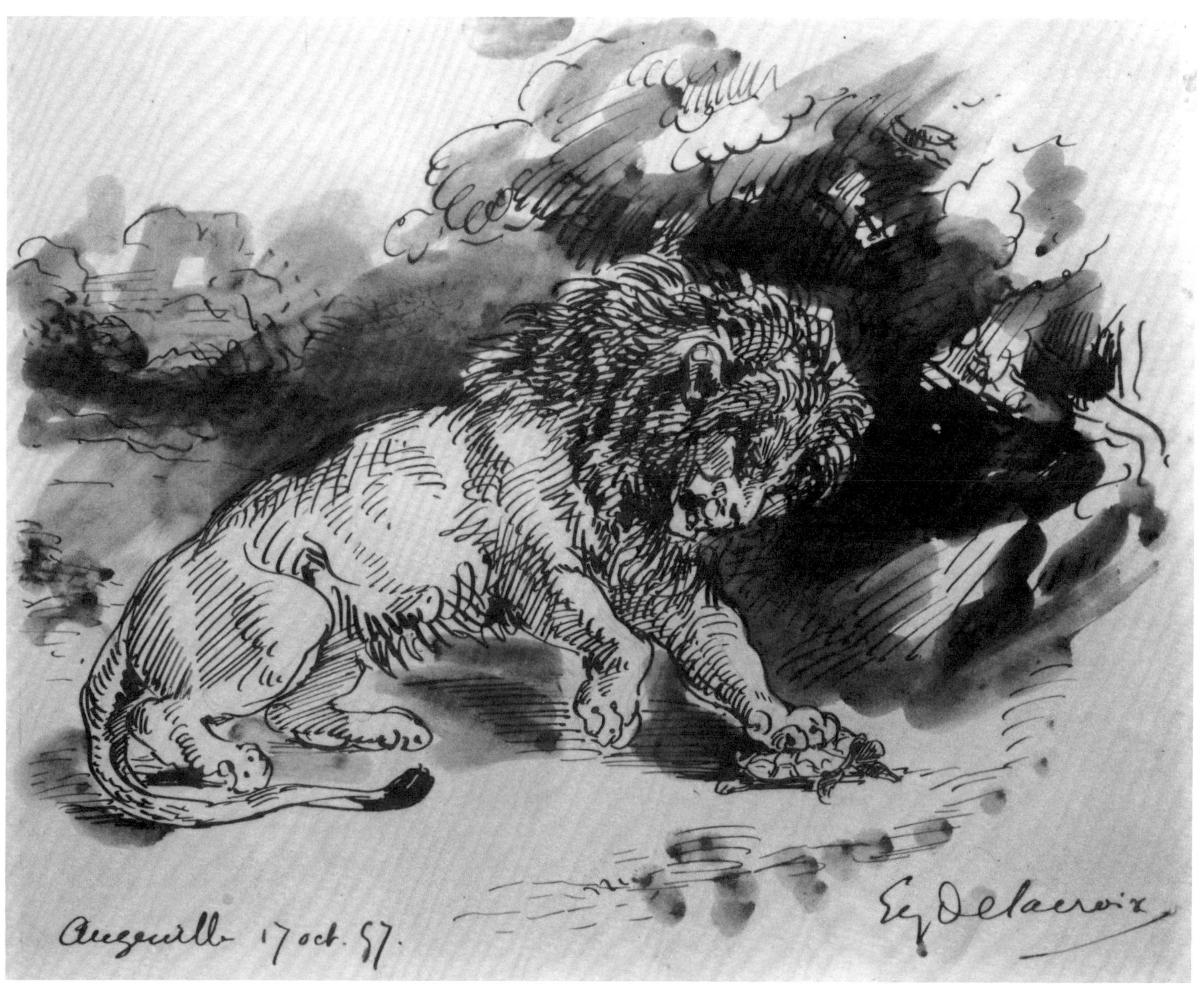

48   *Lion Playing with a Turtle*

THÉODORE GERICAULT
Rouen 1791–Paris 1824

49

Studies of the Head of a Barking Dog

F II 66
Verso in pen and brown ink: Wounded soldiers in a cart
Pen and brown ink; 138 × 215 mm
Inscribed in pencil: *Gericault*
Provenance: F. Koenigs; given by D. G. van Beuningen to the Museum Boymans Foundation, 1940
Literature: Rotterdam 1968, cat. no. 139 (ill.); Eitner 1983, p. 53 (ill.)

This sheet, with drawings on both sides, doubtlessly belonged to one of the many sketchbooks by Gericault that were auctioned off in Paris in 1824 after the artist's death. Of the thirty-three sketchbooks sold at that time, three have been preserved more or less in their entirety; the rest have been broken up and dispersed, ending up in various private collections and museums (L. Eitner, "The Sale of Géricault's Studio in 1824," *Gazette des Beaux-Arts* 53 [1959], pp. 115ff.).

Gericault made sketches on this sheet at two different times. Both recto and verso show small pencil sketches beneath the later pen and ink drawings: the verso has a horse lying down, a man on horseback, and the head of a greyhound adjacent to the detail of a dog's eyes. These pencil sketches are drawn in the "little manner," as Eitner calls it (exhib. cat., Los Angeles 1971, p. 49), and resemble in both style of drawing and subject matter the studies in a sketchbook now in Chicago that Gericault used from 1812 to 1814, before his trip to Italy in 1816/17 (L. Eitner, *Géricault: An Album of Drawings in The Art Institute of Chicago,* Chicago 1960, e.g. pp. 52 [the dog's head], 57 [the man on horseback]).

The pen drawings by contrast are related to paintings from the period around 1818 and therefore must have been sketched after the artist's return from Italy. The central of the five studies of the barking dog appears again in the painted portrait of five-year-old Dominique-Louis-Olivier Bro de Comères (born 1813) now in the A. K. Solomon collection, Cambridge, Massachusetts (K. Berger, *Gericault und sein Werk,* Vienna 1952, no. 60 [ill.]). The Bro de Comères family was among Gericault's close acquaintances in Paris.

The sketch of wounded soldiers in a cart on the verso may be considered a preliminary study for the painting of the same subject now in the Fitzwilliam Museum, Cambridge (*Annual Report 1964,* Cambridge University, 1965, ill. XI). The painting, which differs from the Rotterdam drawing in several details, can probably be dated around 1818; its subject is related to that in the watercolor and lithograph of *The Retreat from Russia,* likewise from 1818. Gericault, even in later years, was fascinated with the defeat of the "Grande Armée" and its retreat from Russia in 1812/13 (exhib. cat., New York 1985, no. 56 [ill.]).

A.M.

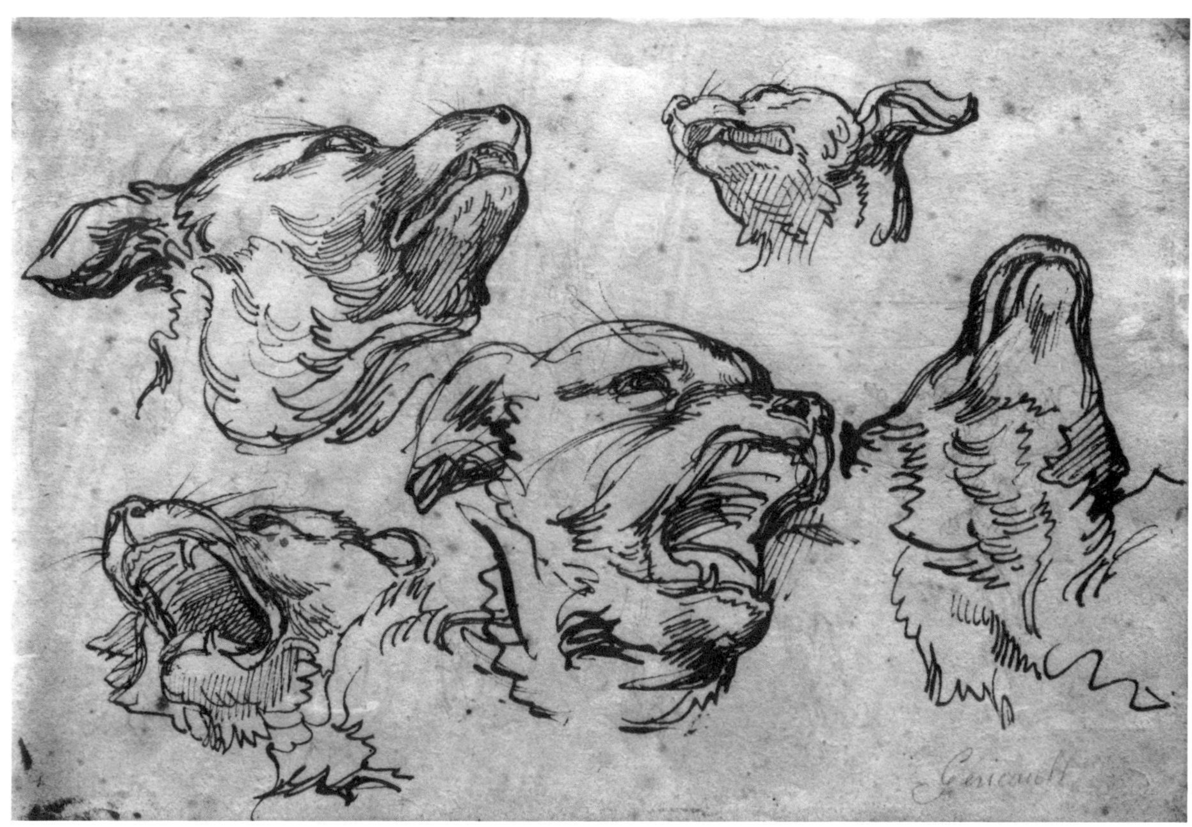

49   *Studies of the Head of a Barking Dog*

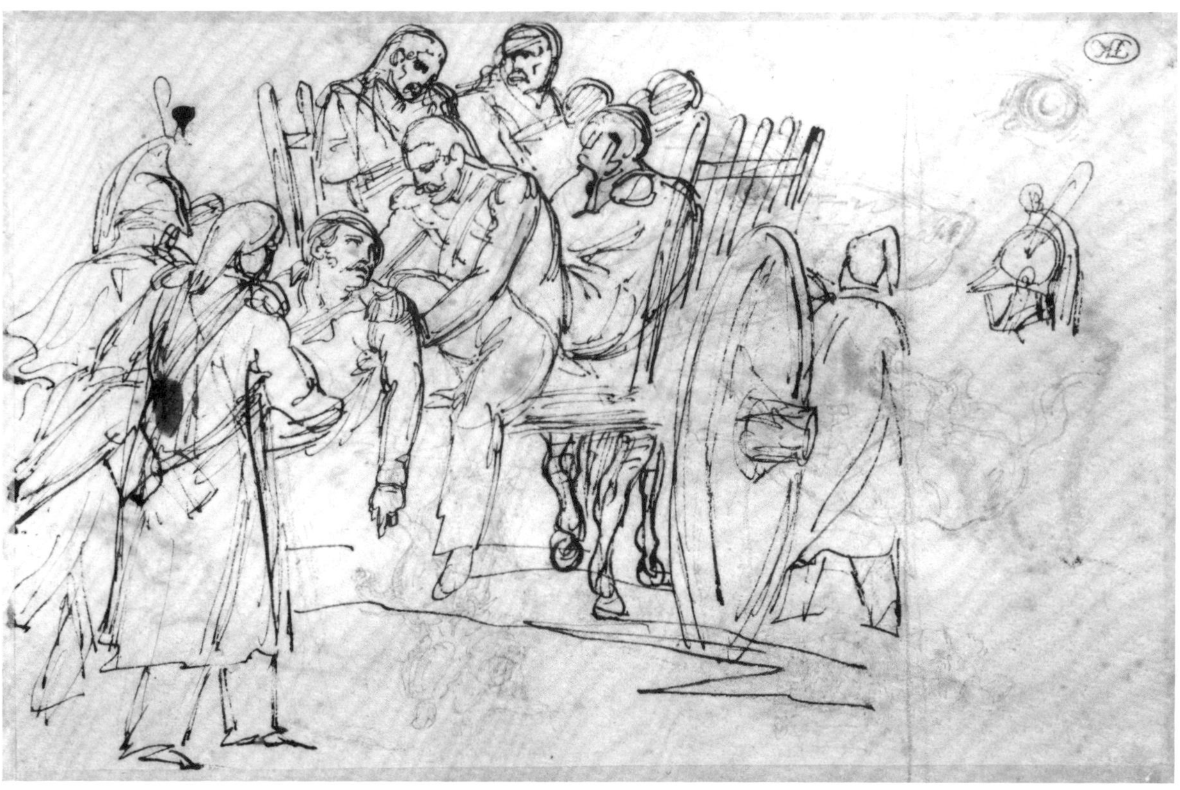

Verso

50

Horse Attacked by a Lion

F II 91
Verso: Two studies of a horse's head
Pencil, brown and gray wash; 207 × 255 mm
Provenance: F. Koenigs; given by D. G. van Beuningen to the Museum Boymans Foundation, 1940
Literature: Rotterdam 1968, cat. no. 140 (ill.); exhib. cat., Los Angeles 1971, no. 102 (ill.); exhib. cat., New York 1985,
    no. 95 (ill.)

Gericault was one of the first artists to use lithography as an artistic medium, with his first prints being published in 1817. Until that time the lithograph, invented in 1796 by Loys Senefelder, had been popular primarily with amateurs and printers of sheet music.

During 1820 and 1821 Gericault stayed in England, where he created around twenty lithographs (Delteil nos. 22–24). Some of these were so-called pen lithographs on "carton autographique" or "stone paper," developed by Senefelder as an alternative for the heavy "lithographic" stone (Delteil no. 22). The method consisted of drawing with a pen on cardboard that had been covered with a layer of a plasterlike substance imitating the surface of lithographic stone. It had the disadvantage of yielding only a few good prints, since the support was apt to crack rather soon (*The Graphic Art of Géricault,* exhib. cat., New Haven 1969, p. 25). Gericault made such a lithograph in London using this drawing from Rotterdam (the watermark in the paper shows the year 1820), but only two prints of the lithograph are known (Delteil no. 42). It is apparent under the gray wash that the left foreleg of the horse in the drawing was originally extended further forward.

A somewhat different version of this subject can be seen in a drawing in the Louvre in Paris (A. del Guercio, *Géricault,* 1963, ill. 62).

A.M.

51

Young Woman on a Dapple-Gray Horse

F II 184
Watercolor over pencil; 282 × 251 mm
Provenance: F. Koenigs; given by D. G. van Beuningen to the Museum Boymans Foundation, 1940
Literature: Rotterdam 1968, cat. no. 141 (ill.); exhib. cat., Los Angeles 1971, no. 99 (ill.); *Géricault,* exhib. cat., Villa Medici,
    Rome 1979/80, under no. 32 (ill.); Eitner 1983, p. 237; exhib. cat., New York 1985, no. 82 (ill.)

For this watercolor Gericault used the same paper as for the drawing in cat. no. 50; the watermark in both reads *J. Whatman 1820.* Therefore both compositions were presumably sketched during Gericault's stay in England in 1820/21.

In London Gericault became friendly with A. Elmore, a horse trader, with whom he also stayed as a house guest for some time. Through Elmore, Gericault was introduced into the equestrian world of riding, racing, and hunting, which undoubtedly included the affluent bourgeoisie and the nobility (S. Lodge, "Géricault in England," *The Burlington Magazine* 107 [1965], p. 617). The young woman depicted here most probably was a member of these circles.

This woman also appears in a painting by Gericault, formerly in a private collection in Paris (exhib. cat., Rome 1979/80, no. 32 [ill.]), where she is represented in the same pose and dressed in the same black riding habit but riding a piebald horse. This painting provides an explanation for the position of the woman's right arm in the watercolor: she was meant to hold a riding crop. The fact that this important detail is absent in the watercolor may suggest that the drawing served as a kind of *modello* for the patron of the painting.

The identity of the sitter is not known, although the painting was entitled *Miss Clarke on Horseback* in the Goldschmidt auction (Paris, 17 May 1888, no. 41).

A.M.

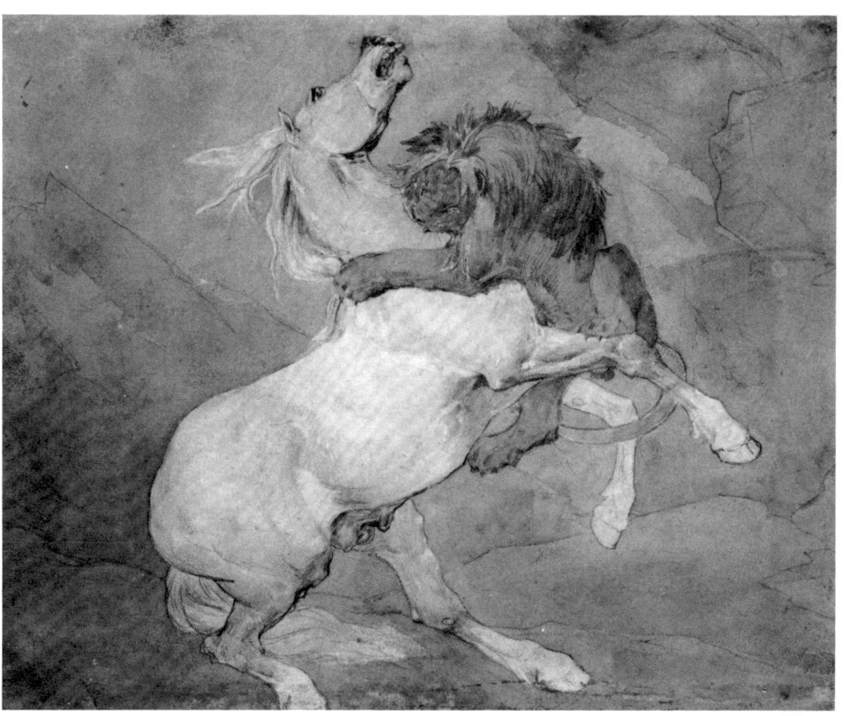

50   Horse Attacked by a Lion (see also color plate 5)

51   Young Woman on a Dapple-Gray Horse

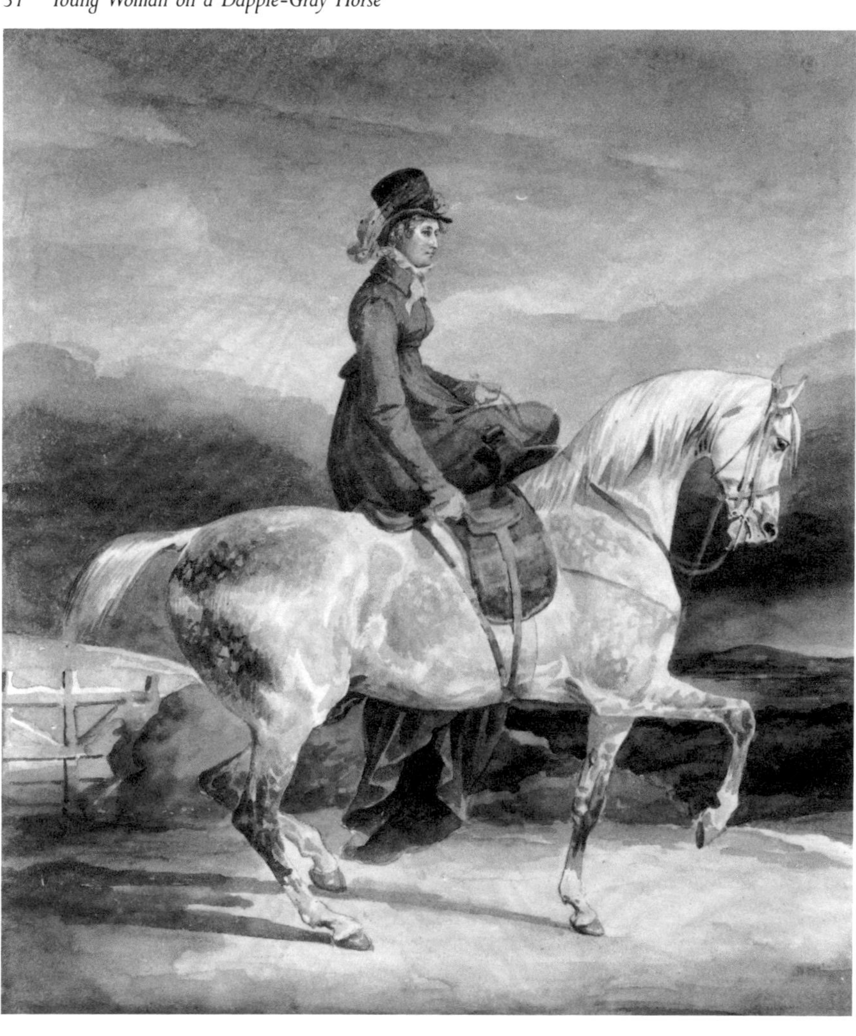

CONSTANTIN GUYS
Flushing 1802–Paris 1892

52
Two Spanish Women Talking

> F II 181
> Pen and brown ink, watercolor; 185 × 155 mm
> Signed and dated with pen in brown ink: *CG/Seville 1847*
> *Provenance:* F. Koenigs; given by D. G. van Beuningen to the Museum Boymans Foundation, 1940
> *Literature:* Rotterdam 1968, cat. no. 147 (ill.); exhib. cat., Rome 1980, ill. IX, p. 19

This drawing shows two Spanish women in gaily colored dresses conversing in the street. The woman on the left, shown from the back, wears a large shawl over her head and shoulders; the second woman, seen from the front and holding an open fan in her right hand, wears flowers in her hair and a dress with a low neckline. Two other women and two men stroll in the middle distance before a backdrop of several buildings.

We know of few signed works by Guys, and even fewer that are dated; this drawing is the only certain indication that the artist was in Spain in 1847. He had been staying in London from 1842 through 1847, working for the *Illustrated London News.*

Haverkamp Begemann compares the Rotterdam drawing to the undated but initialed drawing *Amelia Masi* in Williamstown, Massachusetts (E. Haverkamp Begemann, S. D. Lawder, and Ch. W. Talbot, *Drawings from the Clark Institute,* New Haven/London 1964, no. 207 [ill.]). The drawing from Rotterdam is also related to a drawing in Paris of two Spanish women, likewise dated around 1847 (exhib. cat., Rome 1980, no. 12 [ill.]).

J.P.

53
Two Women on a Balcony

> F II 207
> Pen and brown ink, watercolor; 175 × 134 mm
> *Provenance:* F. Koenigs; given by D. G. van Beuningen to the Museum Boymans Foundation, 1940
> *Literature:* Rotterdam 1968, cat. no. 149 (ill.)

The two women in this drawing, attired in full-skirted dresses with high necklines, are leaning on the balustrade of a balcony and looking out on activity in the street below, not shown in the drawing. The balcony is apparently located at a street corner, for on the left the vague shape of a dome is visible in the background.

Although few signed works by Guy are known, the artist's technique is unmistakable. First the scene is lightly sketched; then ink or watercolor washes are applied in gradations of tone. Finally, the contours are defined with a few bold pen lines. The drawings suggest spontaneity of execution, but Guys usually worked on them for quite a long time in his studio. Often he worked on several drawings simultaneously, culling his memories of what he had seen in the streets.

It is impossible to give an exact date to the sheet, but it seems to have been drawn later than the washed pen and ink drawing in Paris of *Two Spanish Women on a Balcony,* which is dated around 1847 (exhib. cat., Rome 1980, no. 11 [ill.]).

J.P.

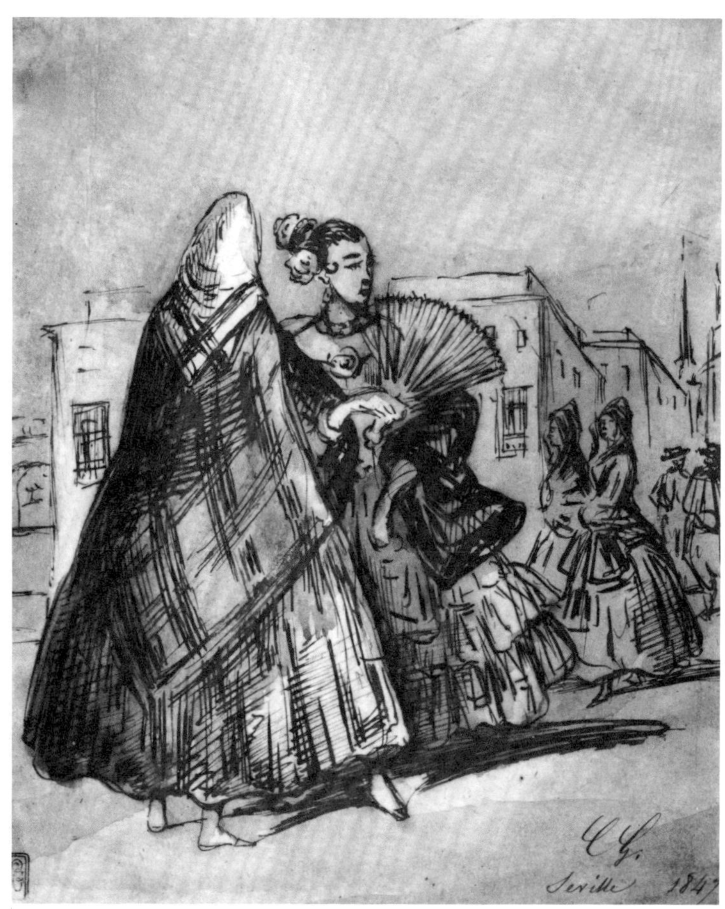

52   Two Spanish Women Talking

53   Two Women on a Balcony

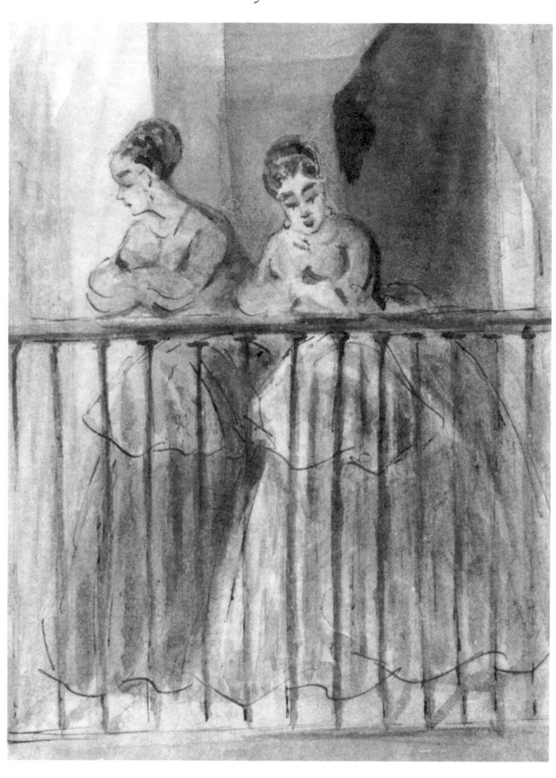

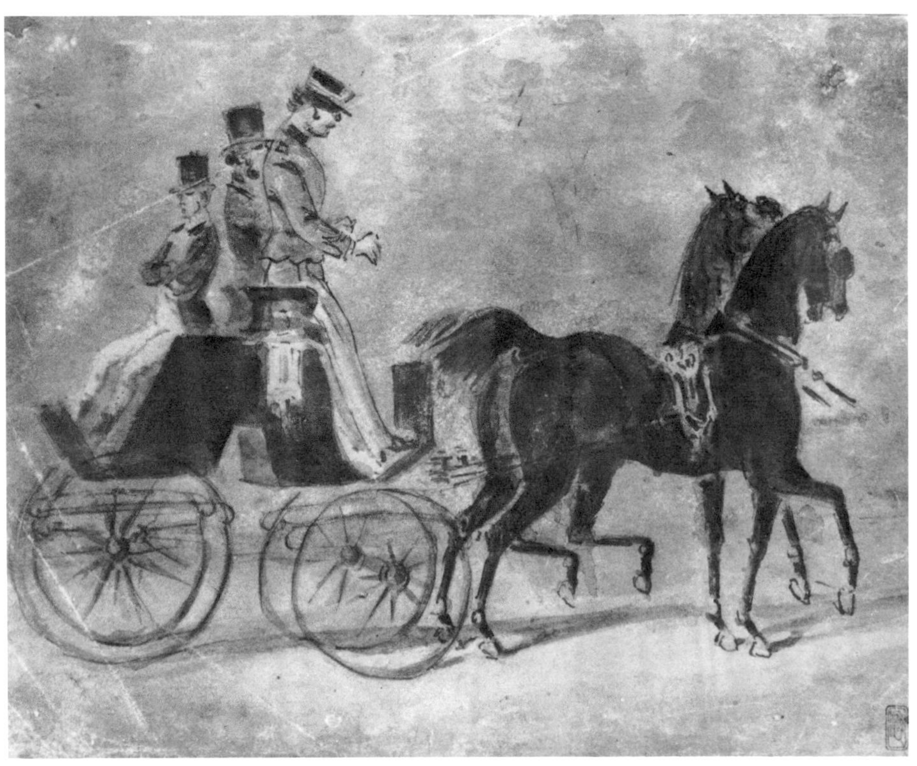

54 Coach with Two Horses

55 Standing Women with a Veil

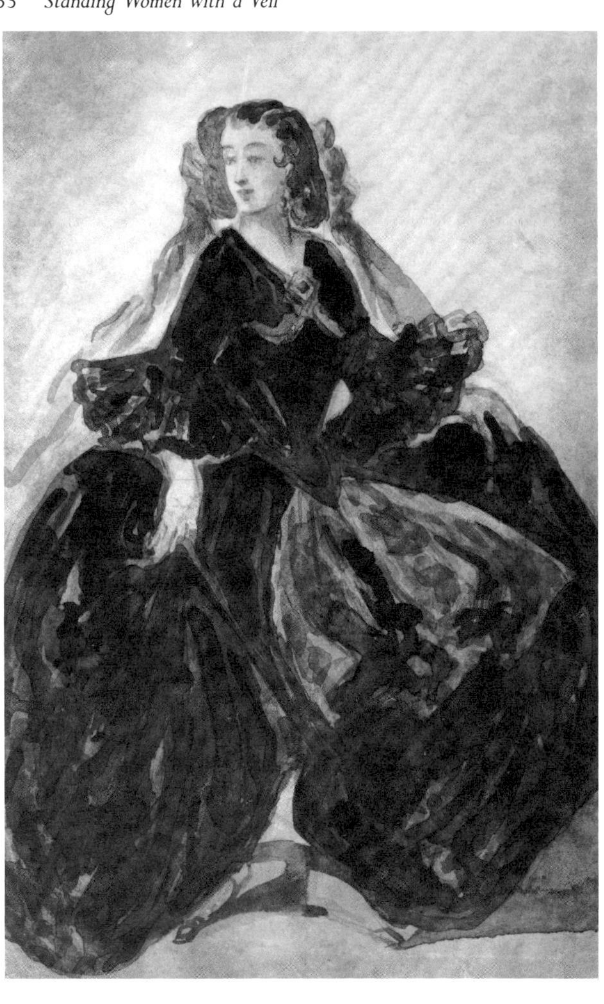

54
Coach with Two Horses

F II 151
Pencil, pen and brown ink, brush in black and gray ink; laid down; 170 × 217 mm
Provenance: F. Koenigs; given by D. G. van Beuningen to the Museum Boymans Foundation, 1940
Literature: Rotterdam 1968, cat. no. 145 (ill.)

A small carriage with two horses is shown bearing three figures, two of whom are seated on the box. Guys had a great gift for observation, which stood him in good stead in his job as illustrator-journalist for the *Illustrated London News.* His detailed knowledge about horses and carriages—and the uniforms, poses, and gestures of their riders—probably dated from his time with the cavalry (exhib. cat., Rome 1980, p. 71).

Unlike the pen and watercolor drawing *L'Impératrice au bois,* dated around 1860/62, where the carriage has been placed in a clearly defined space, Guys concentrated his attention in the Rotterdam drawing on the small carriage in the foreground (Gobin 1960, Guys ill. 4). The latter work seems to be more closely related to the pencil and watercolor drawing *Two Women in a Calash* now in Paris, which is usually dated around 1857/58 (exhib. cat., Rome 1980, no. 44 [ill.]).

J.P.

55
Standing Woman with a Veil

F II 109
Pen and black ink, watercolor; 367 × 240 mm
Provenance: F. Koenigs; given by D. G. van Beuningen to the Museum Boymans Foundation, 1940
Literature: Rotterdam 1968, cat. no. 144 (ill.)

This drawing of a woman nearly fills the entire sheet. The woman is turned slightly to the right, but has turned her head to the left. She wears a dark dress, ornamented with a blue front; the neckline is fairly high and the sleeves are ruffled. She also wears a blue veil fastened in her hair at the back of her head and holds up her crinoline with both hands in a graceful gesture, showing part of her petticoat and her feet.

In his essay "The Painter of Modern Life," Charles Baudelaire discusses the great interest that "Monsieur C. G." (Constantin Guys) had in the contemporary woman (Ch. Baudelaire, *The Painter of Modern Life and Other Essays,* trans. and ed. J. Mayne, London 1964), and particularly the role that ladies of the demi-monde played in the lives of gentlemen of social standing. These women were often depicted by Constantin Guys.

The identity of the subject in this drawing is not known. Her gesture is clearly less risqué than those of women in other drawings by Guys. See, for instance, some Parisian drawings of demi-mondaines, where women display a distinctly more daring décolleté (exhib. cat., Rome 1980, nos. 39, 63, 66 [ill.]).

Hoetink dates the drawing between 1855 and 1863 on the basis of the woman's dress; this corresponds to the date of a pen and watercolor drawing reproduced by Gobin, where the woman also has ruffles on her sleeves (Gobin 1960, ill. 3).

J.P.

JEAN-AUGUSTE-DOMINIQUE INGRES
Montauban 1780–Paris 1867

56

Mlle Harvey Writing, Seen in Three-Quarters from Behind

F II 98

Pencil; 197 × 120 mm

Inscribed on the verso with pencil: *Mlle Harweij volte Subito*

Provenance: F. Koenigs; given by D. G. van Beuningen to the Museum Boymans Foundation, 1940

Literature: Rotterdam 1968, cat. no. 155 (ill.); *Ingres et son temps,* exhib. cat., Montauban 1967, under no. 10; H. Naef, "Ingres
et les demoiselles Harvey," *Bulletin du Musée Ingres* 22 (1967), p. 9; exhib. cat., Paris 1967, under no. 9; H. Naef,
"Henrietta Harvey and Elisabeth Norton: Two English Artists," *The Burlington Magazine* 113 (1971), pp. 79ff., ill. 15;
Naef, I, pp. 106ff., ill. p. 109

A woman is shown sitting on a low stool on a porch and looking out over a walled garden. She is
writing in a fairly thick notebook that rests in her lap and has turned her head to the left—with a
sudden motion, according to the inscription on the verso—so that her profile is not visible.

The same inscription identifies the subject as "Mlle Harvey." Two English artists by that name
belonged to Ingres's circle of acquaintances in Paris: the half-sisters Henrietta and Elizabeth Harvey. The
latter was officially named Elizabeth Norton after her natural father, William Norton. But following a
sojourn in Italy, the two half-sisters and their mother, Elizabeth Harvey-Hill, settled in Paris around
1802, where Elizabeth Norton exhibited her paintings in several Salons between 1804 and 1812, under
the name "Harvey."

Ingres made a full-length portrait of the two sisters in a drawing from 1804, now in the Louvre in
Paris (Naef, IV, no. 31). The Rotterdam sheet must date from around the same time, that is, shortly
before Ingres's departure for Rome in October of 1806. Ingres remained in Rome until 1820, at first as a
student at the Académie and later as an independent artist.

Because the inscriptions on the two drawings do not mention first names, it is impossible to
distinguish between the two sisters. However, the Rotterdam drawing shows a woman writing and thus
may represent Henrietta, who is known to have read poetry and who may also have written poetry
herself (Naef, I, p. 111).

A.M.

57

Portrait of an Unknown Man

F II 161

Pencil; 290 × 220 mm

Signed with pencil: *Ingres*

Provenance: F. Koenigs; given by D. G. can Beuningen to the Museum Boymans Foundation, 1940

Literature: Rotterdam 1968, cat. no. 156 (ill.); exhib. cat., Paris 1967, no. 77 (ill.); exhib. cat., Cambridge 1967, under no. 26;
exhib. cat., Rome 1968, no. 50 (ill.); R. Beyer, "Un modèle d'Ingres: Le chevalier Artaud," *Publications du Collège Littéraire
Universitaire de Muhlhouse,* II, Muhlhouse 1969; Naef, I, pp. 351ff., Naef, IV, no. 129 (ill.)

A man is represented standing beside a table with a book. His left hand rests on the back of a chair,
while his right hand is tucked into the front of his coat—a gesture typical of this period. This work is
generally assumed to be the companion to a portrait drawing of an unknown woman, now in the
Metropolitan Museum, New York (Naef, IV, no. 130 [ill.]). Both sheets have the same dimensions, and
both come from the collection of Henry Lapauze, a connoisseur and collector of Ingres's works; they
appear in the auction catalogue of Lapauze's collection under numbers 18 and 19 (Naef, IV). Ingres

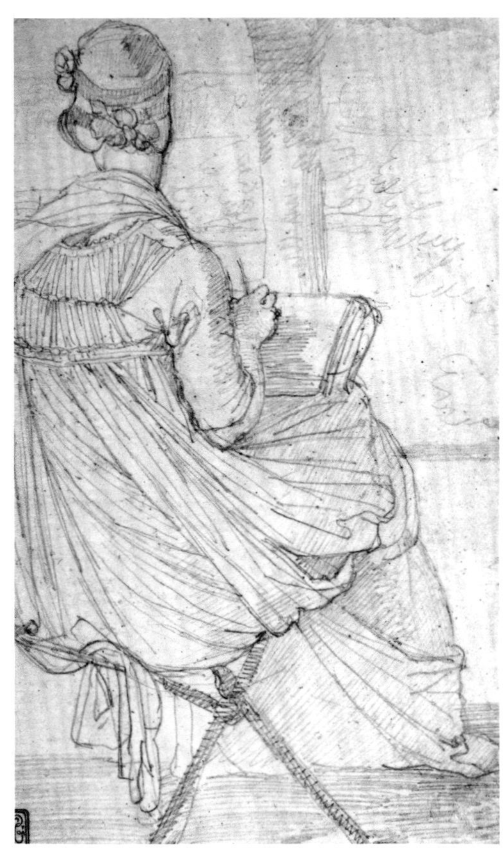

56 *Mlle Harvey Writing; Seen in Three-Quarters from Behind*

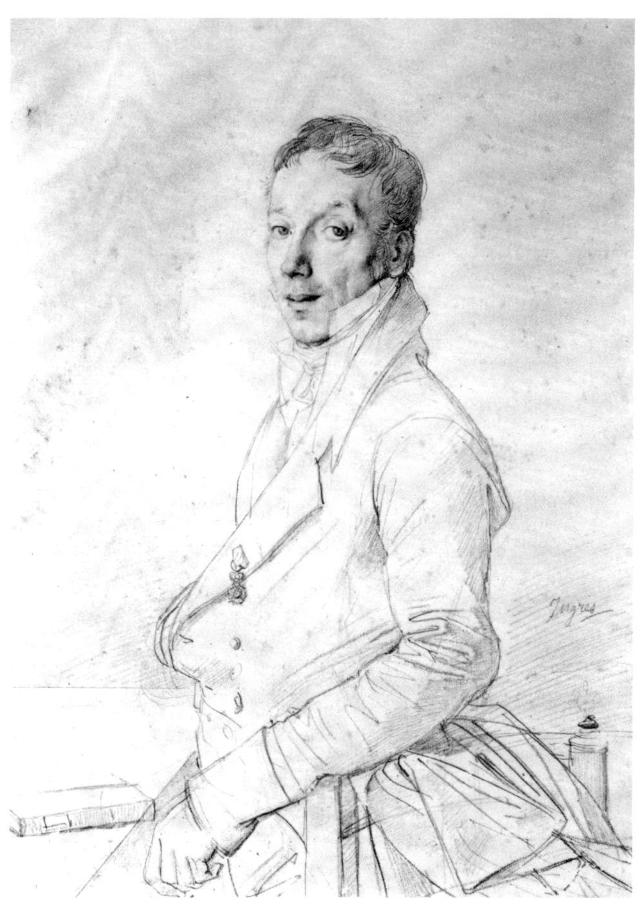

57 *Portrait of an Unknown Man*

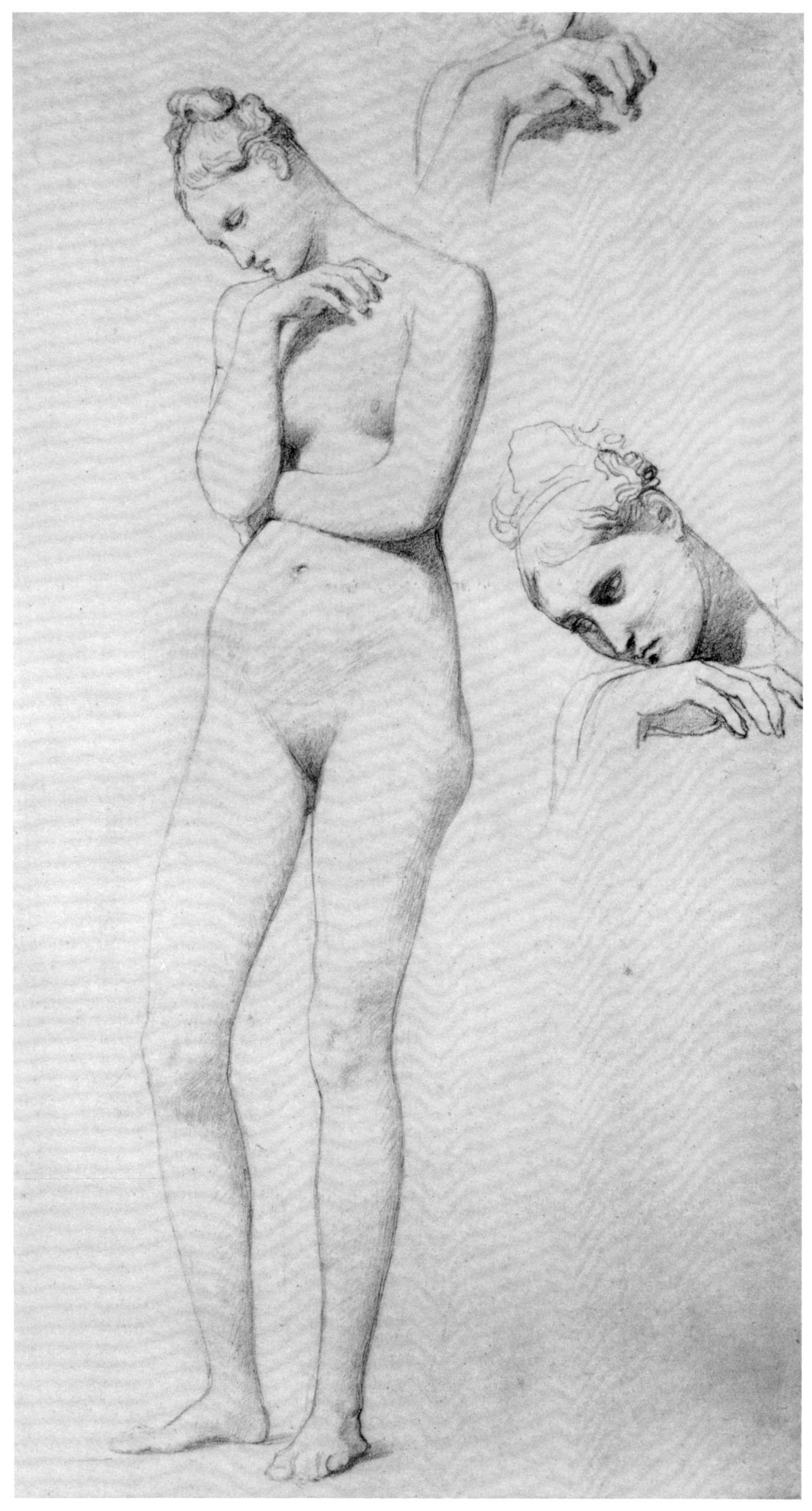

58   *Studies for Stratonica*

dated the New York drawing 1814, which suggests that the Rotterdam portrait was drawn in the same year.

During his first sojourn in Italy—he stayed in Rome from 1806 until 1820, and in Florence from 1820 to 1824—Ingres made more than two hundred portrait drawings of English and French visitors and Italian citizens. He drew these portraits on commission in part, in order to earn a living; and such drawings bear his formal signature as well as the place and date of execution. Ingres also drew portraits of his friends and acquaintances, which often bear only his name, sometimes with a dedication. The man in the Rotterdam drawing probably belonged to Ingres's circle of acquaintances, but attempts to identify the man have as yet been unsuccessful.

A.M.

58
Studies for Stratonica

F II 36
Pencil; 397 × 222 mm
Provenance: F. Koenigs; given by D. G. van Beuningen to the Museum Boymans Foundation, 1940
Literature: Rotterdam 1968, cat. no. 153 (ill.); W. Stechow, "The Love of Antiochus with Faire Stratonica," *The Art Bulletin* 27 (1945), p. 235; exhib. cat., Paris 1967, no. 184; H. S. Francis, "Jean Auguste Dominique Ingres," *The Bulletin of the Cleveland Museum of Art* (1968), p. 109, ill. 4; exhib. cat., Rome 1968, no. 113 (ill.); *The Age of Neo-Classicism,* exhib. cat., The Royal Academy and The Victoria & Albert Museum, London 1972, no. 669

On the left in this drawing a nude female figure stands with her head bowed and resting on the back of her right hand, her eyes downcast; on the right the woman's head is repeated, but with open eyes. The hand is sketched separately in the upper part of the sheet.

This drawing is a preliminary study for the figure of Stratonica in the painting *Antiochus and Stratonica* in the Musée Condé, Chantilly (Wildenstein 1954, cat. no. 232, ill. 82). Ingres made numerous studies for this painting—of the figure of Stratonica as well as of Antiochus. A study for the torso of Stratonica exists in the Musée Ingres at Montauban (*Ingres,* exhib. cat., Arts Council of Great Britain, London 1979, ill. 60), and a study of a nude in the Musée des Beaux-Arts in Tours is closely related to the Rotterdam drawing (exhib. cat., Rome 1968, no. 112). Another drawing of Stratonica, dressed in a classical garment, is in the collection of the Metropolitan Museum in New York (exhib. cat., Cambridge 1967, no. 79).

The story of Antiochus and Stratonica takes place in Syria in the third century B.C., with Antiochus, the son of king Seleucus, falling in love with the second wife of his father, who is much younger than her husband. Tormented by this hopeless love, Antiochus falls seriously ill, to the point of death. But the physician Erasistratus discovers the cause of his ailment and succeeds in persuading Seleucus to give up Stratonica in favor of his son, after which Antiochus recuperates (Stechow, "The Love of Antiochus with Faire Stratonica").

The painting was commissioned in 1834 by Ferdinand-Philippe, duke of Orléans and son of Louis-Philippe, the king of France. In that same year Ingres was appointed director of the Académie de France in the Villa Medici in Rome, a position that he held until 1841. Ingres completed the painting now in Chantilly when he was in Rome in 1840, which suggests that the drawing was also prepared in Italy around 1835/40. The painting was transported to Paris, where it immediately attracted great interest and was extremely well received.

The love story of Antiochus and Stratonica was a favored theme in the arts around 1800—in music and literature as well as in painting—and Ingres even owned a score of Nicholas Mehul's opera "Stratonica" from 1792 (N. Schlenoff, *Ingres: Ses Sources littéraires,* Paris 1956, pp. 242–244). Ingres himself explored this subject at that early time, as evidenced by a recently rediscovered drawing from around 1805 in the Musée des Beaux-Arts in Boulogne-sur-Mer (H. Toussaint, "Remise en cause de deux célèbres dessins du Louvre," *Ingres et son influence,* Bulletin spécial des Amis du Musée Ingres, September 1980, pp. 164ff., ill. no. 4).

A.M.

59

Portrait of Mme Hortense Reiset and Her Daughter Marie

F II 168
Pencil, heightened with white, on vergé paper; laid down; 308 × 245 mm
Signed and dated with pencil: *Ingres Del/à Monsieur/Reiset/1844*
Provenance: F. Koenigs; given by D. G. van Beuningen to the Museum Boymans Foundation, 1940
Literature: Rotterdam 1968, cat. no. 157 (ill.); Naef, III, pp. 348ff., ill. p. 351, no. 5; Naef, V, no. 400 (ill.)

In November 1835 Augustine-Modeste-Hortense Reiset married her twenty-year-old cousin Frédéric Reiset. Then in 1836 the newly married couple visited Rome, where they met Ingres, the newly appointed director of the Académie de France. This visit was the beginning of a long-standing friendship between Ingres and the Reiset family.

In August 1836 after their return to France, the Reisets' only child was born, a daughter named Thérèse-Hortense-Marie, nicknamed "Bibiche." She is pictured in this drawing dated 1844.

The Reisets had a summer home on Lake Enghien north of Paris, where Ingres was a regular guest. Ingres made a total of four portrait drawings of the Reiset family in 1844: one of Hortense's father, Louis Reiset; two of Hortense; and one of Frédéric (Naef, V, nos. 397–400). In 1850 Ingres recommended Frédéric Reiset to become the first curator of drawings at the Louvre; and in this position, Reiset catalogued more than 30,000 drawings by old masters, which had barely received any attention before. Ten years later Reiset was appointed curator of paintings at the Louvre, and finally in 1874 he became the director of the National Museums. He died in Paris in 1891, two years before Hortense.

A.M.

60

Two Studies of a Girl Writing and a Study of a Hand

F II 37
Pencil and black chalk, squared in black chalk; laid down; 294 × 368 mm
Signed with pencil: *Ingres*
Provenance: F. Koenigs; given by D. G. van Beuningen to the Museum Boymans Foundation, 1940
Literature: Rotterdam 1968, cat. no. 154 (ill.)

This sheet, consisting of two pieces of paper glued together, shows two studies of the same female model, nude at left, dressed at right. The model has a writing tablet in her lap and holds a stylus in her right hand. The upper part of the sheet contains a separate study of a resting hand.

These three studies are among the more than one hundred sketches made by Ingres, in pencil on paper and in oil on canvas, for the painting in the Musée Ingres at Montauban, entitled *Christ Among the Doctors* (Wildenstein 1954, cat. no. 302, ill. 193). The painting was commissioned in 1842 by Louis-Philippe, king of France, and his consort, Queen Marie-Amélie; it was intended for the royal chapel of Château de Bizy. The subject of the painting is taken from the Gospel of St. Luke (2:46–52), which tells how the twelve-year-old Jesus stayed behind in Jerusalem when his parents, believing he was with them, returned to Nazareth after the feast of the Passover; they found him three days later in the temple at Jerusalem sitting among the doctors, who were amazed by his wisdom. Ingres started the painting in 1843, but he completed it as late as 1862, after acquiring the right to dispose of it as he saw fit.

The Rotterdam drawing is a study for the second doctor on the left side of the painting, but it more closely resembles the oil sketch and the composition sketch that Ingres made for this figure (Wildenstein 1954, cat. no. 305, ill. 186; and Lapauze 1911, p. 519). In both the sketches and in the drawing the doctor is shown writing, whereas in the painting the doctor is represented with the writing tablet in his left hand and his right hand resting on his knee—in the same position shown in the study of the hand in the upper part of this sheet. This drawing is a good example of Ingres's practice of using female models even for male subjects (Lapauze 1911, p. 538).

A.M.

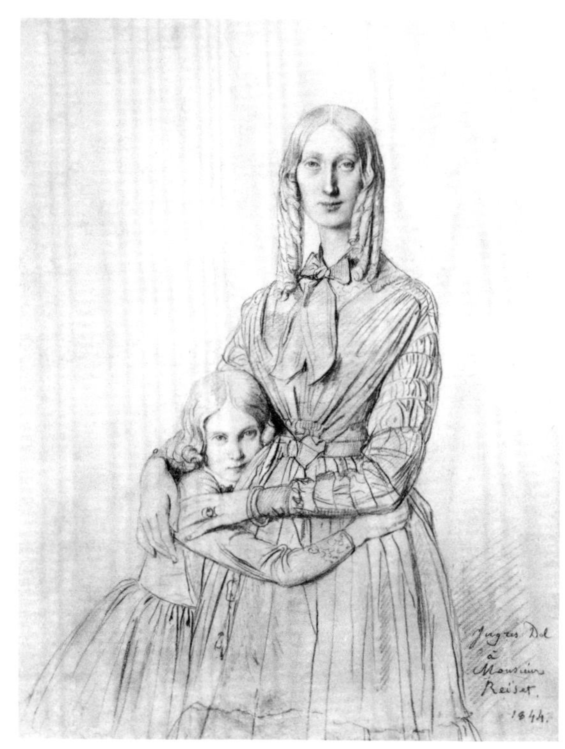

59   *Portrait of Mme Hortense Reiset and Her Daughter Marie*
(see also color plate 6)

60   *Two Studies of a Girl Writing and a Study of a Hand*

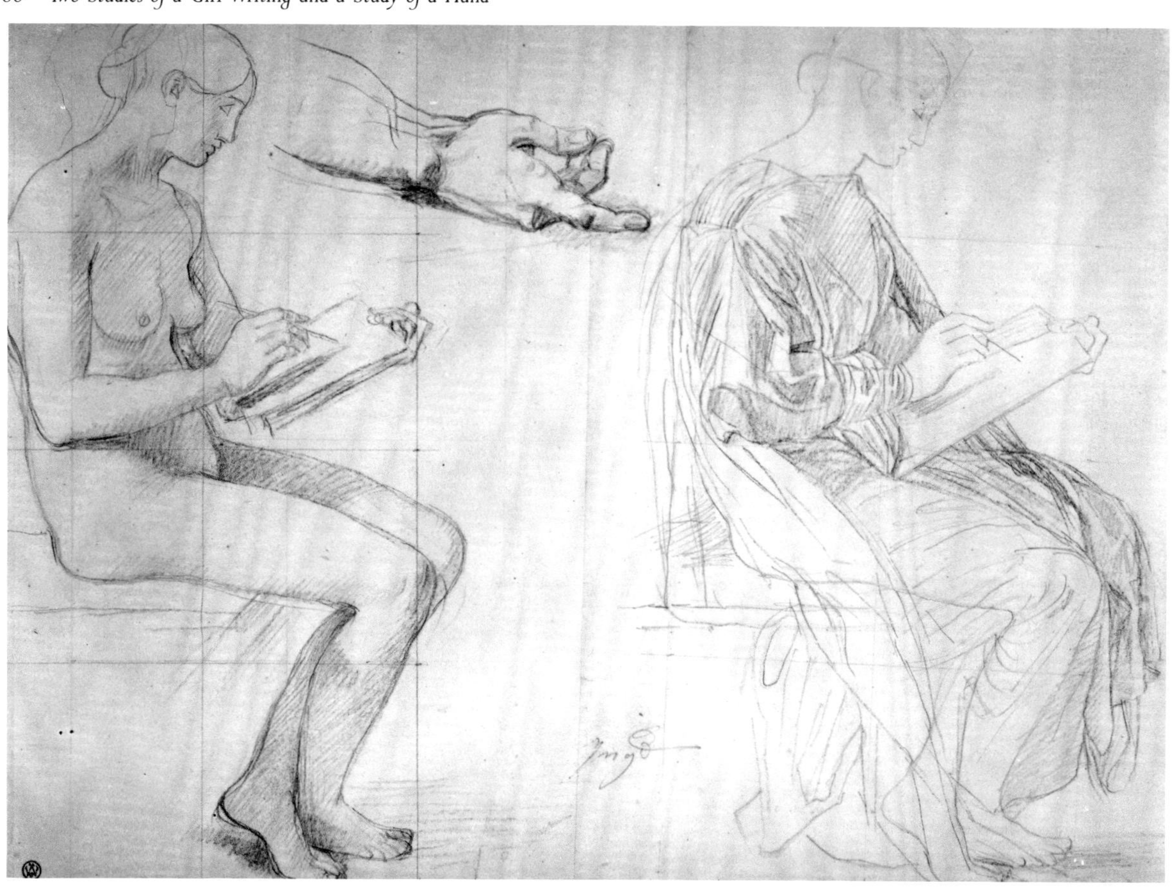

HENRI LE SIDANER
Port Louis, Mauritius, 1862–Versailles 1939

61
Mother and Child

St 98
Black, red, and yellow chalk, squared; 335 × 244 mm
Signed: *le Sidaner*
Provenance: Gift from Mrs. A. Brugh Singer to the Museum Boymans Foundation, 1953
Literature: Rotterdam 1968, cat. no. 163 (ill.)

In this drawing a woman shown in profile to the left is clad in a dark skirt and a light blouse. She sits in a straight chair, and a child rests on her lap with its head against her breast.

Henri Le Sidaner was born on the exotic island of Mauritius but lived in Dunkirk in France from the time time he was ten years old. This city gave him a grant to study with Alexandre Cabanel (1824–1889) at the Ecole des Beaux-Arts in Paris. Le Sidaner relinquished his academic style around 1885 under the influence of symbolism, particularly Belgian symbolism. He participated in the Brussels exhibitions of "La Libre Esthétique" in 1898 and 1902 (J. Juffermans, "Henri Le Sidaner, the Refiner of Impressionism," *Tableau,* V [1982/83], p. 196f.).

Le Sidaner developed quite an idiosyncratic style, reflecting the influence of impressionism, pointillism, and divisionism in addition to symbolism. He drew landscapes, city parks, and city gardens, all in soft hues, drawing not from nature but from memory. Representations of people are rather scarce in Le Sidaner's oeuvre, which has led most people to assume that the Rotterdam drawing portrayed the artist's wife and one of his children. Le Sidaner's eldest son, Louis, confirmed this in a letter dated 12 April 1983, saying that it is he who is shown on his mother's lap in the Rotterdam drawing; he dates the drawing around 1908. This identification corresponds with a chalk drawing in Paris, dated around 1900/1901, in which Le Sidaner drew his son at a much younger age (*Henri Le Sidaner, 1862–1939,* exhib. cat., Musée de la Ville, Dunkirk 1974, no. 24 [ill.]).

The drawing bears a studio stamp (not in Lugt) at the bottom on the right-hand side. Otherwise, it seems to be a more elaborate repetition of a drawing, also squared, reproduced by Mauclair (C. Mauclair, *Henri le Sidaner,* Paris 1928, ill. p. 133). The drawing was donated to the museum in 1953 by Mrs. A. Brugh Singer, widow of the American artist William H. Singer (1868–1943), who for a long time lived in the Netherlands and was a friend of Henri Le Sidaner.

J.P.

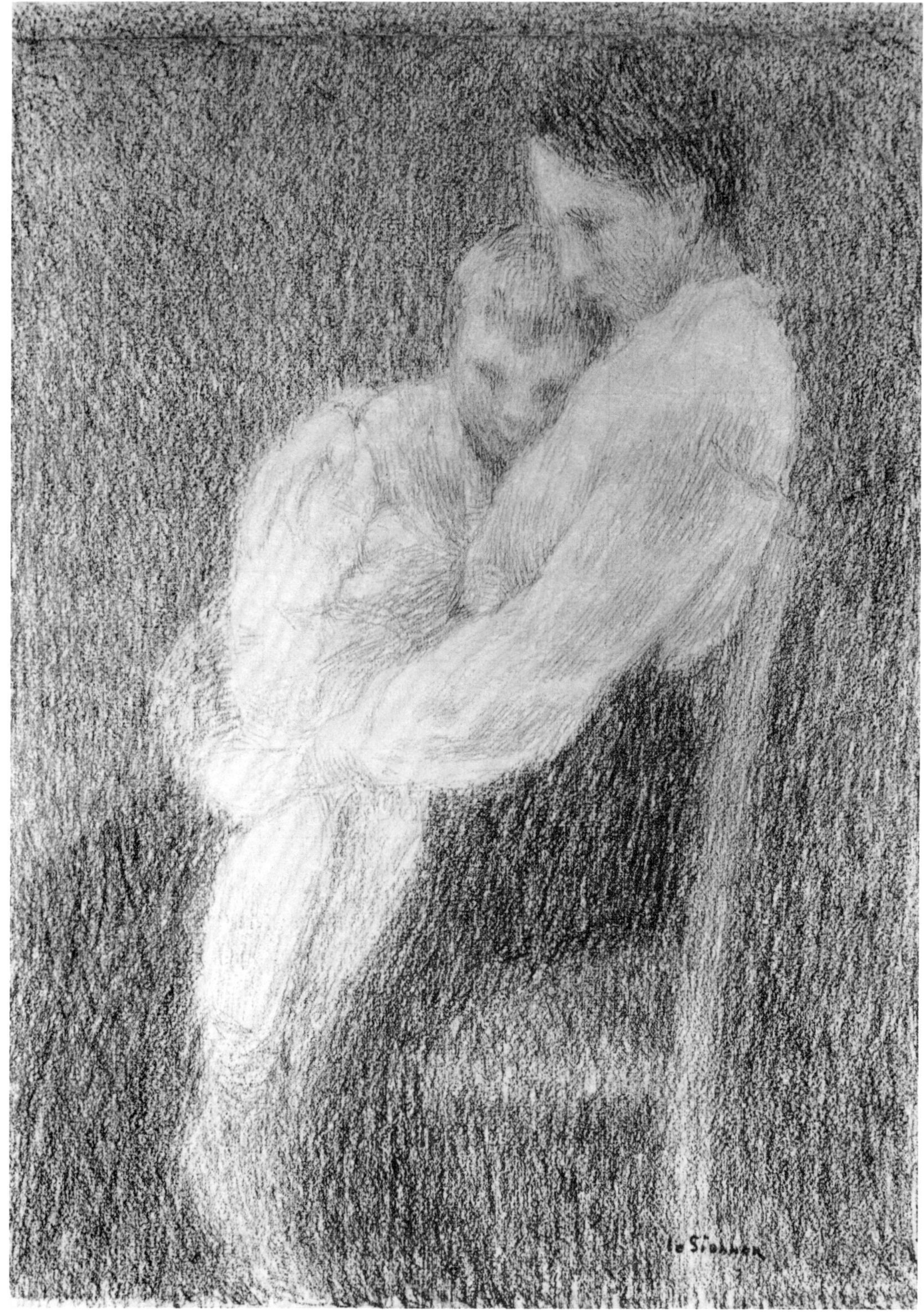

61   *Mother and Child*

ARISTIDE MAILLOL
Banyuls-sur-Mer 1861–Marly-le-Roy 1944

62
Seated Nude, Leaning Forward to the Right

MB 1961/T17
Black chalk on vergé paper; 274 × 226 mm
Provenance: Gift from Mme Dina Vierny to the Museum Boymans-van Beuningen Foundation, 1961
Literature: Rotterdam 1968, cat. no. 165 (ill.)

The bronze "La Méditerranée" by Aristide Maillol is a masterpiece in the collection of twentieth-century sculpture at the Museum Boymans-van Beuningen (Hoetink 1963, pp. 29–55, ill. 1). It was acquired in 1961 as the last casting available in a series of six bronze casts by Alexis Rudier in Paris.

Designated "La Méditerranée" only since 1937, the original sculpture was executed between 1902 and 1905 and was the first in series of robust, nude, mostly seated women, which represent abstract concepts such as "La Nuit" or "La Montagne" (exhib. cat., New York 1975/76, nos. 43 and 98 [ill.]). This series of sculptures was concluded in 1944 with "L'Harmonie" (exhib. cat., Baden Baden 1978, no. 88 [ill.]).

After his studies at the Ecole des Beaux-Arts, Maillol devoted himself to painting and founded a tapestry studio in his native city of Banyuls (exhib. cat., New York 1975/76, nos. 1–14 [ill.]). Somewhat later he also began to make wood carvings and terra cottas (*Maillol,* exhib. cat., Palais des rois de Majorque, Perpignan 1983, ill. pp. 59 and 63; W. Slatkin, "The Early Sculpture of Aristide Maillol, 1895–1900," *Gazette des Beaux-Arts,* VIᶜ per., XCVI [1983], no. 1341, p. 140f. [ill.]). Then during a visit to Paris, Edouard Vuillard put Maillol in touch with the editor/art dealer Ambroise Vollard, who decided to "publish" bronze casts of some of Maillol's terra cottas in multiple copies (U. E. Johnson, *Ambroise Vollard Editeur: Prints, Books, Bronzes,* New York 1977, p. 40 and cat. nos. 218–226). From this time on, Maillol concentrated mainly on sculpting.

This drawing and the one in the following entry (cat. no. 63) belong to a series of eleven preparatory studies for "La Méditerranée" that were donated to the Museum in 1961 on the occasion of the acquisition of the sculpture, by Madame Dina Vierny, the executor of Maillol's estate and since 1935 his model and lifelong companion.

J.P.

63
Squatting Nude with Left Arm Around Left Knee

MB 1961/T27
Verso: Four standing women
Black chalk on rugged gray paper; 279 × 215 mm
Provenance: Gift from Mme Dina Vierny to the Museum Boymans-van Beuningen Foundation, 1961
Literature: Rotterdam 1968, cat. no. 175 (ill.)

This sketch, like the one in the preceding entry (cat. no. 62), belongs to a series of eleven preparatory drawings for Maillol's statue "La Méditerranée" (1902–1905), that can be found along with the sculpture in the collections of the Museum Boymans-van Beuningen (Rotterdam 1968, cat. nos. 165–175 [ill.]; Hoetink 1963, ill. 1). According to Madame Dina Vierny, the drawings were done around 1902, with the artist's wife, Clotilde, and her sister Angélique serving as models (Hoetink 1963, note 41, pp. 47–48, and note 49, p. 52).

Maillol sketched many nudes, mainly female, and his interest was in pose, form, and mass rather than in movement or details of the head and face (E. Gradmann, *Maillol as Zeichner,* exhib. cat., Baden Baden

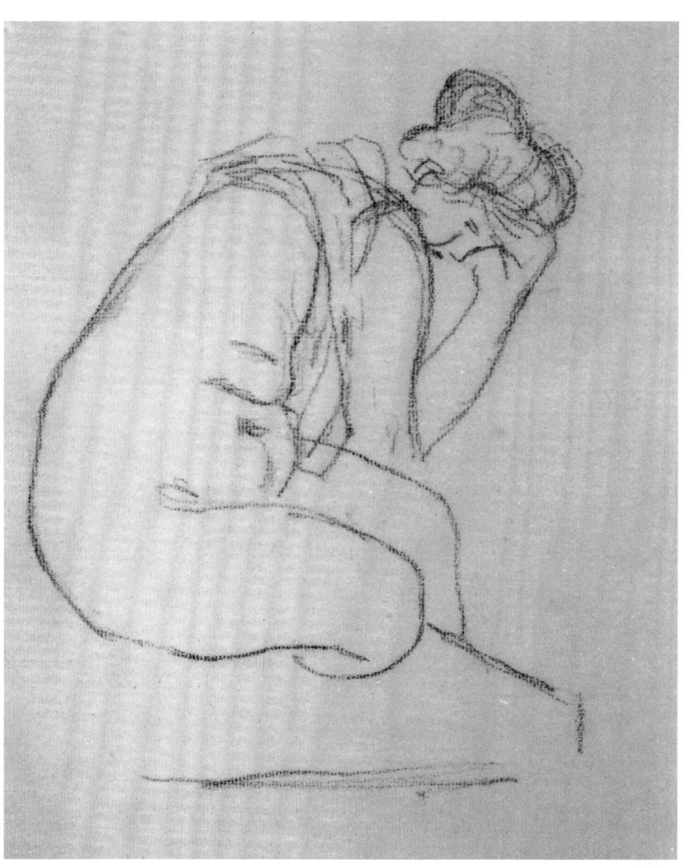

62   Seated Nude, Leaning Forward to the Right

63   Squatting Nude with Left Arm Around Left Knee

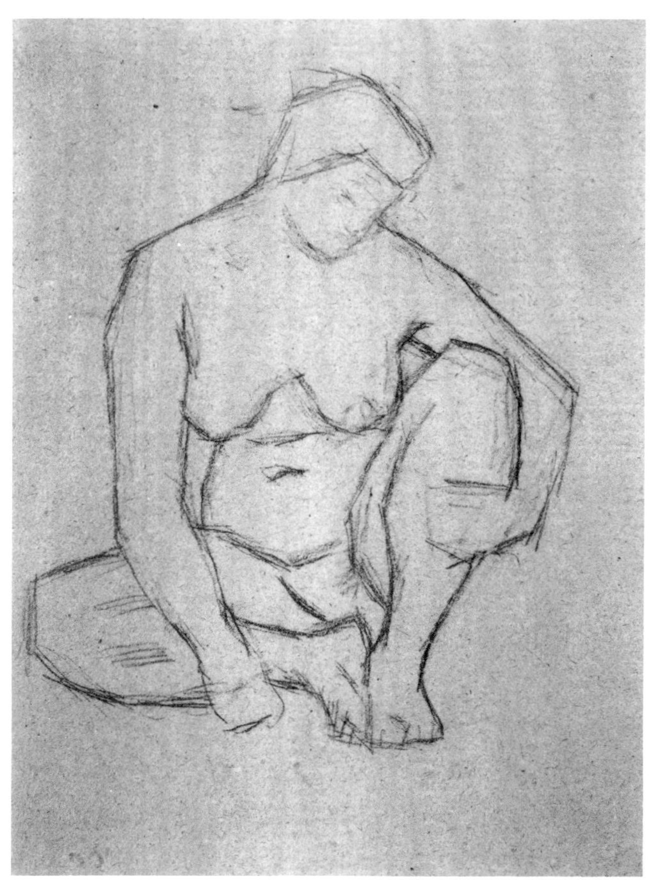

1978, pp. 157–158). Starting with a drawing done from life, such as that in the previous entry, Maillol elaborated his thoughts in further sketches and then modeled in clay (see Hoetink 1963, pp. 29–55, for the development of the sculpture "La Méditerranée"). The first sketch shows the model seated on some object and still includes details of clothing, coiffure, and individual features. Yet in the drawing exhibited here, Maillol's attention to the body mass—resulting in some distortion—already makes it typical of a sculptor's drawing. In the subsequent sketches of the series, the models seem to float on the plane of the paper, individual features have almost disappeared, and the artist confines himself to sketching in large, simple planes, related to the forms of the sculpture. Among the series of sketches for "La Méditerranée" that are in the Museum Boymans-van Beuningen collection, the present drawing was the last one done before the modeling of the sculpture in plaster, stone, and marble.

The sketch on the verso seems related to the theme of women in a park, which occurs in paintings as well as in tapestries by Maillol (exhib. cat., New York 1975/76, no. 8 [ill.]). According to Madame Vierny, Maillol drew this subject repeatedly in the period around 1896 (Hoetink 1963, p. 48).
J.P.

EDOUARD MANET
Paris 1832–1883

64
The Finding of Moses

F II 105
Pen and brush and brown ink over pencil, squared in red, on vergé paper; laid down; studio stamp in red (Lugt 880);
    333 × 280 mm
Provenance: F. Koenigs; given by D. G. van Beuningen to the Museum Boymans Foundation, 1940
Literature: Rotterdam 1968, cat. no. 183 (ill.); exhib. cat., Philadelphia/Chicago 1966/67, no. 14 (ill.); De Leiris 1969, no. 144,
    ill. 41; Wilson Bareau 1986, pp. 28–29, ill. 24.3

In this drawing a young woman kneels on the wooded bank of a river, which winds its way into the distance behind her. She wears a simple garment, and her hair is pulled back in a bun. Looking over her right shoulder, she raises her right arm in surprise to see a basket with a baby afloat on the water.

The entire sheet, which represents *The Finding of Moses* (Exodus 2:5–6), has been squared in red, which suggests that the drawing was preparatory for an unknown painting. Antonin Proust mentioned that Manet was working on such a painting around 1859 (A. Proust, "Edouard Manet, Souvenirs," *La Revue Blanche,* February–May 1897; exhib. cat., Paris/New York 1983, no. 19). Wilson Bareau relates this to an oil sketch now in Oslo for the painting *The Surprised Nymph* in Buenos Aires (Wilson Bareau 1986, pp. 26–36 [ill.]; exhib. cat., Paris/New York 1983, nos. 20 and 19 [ill.]).

According to De Leiris, the Rotterdam drawing is still strongly reminiscent of Manet's early drawings after other artists (De Leiris 1969, p. 40). Wilson Bareau concurs, and reproduces two prints after paintings by Italian artists to illustrate Manet's possible source of inspiration for the figures in the Rotterdam drawing (Wilson Bareau 1986, ill. 22 and 23). The scenery in the background resembles that in the New York painting *La Pêche* of 1861/63; a watercolor related to that painting belongs to the collection of the Museum Boymans-van Beuningen (exhib. cat., Philadelphia/Chicago 1966/67, no. 11; Rotterdam 1968, cat. no. 186 [ill.]). This landscape is believed to be drawn from the banks of the Seine near the Ile Saint-Ouen (Gennevilliers), where the Manet family owned property.
J.P.

65
Léon Koëlla-Leenhoff, Standing

F II 104
Red chalk; 325 × 232 mm
Signed with red chalk: *Ed. Manet*
Provenance: F. Koenigs; given by D. G. van Beuningen to the Museum Boymans Foundation, 1940
Literature: Rotterdam 1968, cat. no. 182 (ill.); De Leiris 1969, no. 232, ill. 247; Rouart/Wildenstein 1975, II, no. 465 (ill.);
    exhib. cat., Paris/New York 1983, no. 110 (ill.); Hofmann 1985, ill. 12

This is a three-quarter-length portrait of a young man with rather short hair, seen from the front. He wears a vested suit and stands casually with his hands in the pockets of his trousers.

The drawing has been related to the 1868 painting *Le Déjeuner dans l'Atelier* now in Munich (Hofmann 1985), for which the model was Léon Koëlla-Leenhoff (1852–1927), Manet's son with Dutch pianist Suzanne Leenhoff, whom the artist married in 1863. The young man also appears in the New York painting *La Pêche,* dated 1861/63, a landscape after the manner of Rubens in which Manet included himself, Suzanne Leenhoff, and their son (exhib. cat., Paris/New York 1983, no. 12 [ill.]). Although Manet never legitimatized Léon, the latter lived with his mother in Manet's parental home from 1867, and after the artist's death he was one of the heirs (according to Manet's will of 30 September 1882, in

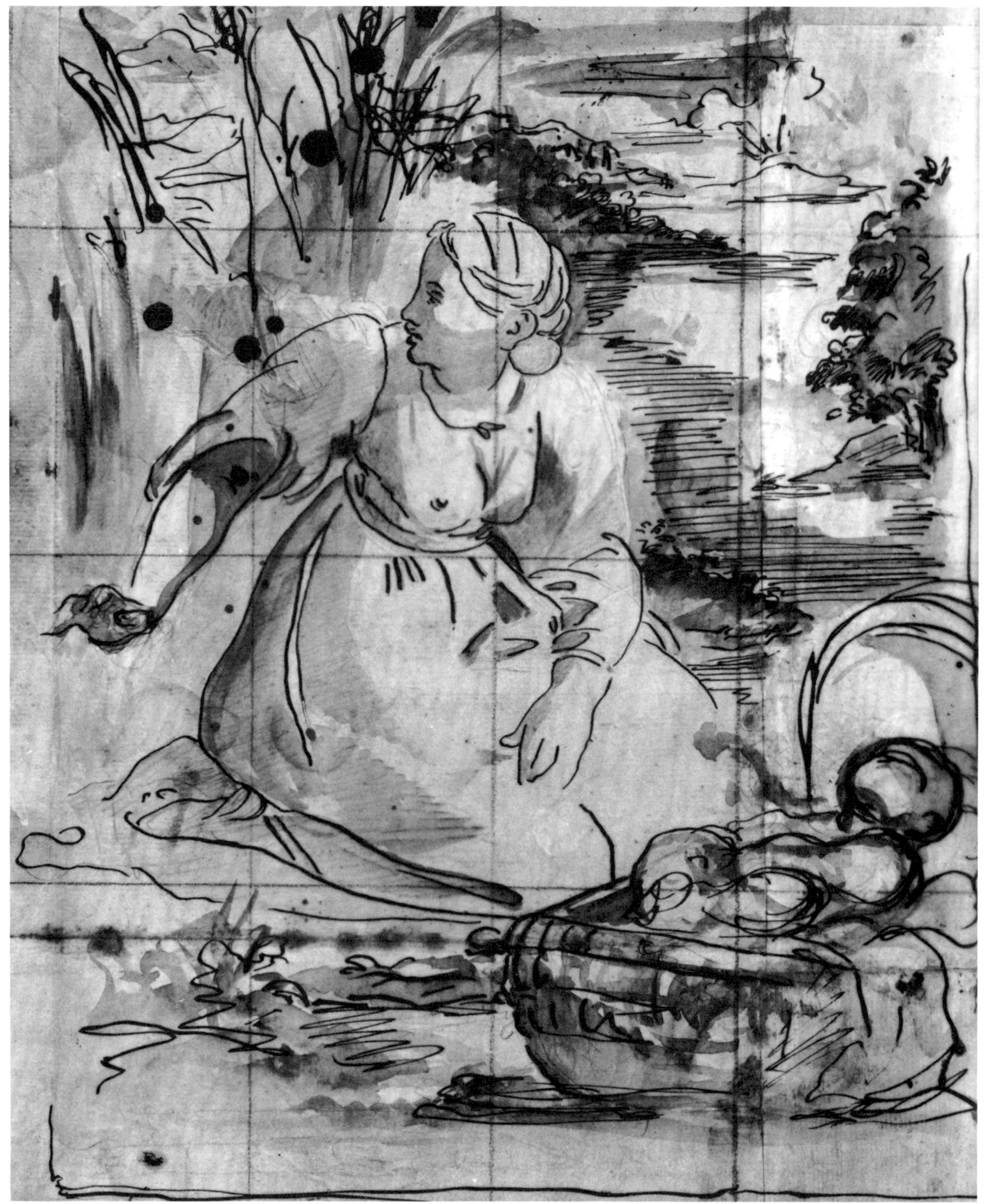

64　*The Finding of Moses*

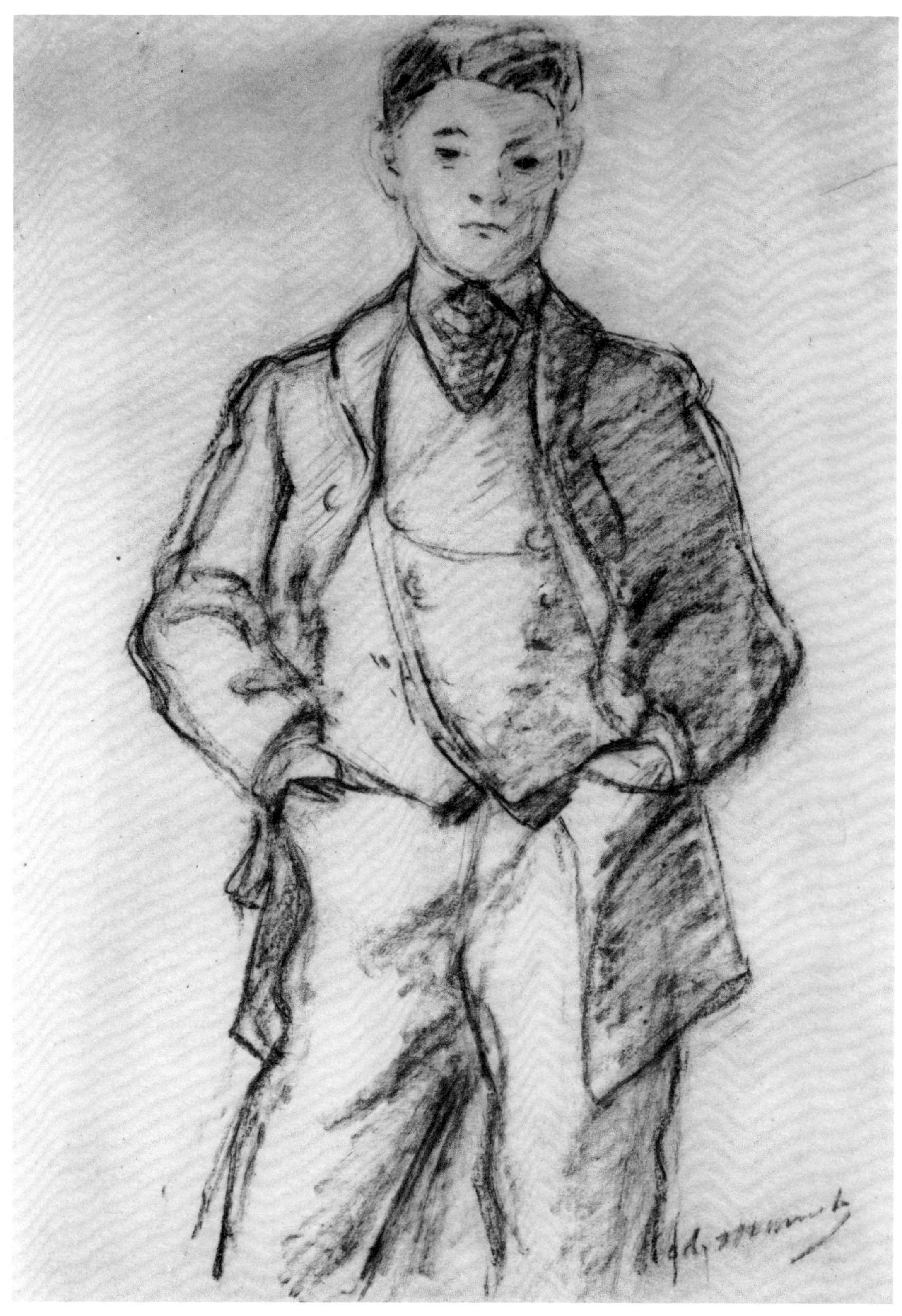

65   *Léon Koëlla-Leenhoff, Standing*

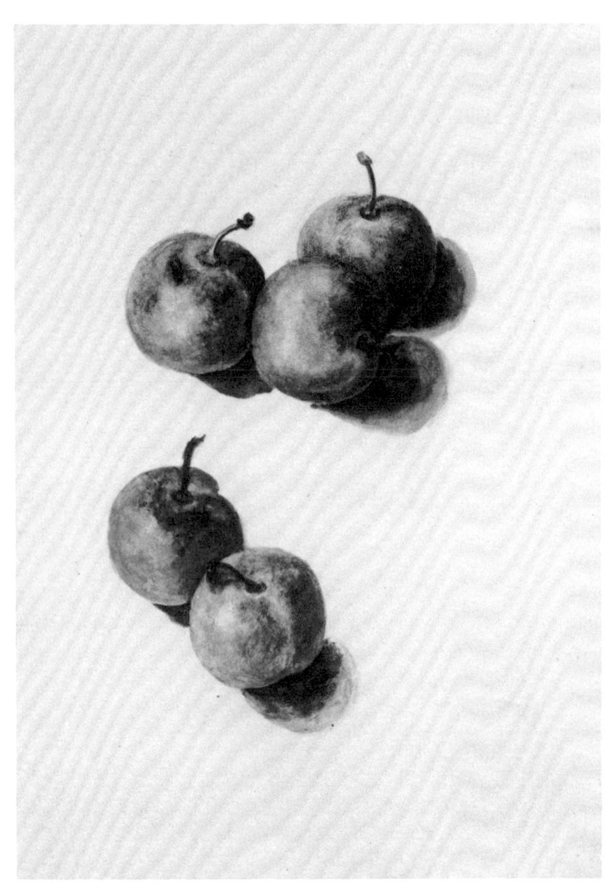

66   *Five Plums (see also color plate 7)*

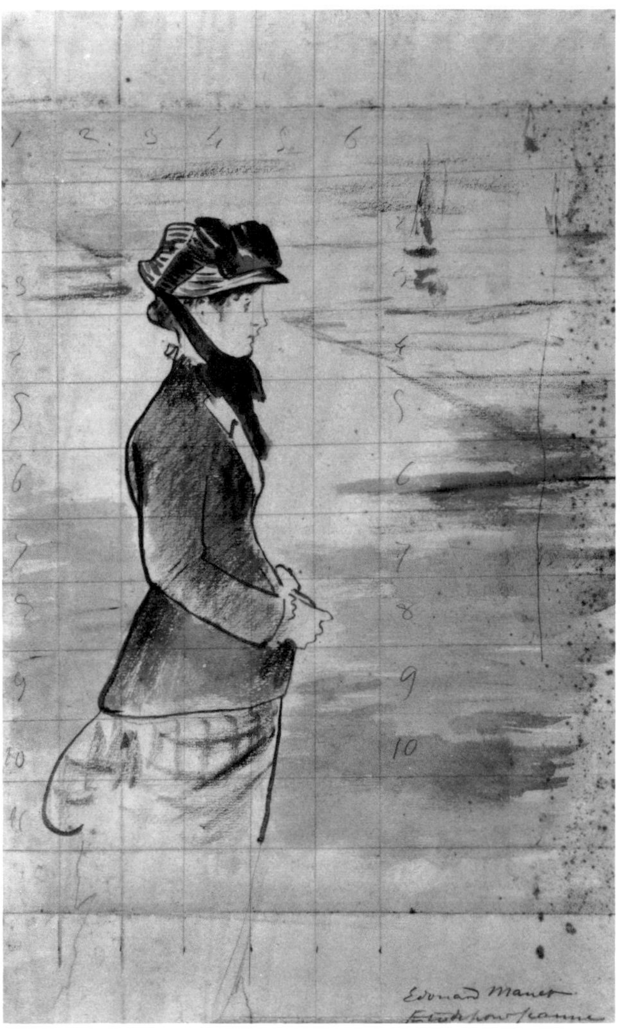

67   *Woman Standing to the Right*

Rouart/Wildenstein 1975, I, p. 25). Léon often served as a model for Manet, appearing in several etchings even as a child (J. Leymarie and M. Melot, *Les Gravures des impressionistes,* Paris 1971, nos 21–26, 57 [ill.]).

Doubt is sometimes cast upon the authenticity of the Rotterdam drawing as well as on a drawing in Chicago, probably also of Léon Koëlla-Leenhoff (Joachim 1974, no. 72 [ill.]). Despite some differences in the dress and pose of the young man in the Rotterdam drawing and the young man in the Munich painting, a great similarity exists between the two, particularly in their facial features (see P. Schneider, *The World of Manet, 1832–1883,* New York 1968, p. 66, for a photograph of Léon Koëlla-Leenhoff). A drawing in Keswick, England, is generally considered a work after the painting (Hofmann 1985, ill. 4).

The apparent age of the young man in the Rotterdam drawing and in the Munich painting is consistent with Léon's age in 1868. In that year, at the age of sixteen, he went to work for the banking firm of Edgar Degas's father (Hofmann 1985, p. 24). The Chicago drawing is dated around 1865, when Léon was thirteen (Joachim 1974, no. 72 [ill.]). Accordingly, he would be fifteen years old in the Lisbon painting *Soap Bubbles* from 1867 (exhib. cat., Paris/New York 1983, no. 102 [ill.]), and seventeen in the 1869 painting in Stockholm, with his first growth of beard (*Manet, Närbild,* exhib. cat., Nationalmuseum, Stockholm 1985, no. 64 [ill.]).

J.P.

66
Five Plums

F II 72
Watercolor on white cardboard; 224 × 160 mm
Provenance: F. Koenigs; given by D. B. van Beuningen to the Museum Boymans Foundation, 1940
Literature: Rotterdam 1968, cat. no. 180 (ill.)

Around October 1880 Manet spent some time in Bellevue, where he had rented a house in order to recuperate from an illness. For his amusement, he made watercolors of flowers and fruits from the garden, and he used these to decorate letters he wrote to his friends in Paris.

Manet wrote to a certain Isabelle Lemonnier, for instance, whom he always addressed as "Mademoiselle" (Rouart/Wildenstein 1975, II, no. 587 [ill.]; for her portrait, see Rotterdam 1968, cat. no. 184 [ill.]). Another letter, adorned with a plum, is in the collections of the Museum Boymans-van Beuningen (Rotterdam 1968, cat. no. 181 [ill.]). This letter uses "Madame" and was probably intended for Mrs. Jules Guillemet, an American by birth, who ran a sumptuous fashion boutique on the Faubourg St. Honoré in Paris with her French husband (E. M. Zafran, *Master Drawings from Titian to Picasso: The Curtis O. Bear Collection,* Atlanta 1985, no. 82B [ill.]; see Rouart/Wildenstein 1975, I, no. 289 [ill.], for her portrait). This assumption is supported by the fact that the letter as well as the drawing with five plums belonged to Mrs. Jules Guillemet's collection.

Manet also painted flowers and fruits in oil; a painting with five plums, dated approximately 1880, exists in Houston, Texas (Rouart/Wildenstein, 1975, I, no, 363 [ill.]).

J.P.

67
Woman Standing to the Right

F II 20
Brush and gray ink over pencil, squared and numbered with pencil, on vergé paper (Arches); 462 × 290 mm
Signed and inscribed with pencil: *Edouard Manet/Etude pour Jeanne*
Provenance: F. Koenigs; given by D. G. van Beuningen to the Museum Boymans Foundation, 1940
Literature: Rotterdam 1968, cat. no. 176 (ill.); exhib. cat., Philadelphia/Chicago 1966/67, no. 136 (ill.); De Leiris 1969, no. 591, ill. 429; Rouart/Wildenstein 1975, II, no. 435 (ill.); exhib. cat., Paris/New York 1983, no. 152 (ill.)

This drawing shows a young woman in profile, dressed in a hip-length jacket, a plaid skirt, and a hat with a large bow and a ribbon under her chin. She stands on the shore gazing at the sea to the right, with some small sailboats in the background.

In 1881 Stéphane Mallarmé asked his friend Manet to draw illustrations for his translation of poems by Edgar Allan Poe (Rouart/Wildenstein 1975, II, no. 437). The first edition (1888) contains no illustrations by or after Manet, but Mallarmé dedicated the volume to Manet in any case (exhib. cat., Philadelphia/Chicago 1966/67, p. 151).

Manet was definitely interested in this project, but its execution was impeded by his ill health. Nevertheless, he designed illustrations for a few of Poe's poems—for instance, a drawing now in New Haven, Connecticut, for "The City in the Sea" (De Leiris 1969, no. 595 [ill.]). The Rotterdam drawing is related to Poe's poem "Annabel Lee," but Manet was not faithful to the letter of the poem. Instead, he referred for his image back to his 1879 painting *Jeune femme dans un jardin,* now in Merion, Pennsylvania (Rouart/Wildenstein 1975, I, no. 315 [ill.]). Four drawings are known in which the young woman from this painting is shown not in a garden but at the seaside (Rouart/Wildenstein, 1975, II, nos. 435–438 [ill.]). The fact that the squaring in the Rotterdam sheet is underneath the drawing of the female figure suggests that this is the first drawing of the theme. The second and third drawings are in New York and Buenos Aires (Rouart/Wildenstein 1975, II, nos. 435 and 436 [ill.]). The fourth drawing, now in Copenhagen, shows the girl lying on the beach (Rouart/Wildenstein 1975, II, no. 438 [ill.]). An illustration after this motif occurs in Mallarmé's second edition of the poems by Poe (1889).

Because of the inscription, Rouart and Wildenstein believe that Jeanne Demarcy served as the model for the painting and the drawings. She was a young actress who also posed for the 1881 painting *Le Printemps* now in New York (Rouart/Wildenstein 1975, I, no. 372 [ill.]). Others believe that the "Jeanne" in this drawing is the younger sister of Manet's student Eva Gonzales (for Eva Gonzales and her relatives, see *Manet: Dessins, aquarelles, eaux-fortes, lithographies, correspondance,* exhib. cat., Huguette Beres, Paris 1978, no. 107). This seems unlikely when one compares the apparent age of Jeanne Gonzales in the painting *La Partie de Croques* from 1871 with the age of the young woman in the illustrations to "Annabel Lee" of 1889 (Rouart/Wildenstein 1975, I, no. 173 [ill.]).

Manet had worked earlier on the theme of a young woman by the sea, in a watercolor in Paris. According to Rouart and Wildenstein, who date this sheet 1880, Mrs. Jules Guillemet's younger sister Marguérite was the model (cat. no. 66; Rouart/Wildenstein 1975, II, no. 414 [ill.]).
J.P.

FRÉDÉRIC BOURGEOIS DE MERCEY
Paris 1805–La Faloise 1860

68
View on the Emperor's Palace, Rome

MB 1981/T9
Black chalk; 420 × 583 mm
Inscribed with pencil: *vue du Palais des empereurs près du Collisée*
Provenance: Studio stamp F. de Mercey (not in Lugt); auction, London, 14 June 1973, no. 115 (ill.); acquired 1981

According to the inscription at the bottom left and right of this sheet, the drawing is of the ruins of the imperial palace on the Palatine Hill in Rome. This palace was built by the emperor Domitian at the end of the first century A.D., and it served for a long time as the seat of the Roman emperors. De Mercey, an artist of whom little is known nowadays, was the son a high official in the Napoleonic administration in Italy ("Gavarni," *Dessins originaux,* cat., Paul Prouté, Paris 1969, p. 28). Known primarily as a landscape painter, de Mercey made his artistic debut in Paris in 1831 at the age of twenty-six, with a view of Venice. He was also recognized as a writer.

In the years before 1831 de Mercey was probably a student at the Académie de France in Rome. This is suggested by the drawing he did of the Villa Medici, where the Academy was housed (Paris, Fondation Custodia, coll. F. Lugt, inv. no. 1976-T-21), a drawing that shows the same technique and dimensions as the one in Rotterdam.

The small initials on the bottom, just to the right of the center, appear in both drawings and may be read as "MF" (or "Mercey fecit").
A.M.

68   *View on the Emperor's Palace, Rome*

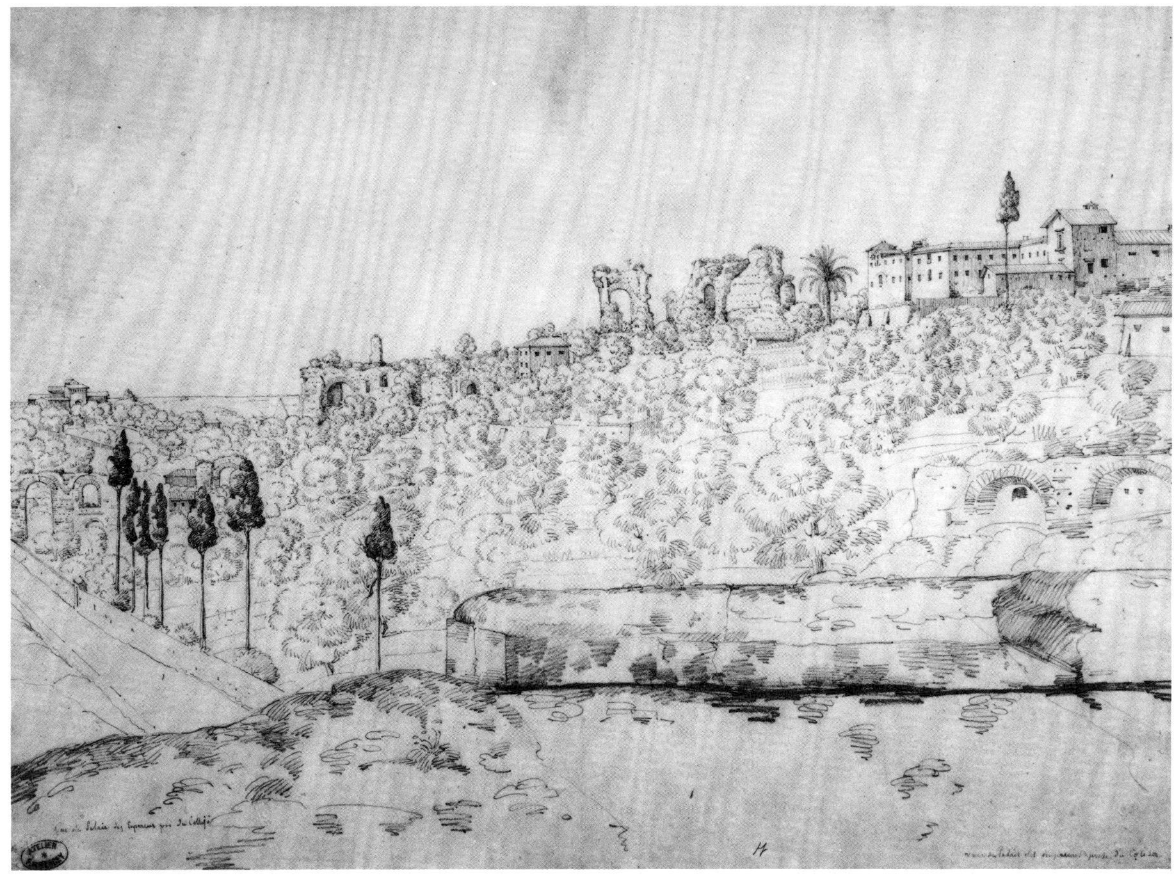

JEAN-FRANÇOIS MILLET
Gruchy (Greville) 1814–Barbizon 1875

69
Woman Sitting at a Table

F II 11
Pastel on light brown paper; 323 × 266 mm
Signed with black chalk: *F. Millet*
Provenance: F. Koenigs; given by D. G. van Beuningen to the Museum Boymans Foundation, 1940
Literature: Rotterdam 1968, cat. no. 192 (ill.); L. Lepoittevin, *Jean-François Millet, Portraitiste,* Paris 1971, no. 19 (ill.); exhib.
cat., Paris 1975, under no. 2

The woman in this drawing is traditionally identified as Pauline-Virginie Ono, Millet's first wife, to whom he was married for only three years, until her death in 1844. According to R. L. Herbert, however, the identification is incorrect (exhib. cat., Paris 1975). He maintains instead that this is a portrait of Millet's second wife, Catherine Lemaire, comparing this with a strikingly similar portrait of her from 1848/49. Millet lived with Catherine Lemaire from 1845 until his death in 1875 (exhib. cat., Boston 1984, no. 12 [ill.]). If the woman depicted here is indeed Catherine Lemaire, this representation must have been staged, because it is known that she could neither read nor write.

This pastel belongs to Millet's early work, when he was living alternately in Cherbourg, Le Havre, and Paris, and earned his living by painting portraits. The signature *F. Millet* instead of the more usual *J. F. Millet* occurs more frequently on painted portraits dating from this time (Lepoittevin, *Jean-François Millet, Portraitiste,* nos. 85, 89, 90, 92).

A.M.

70
Farmer Leaning on His Spade

F II 96
Black chalk on vergé paper; 304 × 214 mm
Provenance: F. Koenigs; given by D. G. van Beuningen to the Museum Boymans Foundation, 1940
Literature: Rotterdam 1968, cat. no. 196 (ill.); *J. F. Millet,* exhib. cat., Wildenstein & Co., London 1969, under no. 21 (ill.); exhib. cat., Paris 1975, no. 50 (ill.); exhib. cat., London 1976, no. 32 (ill.)

On this sheet a farmer is shown leaning on his spade to rest from ploughing in the field. In the background the roofs of several huts are barely discernible at the edge of a forest.

The rough borders around the image, sketched by Millet himself, suggest that the sheet was a direct compositional study for the painting formerly in the Burke collection (auction cat., New York, Parke-Bernet, 6 November 1983, no. 56 [ill.]; exhib. cat., London 1969, no. 21). The painting differs from the drawing in some details, although the background is the same. In the drawing the man rests both arms on the spade; in the painting he rests his chin on his hands, and a basket, which is absent in the drawing, sits on the ground beside him. The painting was executed around 1850, which suggests that the study was drawn around that time as well.

In 1849 Millet settled permanently in Barbizon, a farming village at the edge of the Bois de Fontainebleau; this was two years after Théodore Rousseau had moved there to live. The two artists became good friends and formed the beginning of what would later be called the "School of Barbizon." Many artists, among them a few Americans, came to Barbizon in future years to practice landscape painting.

A.M.

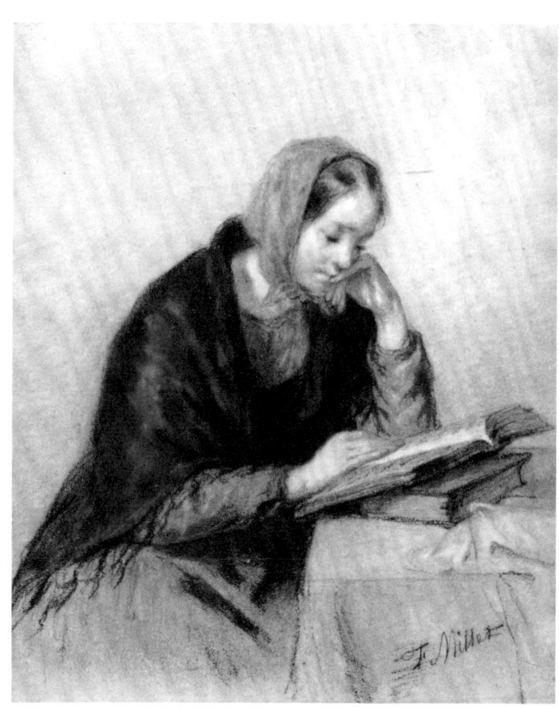

69   Woman Sitting at a Table (see also color plate 8)

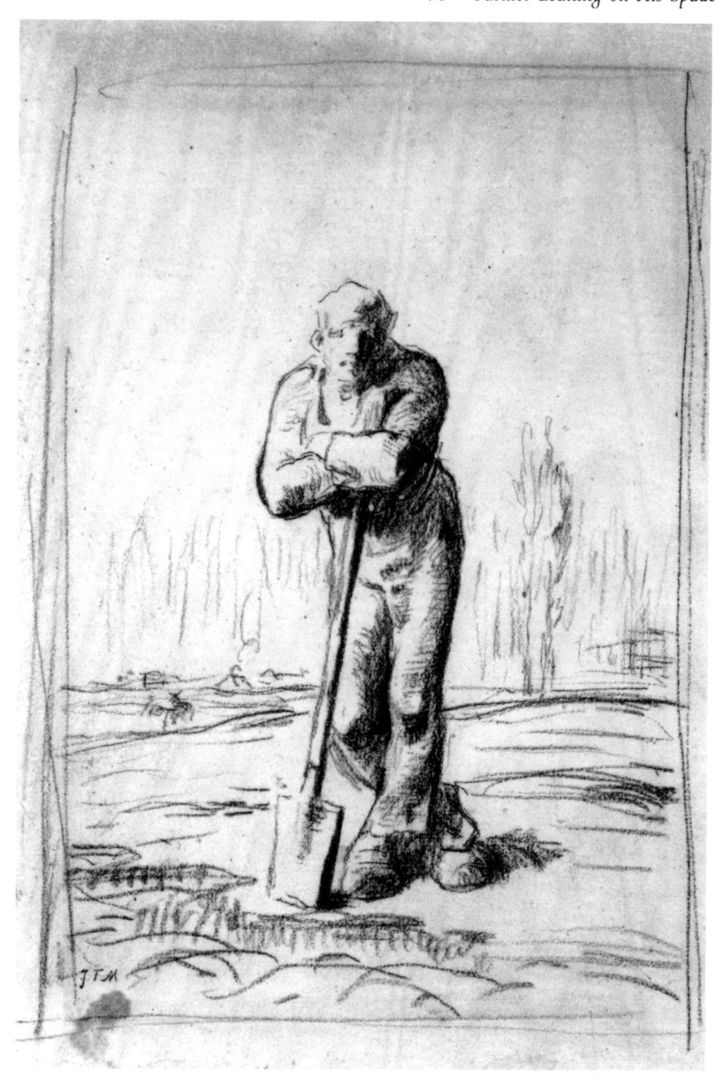

70   Farmer Leaning on His Spade

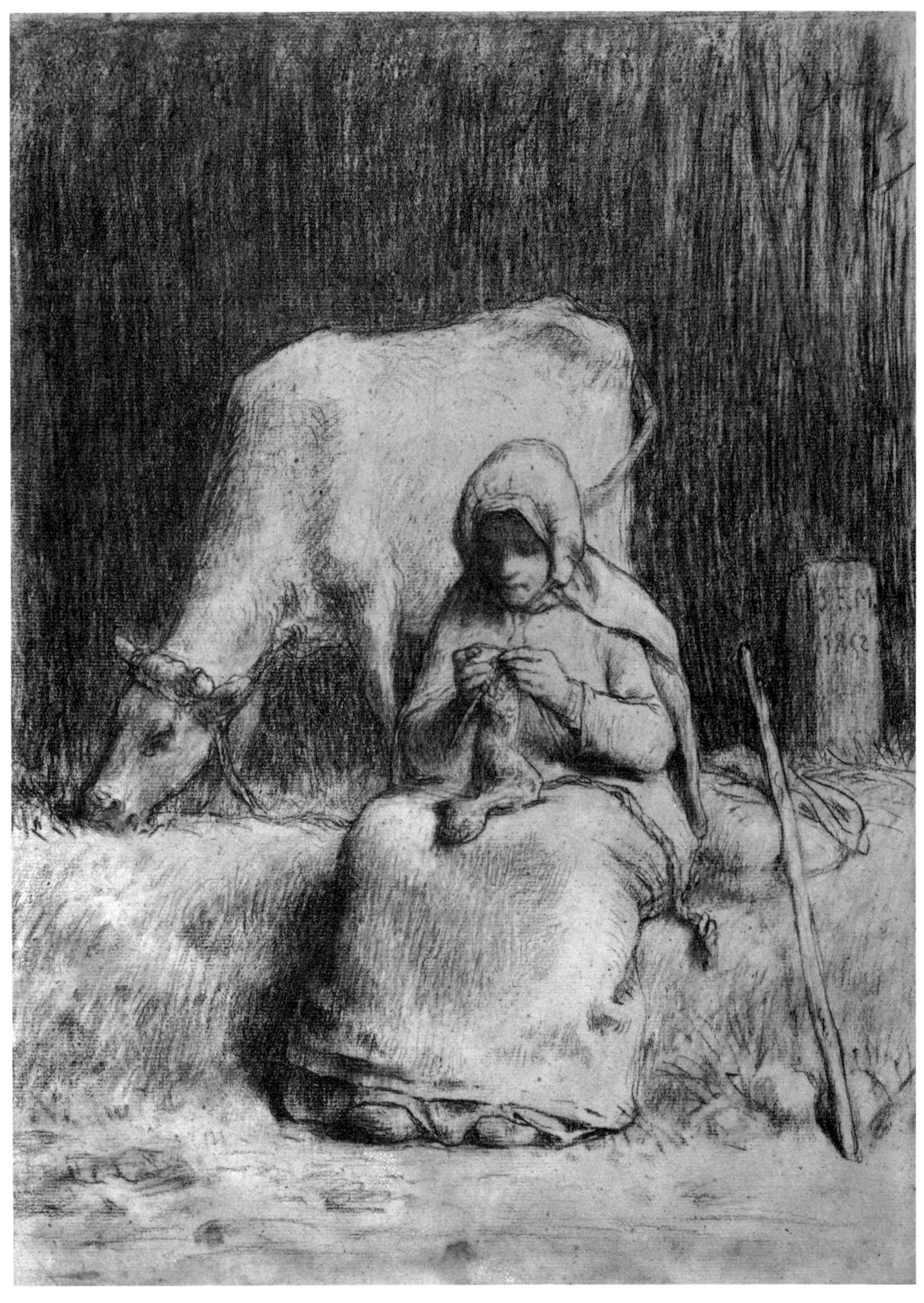

71   *Peasant Girl Watching over Her Cow*

Peasant Girl Watching over Her Cow

F II 10
Black chalk on vergé paper; 415 × 312 mm
Signed and dated with black chalk: *J.F.M. 1852*
Provenance: F. Koenigs; given by D. G. van Beuningen to the Museum Boymans Foundation, 1940
Literature: Rotterdam 1968, cat. no. 191 (ill.); exhib. cat., Paris 1975, no. 89 (ill.); London 1976, no. 69 (ill.), under no. 43;
  The Realist Tradition, exhib. cat., The Cleveland Museum of Art, Cleveland 1980/81, fig. 46 (G. P. Weisberg); *An*
  International Episode: Millet, Monet and Their North American Counterparts, exhib. cat., Memphis 1982, pp. 24 and 94, no. 8,
  ill. 2; exhib. cat., Boston 1984, under no. 28

Through Alfred Sensier, a government employee in Paris and a friend of the artist, Millet received a commission from the government at the end of 1852 to make a painting for the Directeur des Beaux-Arts in Paris. Millet hastily sent Sensier this sketch of a knitting peasant girl who watches over her cow; Millet told Sensier that he had kept a tracing of the sketch (E. Moreau-Nélaton, *Millet raconté par lui-même,* I, Paris 1921, pp. 108, 109). The tracing that Millet mentioned is probably the very summary and squared drawing in the Louvre, which shows only the most elementary details of the composition (see *Cabinet des Dessins du Musée du Louvre, Catalogue Raisonné,* Paris 1938, no. 10586 [ill.]).

The milestone on the right and behind the seated girl, on which Millet so prominently signed his initials and the year 1852, indicates that the girl was grazing her cow on the grassy shoulder along a road. In this way the artist referred to the loss of the right of communal grazing, which was part of the communal farming system, and which allowed French peasants who did not possess farm lands to graze their cows on land belonging to other people. This right was abolished in the first half of the nineteenth century (exhib. cat., Boston 1984, p. 51). Millet eventually fulfilled his commission in 1858 with a painting that completely differed from the drawing in composition, but which had the same tenor: the peasant girl stands with her cow in the wide plain of the Chailly-Barbizon region, on the public road leading between the fields in which she is not allowed to graze her cow (exhib. cat., Paris 1975, no. 67, [ill.]).
A.M.

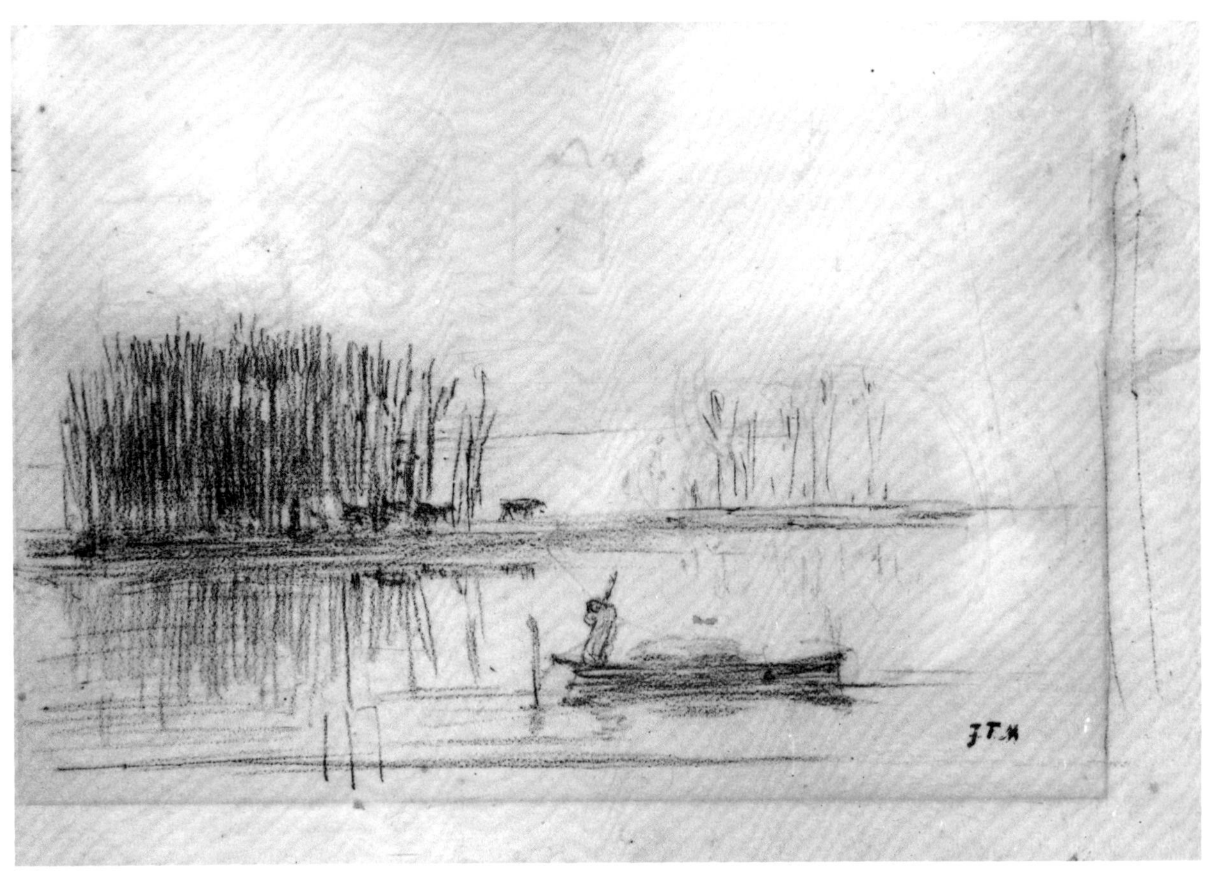

72   *View of a River with a Small Boat*

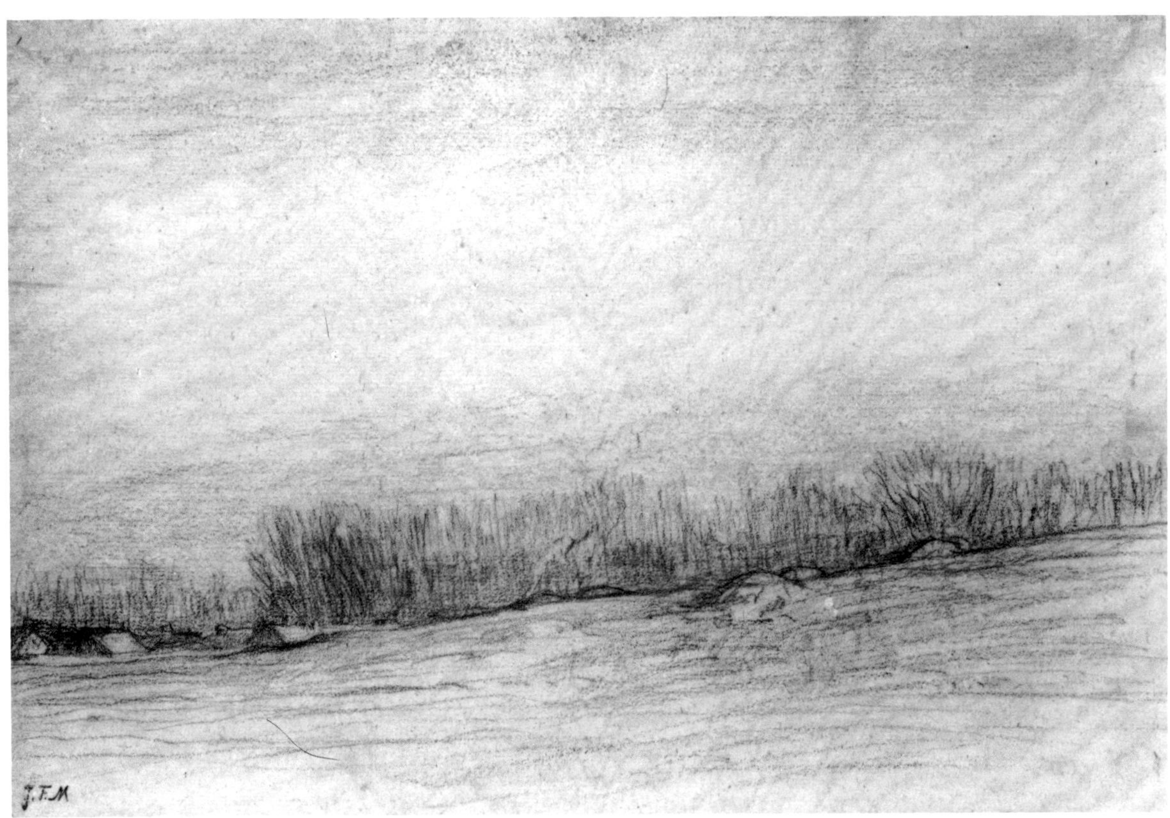

73   *Landscape with the Edge of a Forest*

72
View of a River with a Small Boat

F II 199
Verso: Various sketches
Black and white chalk on thin paper, corrections in white chalk; 190 × 280 mm
Signed in brown ink: *J.F.M.*
Provenance: F. Koenigs; given by D. G. van Beuningen to the Museum Boymans Foundation, 1940
Literature: Rotterdam 1968, cat. no. 200 (ill.); Paris 1975, under no. 78; London 1976, under no. 52; exhib. cat., Boston 1984, under no. 62

A man is depicted at work in his boat, moored between two poles in the middle of a river. On the opposite bank a herd of cows is being driven to the right, out of a small cluster of trees. The same motif can be seen in a fairly large watercolor in the Louvre (R. Bacou, *Millet Dessins,* Paris, 1975, no. 35 [ill.]), although in the foreground of this watercolor, a woman is shown standing with a water jug on her shoulder. Millet used both sheets, together with several other studies, as preparatory sketches for the 1855 painting *The Washerwomen,* now in Boston, Massachusetts (exhib. cat., Boston 1984, no. 62, [ill.]). Specifically, the Rotterdam drawing serves, in modified form, as the background. Because the paper was thin, the sketches on the verso of the sheet were visible on the front; to hide them, Millet covered the sky with a white gouache paint.
A.M.

73
Landscape with the Edge of a Forest

F II 64
Black chalk on vergé paper; 220 × 288 mm
Provenance: F. Koenigs; given by D. G. van Beuningen to the Museum Boymans Foundation, 1940
Literature: Rotterdam 1968, cat. no. 194 (ill.); *Cent dessins français du Fitzwilliam Museum,* exhib. cat., Paris 1976, under no. 68

Millet drew this landscape in the precise manner so characteristic of his work in the 1850s; this style of drawing is also apparent in the preceding sheet (cat. no. 72). In the present work, a sloping field at the edge of a forest descends into a hollow in the background. In the field are several trash piles, two of which have already been burned; and over the edge of the declivity, on the left, the roofs of some farmhouses are barely discernible. This drawing illustrates Millet's interest, unlike Rousseau's, in landscapes that showed signs of human activity.

The verso of a drawing in the Ashmolean Museum, Oxford, contains a sketch comparable to this drawing (exhib. cat., Paris 1976). As mentioned elsewhere, however, neither sheet can be related to paintings by Millet.
A.M.

Country Road with Twisted Trees

F II 176
Pen and brown ink, watercolor, over pencil on vergé paper; laid down; 115 × 186 mm
Provenance: F. Koenigs; given by D. G. van Beuningen to the Museum Boymans Foundation, 1940
Literature: Rotterdam 1968, cat. no. 199 (ill.)

On the advice of their physician, Millet and his wife sojourned in Vichy, the famous French health resort, during the summers of 1866–68, in order to seek a cure for the liver ailment that had troubled Madame Millet for some time. Letters written to Sensier in Paris show that Millet was enchanted by the scenery around Vichy. He wrote that he worked hard in order to assemble as many "documents" (i.e., sketches) as possible, particularly of the scenery, and that he filled in small sketches with watercolor. He did this, he said, in order to recall the colorful scenery in general (E. Moreau-Nélaton, II, pp. 8, 9).

A large number of these small sketches have been preserved (see exhib. cat., Boston 1984, nos. 117–127). Millet drew them in pencil and touched them up later with ink and watercolor, using the color samples he had made on the spot, which can still be seen on some of the sketches. Later he used many of these drawings for his paintings.

The little sketch shown here was done near Vichy in 1866 or 1867—in 1868 Millet was much too ill himself to be able to work. In fact, since the dimensions of this sheet correspond to those of two other sketches in Boston, which are dated 1867, this watercolor can probably be assigned to the same year (exhib. cat., Boston 1984, nos. 123, 124 [ill.]).
A.M.

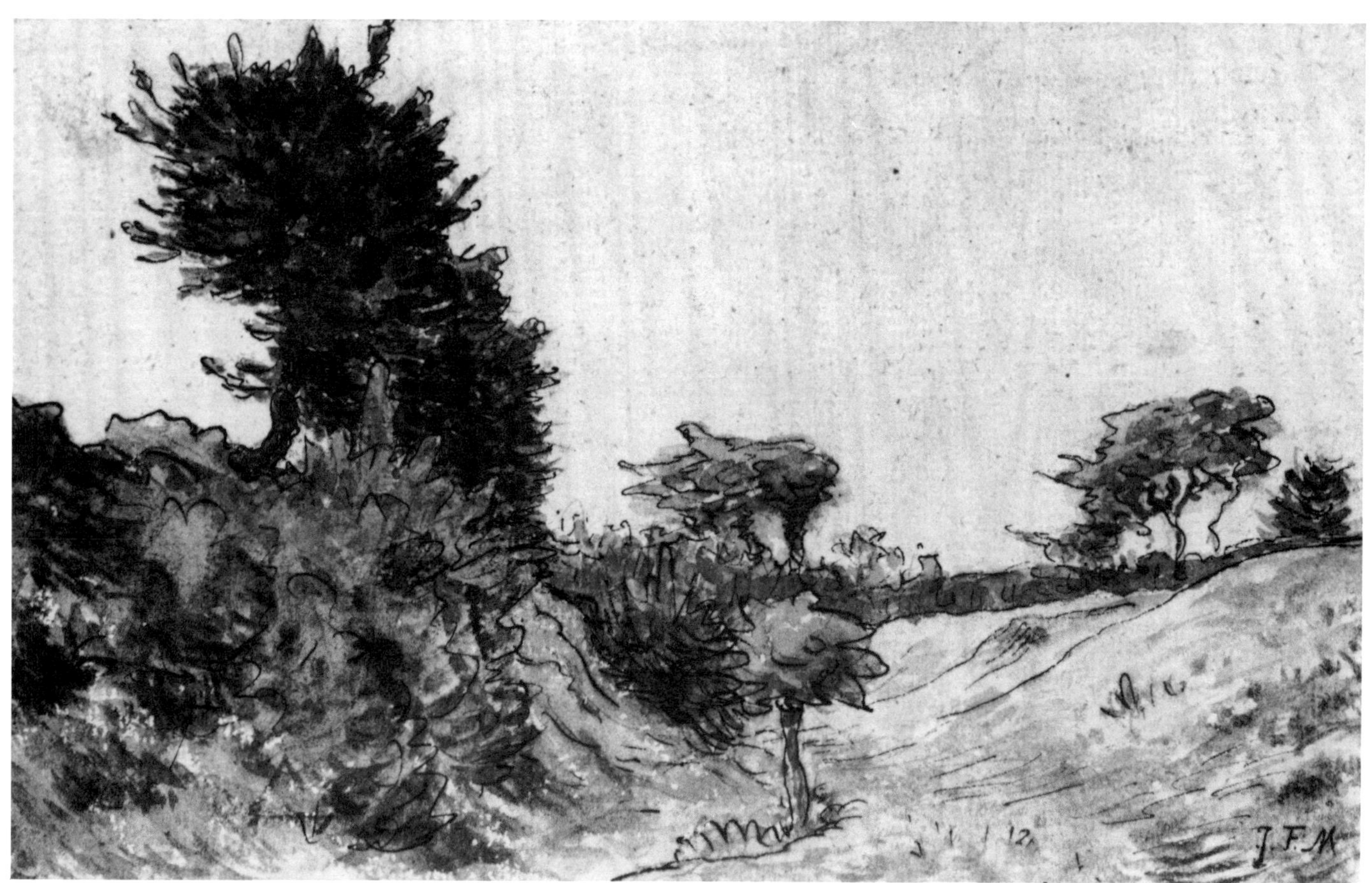

74　Country Road with Twisted Trees

CLAUDE MONET

Paris 1840–Giverny 1926

75
Study of Five Boys

F II 142
Black chalk and pastel on buff paper; 164 × 142 mm
Signed with black chalk: *Cl. Monet*
Provenance: F. Koenigs; given by D. G. van Beuningen to the Museum Boymans Foundation, 1940
Literature: Rotterdam 1968, cat. no. 201 (ill.)

Although Monet started drawing caricatures in Le Havre, and devoted himself to drawing during his first period of study in Paris, on the advice of Constant Troyon (1810–1865) and Eugène Boudin (1825–1898), drawings form only a modest part of Monet's oeuvre (W. C. Seitz, *Claude Monet,* Amsterdam/Antwerp 1963, ill. p. 50; Monet's letter to Boudin dated 19 March 1859; and Wildenstein 1974, I, p. 419). A few composition sketches for the landscapes are known, but sketches of figures are extremely rare; and the few that are known were—in preparation for paintings—almost always enhanced with color (for landscapes at Etretat, for instance, see J. Isaacson, *Claude Monet: Observation and Reflection,* Oxford 1978, ill. nos 77, 79).

The Rotterdam drawing is similar to another pastel, also with five farmboys, whose current whereabouts are unknown (H. Keller, *Claude Monet,* Munich 1985, ill. p. 40). One of the boys in this pastel reappears in the Paris painting *Farmyard in Normandy,* dated approximately 1863/64. Letters written by the artist in 1864 to Frédéric Bazille (1841–1870) show that Monet was in Honfleur and Ste. Andresse in that year (Wildenstein 1974, I, pp. 420–421). Probably the sketches of the figures on the Rotterdam sheet were intended for a similar painting.

J.P.

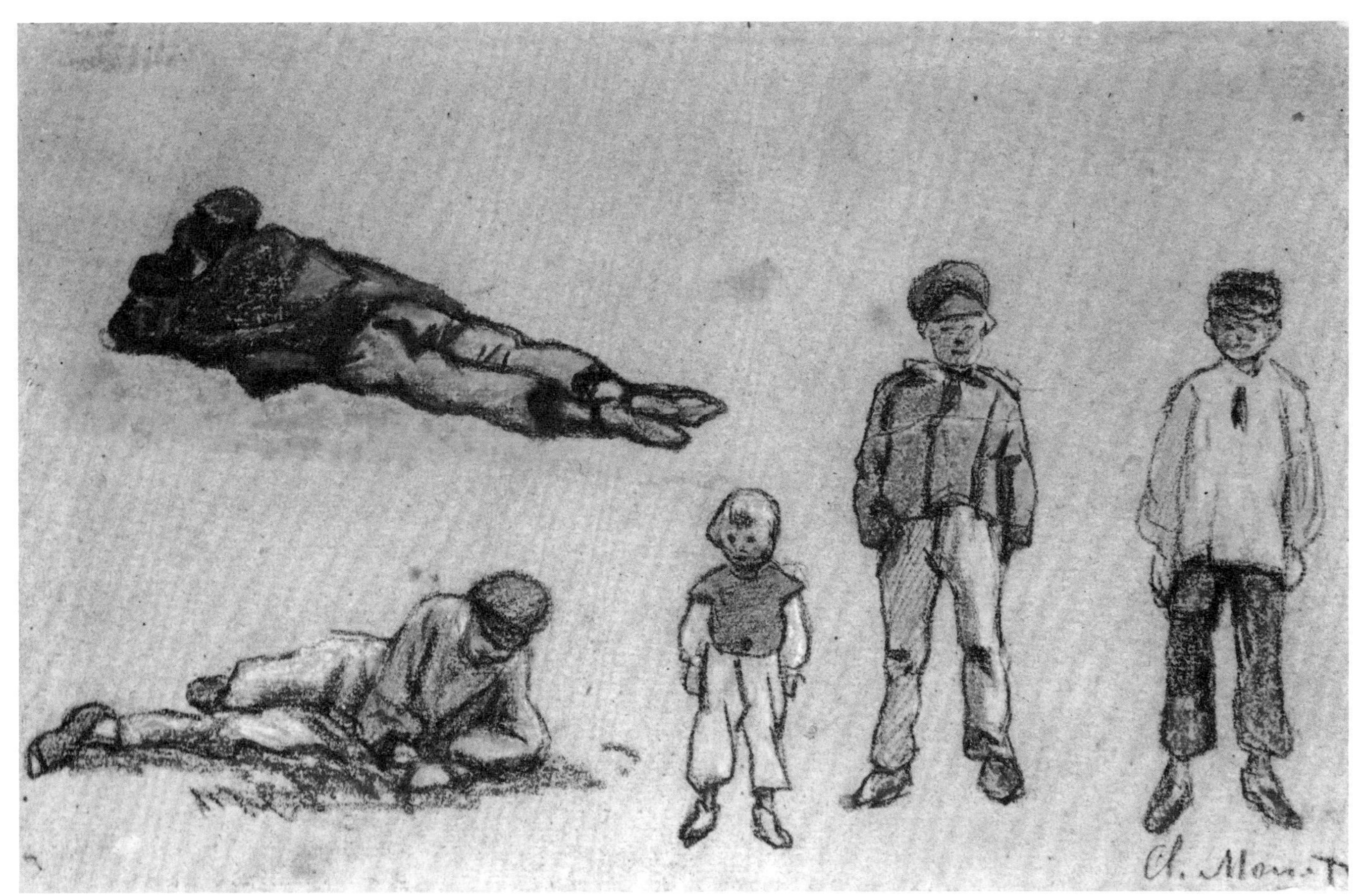

75　*Study of Five Boys*

CAMILLE PISSARRO
St. Thomas 1831–Paris 1903

76
Women on a Merry-Go-Round

F II 140
Black chalk; 215 × 170 mm
Provenance: F. Koenigs; given by D. G. van Beuningen to the Museum Boymans Foundation, 1940
Literature: Rotterdam 1968, cat. no. 213 (ill.)

Three figures in this drawing, two of them recognizable as women, are seated on wooden horses in a merry-go-round, while two men to the left look on. In the background high hills are visible.

Some similarity exists between this chalk drawing in Rotterdam and two pastels and a watercolor that are dated around 1883 (Pissarro/Venturi 1939, nos. 1566, 1567 [ill.]; auction cat., New York, Sotheby Parke Bernet, 7 August 1977, no. 8 [ill.]). One of the pastels and the watercolor bear titles indicating that they represent the fair at Osny, where Pissarro stayed in 1883 and was visited by Paul Gauguin (exhib. cat., London 1980/81, p. 63).

J.P.

77
Market with Public

F II 49
Verso: Sketch of a standing man
Black chalk, gray wash; 165 × 214 mm
Provenance: F. Koenigs; given by D. G. van Beuningen to the Museum Boymans Foundation, 1940
Literature: Rotterdam 1968, cat. no. 205 (ill.)

In the foreground of this drawing, two men wearing bowlers are looking down at something on the ground in front of them, which is not depicted in the drawing. On the right behind these men are two more standing figures, and in the middle distance, a large crowd has gathered. The roofs of small houses or market stalls are visible across the full width of the sheet, including a large tent with a flag on top to the left. The scene looks like a market, with the men in the foreground probably studying merchandise displayed in the ground.

Pissarro sketched many markets in his career: see, for instance, an 1853 drawing now in Caracas and the 1901 painting *The Fair at Dieppe, Sunshine, Afternoon,* in Philadelphia (Brettell/Lloyd 1980, ill. 14; exhib. cat., London 1980/81, no. 88 [ill.]). He also said in a letter to his son Lucien, dated 23 June 1891, that he was planning to paint several markets (Pissarro 1943, p. 177). The composition of the Rotterdam drawing is typical of Pissarro's market scenes, in which a few larger foreground figures guide the viewer's eye into the picture.

The Rotterdam sheet can be associated with two specific markets. Men with similar hats and smocks reappear in the 1885 painting *The Poultry Market at Gisors,* now in Boston (exhib. cat., London 1980/81, no. 61 [ill.]). Gisors was a somewhat large town near Eragny-sur-Epte, where Pissarro lived in 1884. This association would correspond with the date usually assigned to the Rotterdam drawing, around 1885. But the Rotterdam drawing differs from Pissarro's other representations of the market at Gisors in several respects, especially in the forms of the houses. The background of the Rotterdam sheet is more like that in a fan from 1881, in the etchings *Foire de la Sainte à Pontoise* from 1879 and *Chestnut Vendor* from 1881, and in the gouache *Foire de la Sainte-Martin à Pontoise* from 1883 (Delteil, 1923, Pissarro nos. 21, 15 [ill.]); Pissarro/Venturi 1939, no. 1618 [ill.]; exhib. cat., Pontoise 1980/81, no. 11 [ill.]). The

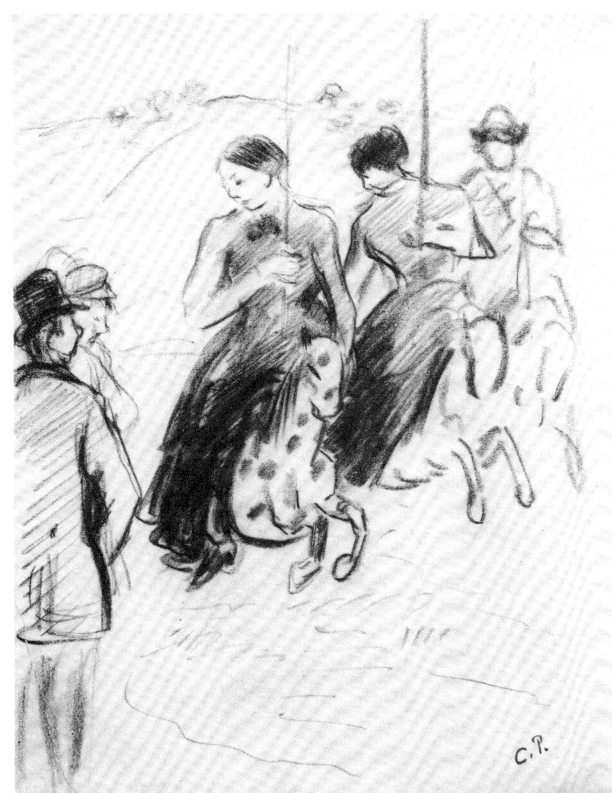

77 *Market with Public*

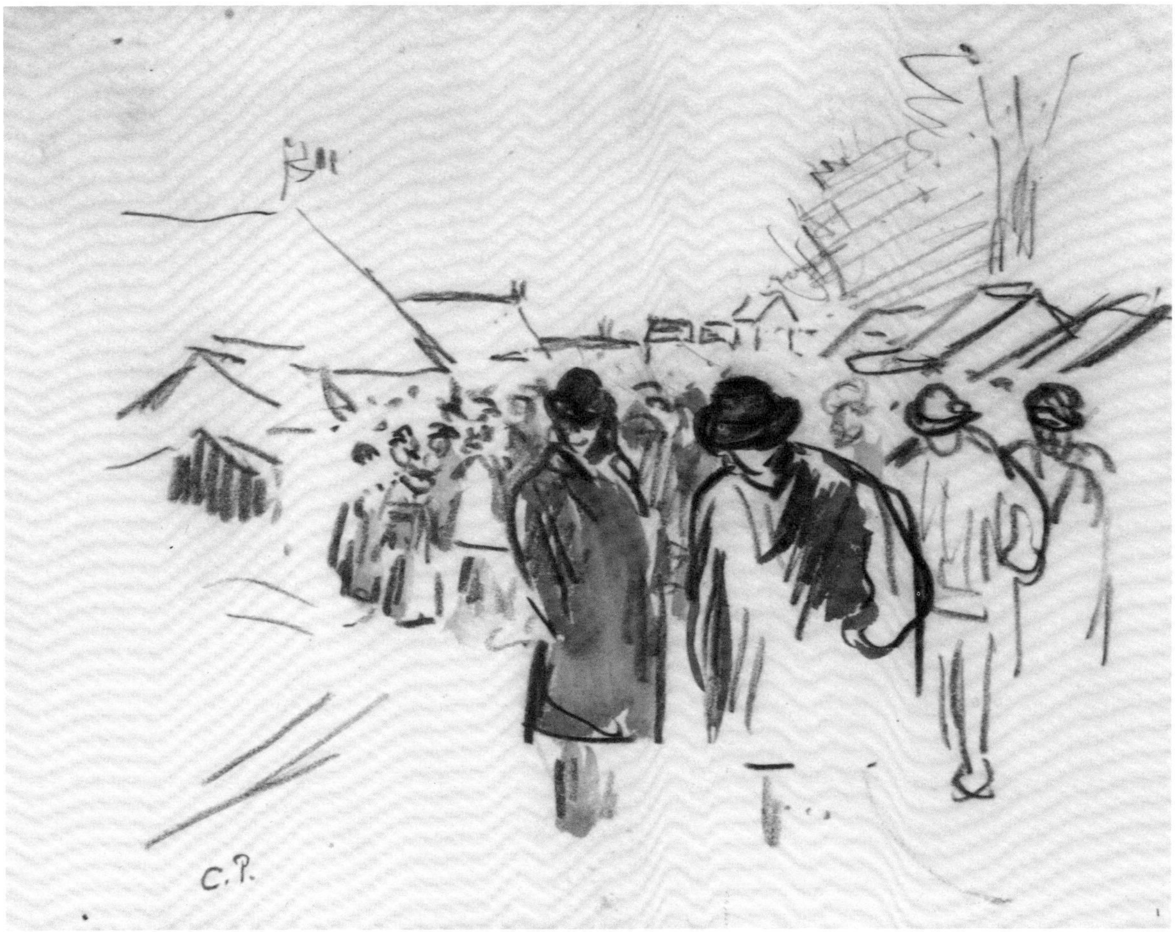

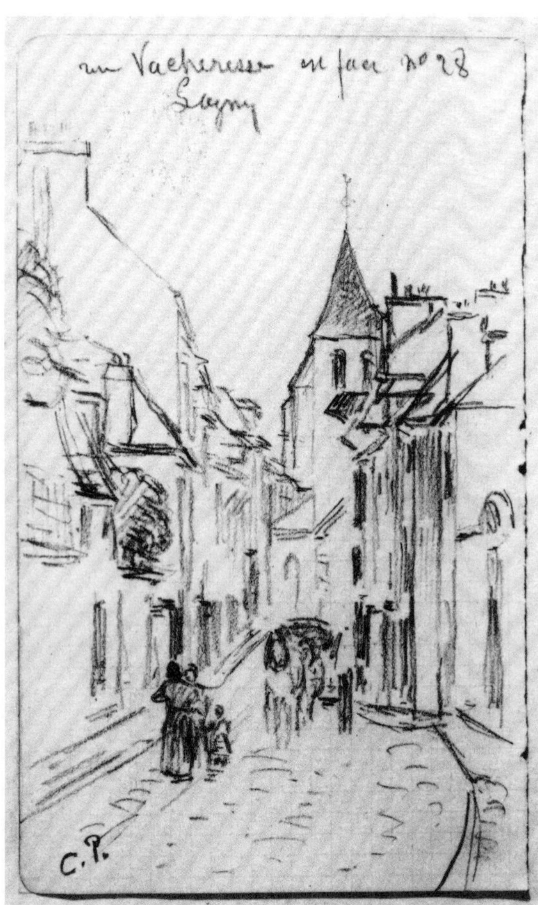

78   *Street in Lagny*

79   *The Rue Notre Dame in Troyes*

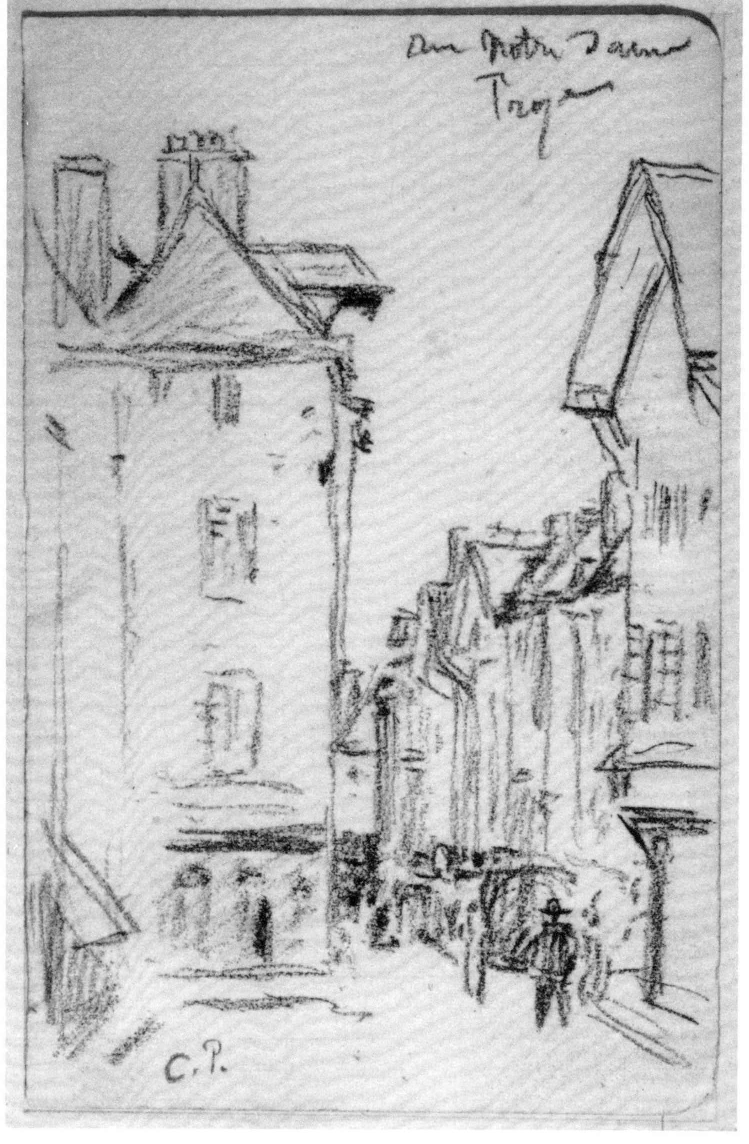

striking lantern hung high on a pole in the etchings, the fan, and the gouache is absent in the
Rotterdam drawing, however.

J.P.

78
Street in Lagny

F II 51
Black chalk on gray-blue lined graphic paper, two left corners rounded; 162 × 100 mm
Inscribed with black chalk: *rue Vacheresse en face no 28/Lagny*
Provenance: F. Koenigs; given by D. G. van Beuningen to the Museum Boymans Foundation, 1940
Literature: Rotterdam 1968, cat. no. 207 (ill.)

According to the inscription, this drawing shows a view of the rue Vacheresse at Lagny. Pissarro wrote
to his son Lucien in a letter dated 23 October 1891 that he was planning to find accommodations in
Pontoise, Lagny, and a number of other places (Pissarro 1943, p. 184). The Musée Pissarro in Pontoise
maintains that Pissarro was also in Lagny in July 1898 (exhib. cat., Pontoise 1980/81, p. 36). There is a
sketch in Oxford of the bridge in Lagny, on the same kind of paper and probably of the same
dimensions before it was cut down (Brettell/Lloyd 1980, no. 160D [ill.]).

J.P.

79
Rue Notre Dame in Troyes

F II 52
Black chalk on gray-blue lined graphic paper, two right corners rounded; 161 × 106 mm
Inscribed with black chalk: *Rue Notre Dame/Troyes*
Provenance: F. Koenigs; given by D. G. van Beuningen to the Museum Boymans Foundation, 1940
Literature: Rotterdam 1968, cat. no. 208 (ill.)

The inscription on this drawing identifies the scene as the rue Notre Dame in Troyes, another city
Pissarro intended to visit in 1891, according to a letter to his son Lucien dated 23 June of that year. In a
letter dated 27 June 1898, again to Lucien, the artist complained about the unsuccessful watercolors he
had painted in Troyes (Pissarro 1943, pp. 177, 326). In addition to Troyes, Pissarro visited Dijon, Macon,
Cluny, and several other cities in June–July 1898 (exhib. cat., London 1980/81, p. 64).

    This sketch of Troyes and the sketch of Lagny discussed in the previous entry (cat. no. 78), were
drawn on quadrille paper, with rounded corners on one side; the dimensions of the two sheets are
identical. This is also the case with a sketch now in Oxford of the *St. Urban at Troyes,* which suggests that
all three of these sheets came from the same or similar sketchbooks (see Brettell/Lloyd 1980, no. 273a
[ill.]). The artist's perspective from the middle of the street in the two sketches in Rotterdam—probably
adopted because the streets were so narrow—recalls that in Pissarro's etchings and lithographs of
Rouen (Delteil 1923, Pissarro nos. 52–54, 68, 173–179 [ill.]).

J.P.

PIERRE PUVIS DE CHAVANNES

Lyon 1824–1898

80
Portrait of a Woman

>F II 147
>Charcoal, black and red chalk on gray vergé paper, squared; 542 × 430 mm
>Inscribed with pencil: *Mme de Veyssière*
>*Provenance:* F. Koenigs; given by D. G. van Beuningen to the Museum Boymans Foundation, 1940
>*Literature:* Rotterdam 1968, cat. no. 219 (ill.); exhib. cat., Ottawa 1977, under no. 34

According to the inscription, this is a portrait of "Mme de Veyssière," but nothing is known about this woman. She appears again in a drawing in Rouen, where her clothes are defined in more detail (exhib. cat., Ottawa 1977, no. 34 [ill.]). Both sheets have been squared twice, once specifically for the woman's features, which suggests that the drawings were intended for an as yet unidentified painting. The Rotterdam drawing is generally dated around 1860 on the basis of its realistic treatment of the subject. A.M.

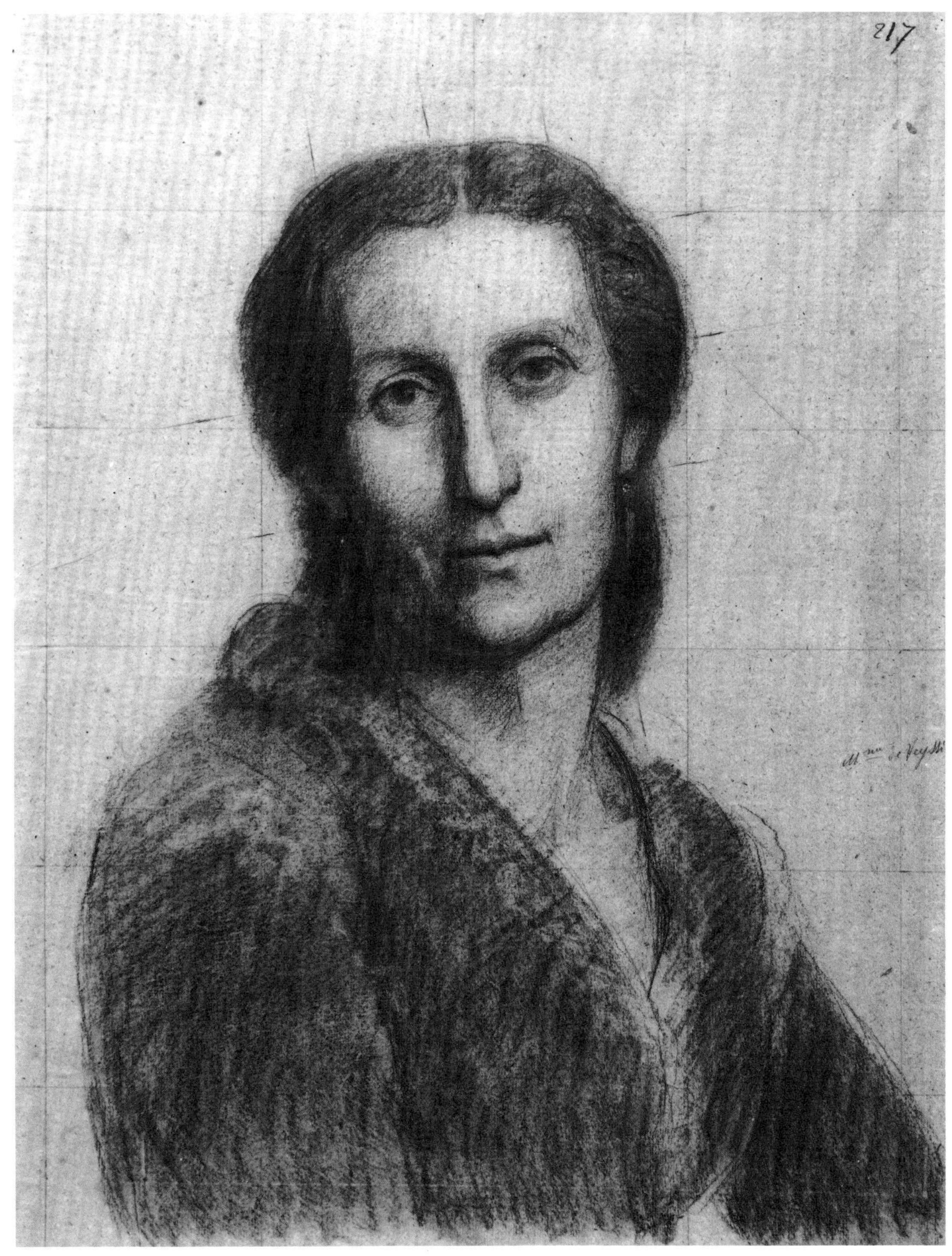

80 *Portrait of a Woman*

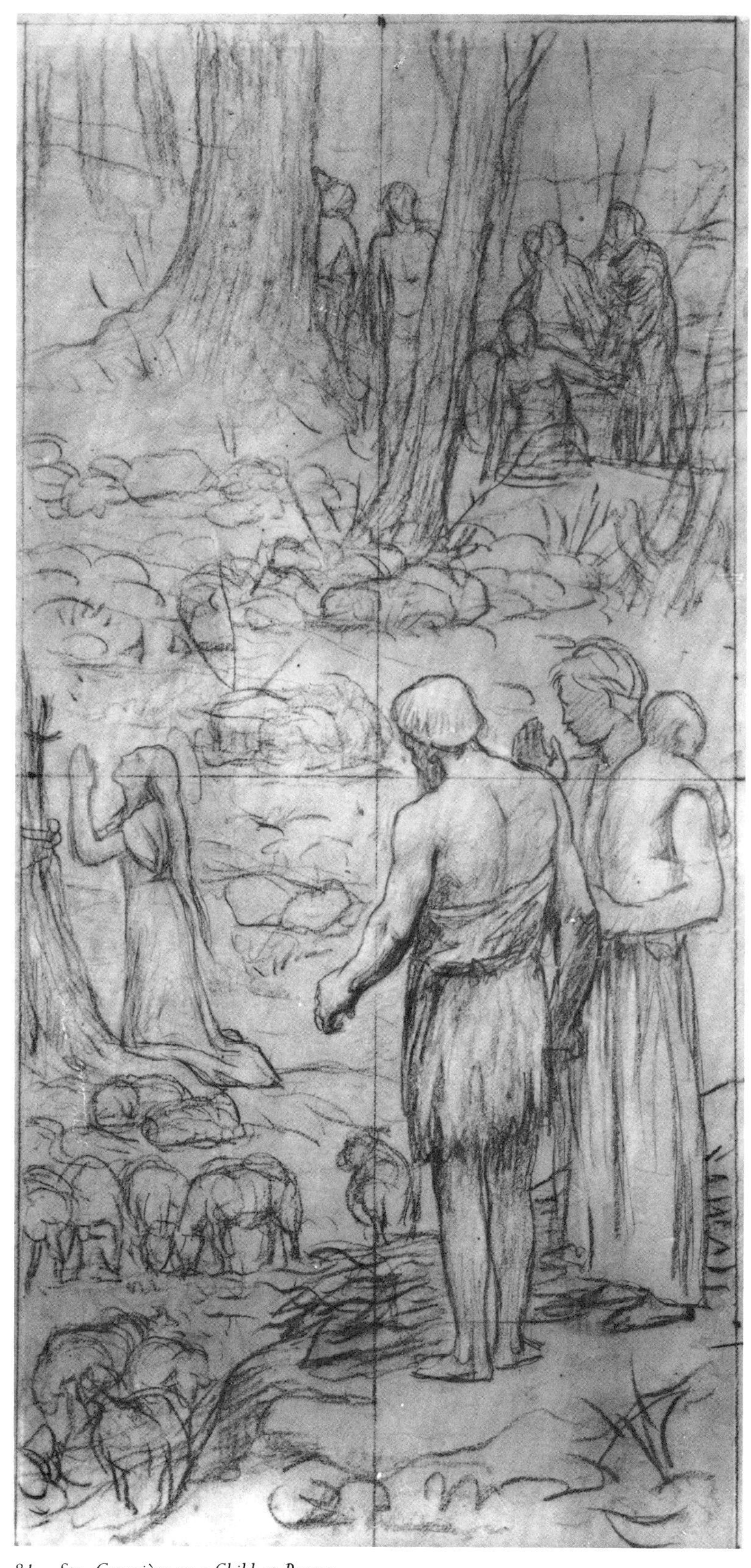

81   *Ste. Geneviève as a Child at Prayer*

Ste. Geneviève as a Child at Prayer

F II 148
Red chalk, some black chalk, squared, partially traced with a needle; 570 × 283 mm
Provenance: F. Koenigs; given by D. G. van Beuningen to the Museum Boymans Foundation, 1940
Literature: Rotterdam 1968, cat. no. 220 (ill.); exhib. cat., Ottawa 1977, p. 133; auction catalogue, Sotheby's, London, 27
    November 1980, under no. 95/96

Ste. Geneviève, the legendary patron saint of the city of Paris, is said to have lived in the fifth century
A.D. and to have protected the city from capture by Attila and his Huns. She was a shepherdess in her
youth and known for her great piety (L. Réau, *Iconographie de l'Art Chrétien,* Paris 1958, III, p. 563).

In 1775 Louis XV decided to have a monumental church built in Paris and dedicated to Ste.
Geneviève. This structure, designed by Jacques Soufflot, was completed in 1789. The church was
secularized and renamed "Panthéon des Grands Hommes" in 1791 during the French Revolution and
was destined to house the remains of the great men of France. But until 1885, when the church became
definitively the Panthéon, the building served alternately an ecclesiastical and secular function.

In 1874, at a time when the edifice was used as a church, Philippe de Chennevières, the director of
the Ecole des Beaux-Arts in Paris and the future cabinet minister, devised an extensive program of
redecoration. Murals were planned to depict the life of Ste. Geneviève as well as episodes in French
history, and many artists were invited to participate. Puvis de Chavannes was commissioned to represent
the story of Geneviève's youth in four large oil paintings on canvas.

The red chalk drawing exhibited here is a study for the painting on the extreme right of this cycle:
according to the artist's own record, a kneeling Geneviève at prayer is watched by a woodcutter and his
wife and baby (exhib. cat., Ottawa 1977, p. 135). Geneviève's flock of sheep graze in the foreground, as
in a watercolor at the Louvre and in its preparatory sketch (*L'Aquarelle en France au XIXᵉ siècle,* exhib. cat.,
Paris 1983, no. 129 [ill.]). The definitive composition in the Panthéon shows that the artist ultimately
decided on an even simpler form, with the foreground left empty, as in two later composition sketches
(auction catalogue, Sotheby's, London 1980)
A.M.

AUGUSTE RENOIR
Limoges 1841–Cagnes 1919

82

Two Girls, Seated Outside

> F II 133
> Black chalk on vergé paper (MBM); 420 × 310 mm
> Signed with black chalk: *R*
> *Provenance:* F. Koenigs; given by D. G. van Beuningen to the Museum Boymans Foundation, 1940
> *Literature:* Rotterdam 1968, cat. no. 226 (ill.)

In this drawing two girls wearing large hats are seated on the ground, gazing off into the distance; they are shown at an oblique angle from the back. A landscape and some figures on the left are very lightly sketched in the background.

These same girls appear in several other drawings as well (see auction catalogues: Lucerne, Fischer, 24 November 1960, no. 680 [ill.] [red chalk]; London, Sotheby's, 22 March 1961, no. 103 [ill.] [pencil]; and Paris, Galleria, 6 December 1975, no. 27 [ill.] [crayon conté]). All of these drawings resemble the painting *Au bord de la mer* from 1894, now in Paris (M. Drucker, *Renoir,* Paris 1944, ill. 113), and particularly recall a detail of the girls on the bottom right in two paintings from 1883 entitled *Baigneuses à Guernsey,* now in Switzerland and Paris (Daulte 1971, I, nos. 452, 453 [ill.]). As is known, Renoir visited the Channel Isles of Jersey and Guernsey in September of 1883 (exhib. cat., London 1985/86, p. 301), so probably this charming sketch originated here. Seen in reverse, these drawings also resemble an etching dated around 1892 (see Delteil 1923, Renoir no. 5 [ill.]).

J.P.

83

Woman with an Iron

> F II 135
> Black chalk on vergé paper (Ed. & Cie); 471 × 310 mm
> Signed with black chalk: *AR*
> *Provenance:* F. Koenigs; given by D. G. van Beuningen to the Museum Boymans Foundation, 1940
> *Literature:* Rotterdam 1968, cat. no. 228 (ill.); M. Blunden and G. Blunden, *Journal de l'Impressionisme,* Geneva 1970, ill. p. 157

The woman in this drawing, dressed in a knee-length skirt and an undershirt, is standing barefoot in front of her ironing. As she bends forward to the right, she braces her right arm against her thigh and leans on the iron in her left hand.

Renoir was well acquainted with the labors of the common people: his father was a tailor and his mother a seamstress; and he himself worked as a porcelain painter for a while. Renoir is also known for his representations of laundresses, which he drew and painted repeatedly, for instance in the 1886 painting *La Blanchisseuse et Son Enfant* in Merion, Pennsylvania (Daulte 1971, I, no. 509 [ill.]). The woman in this painting wears the same kind of shirt as the woman in the Rotterdam drawing, and laundry is hanging in the background. It was painted in Essoyes, where Renoir was staying in 1886 and in the fall of 1888 in order to—as he wrote in a letter to Edouard Manet—"get away from expensive Parisian models . . . [and paint] laundresses, or rather washerwomen on the riverbanks" (exhib. cat., London 1985/86, p. 303).

J.P.

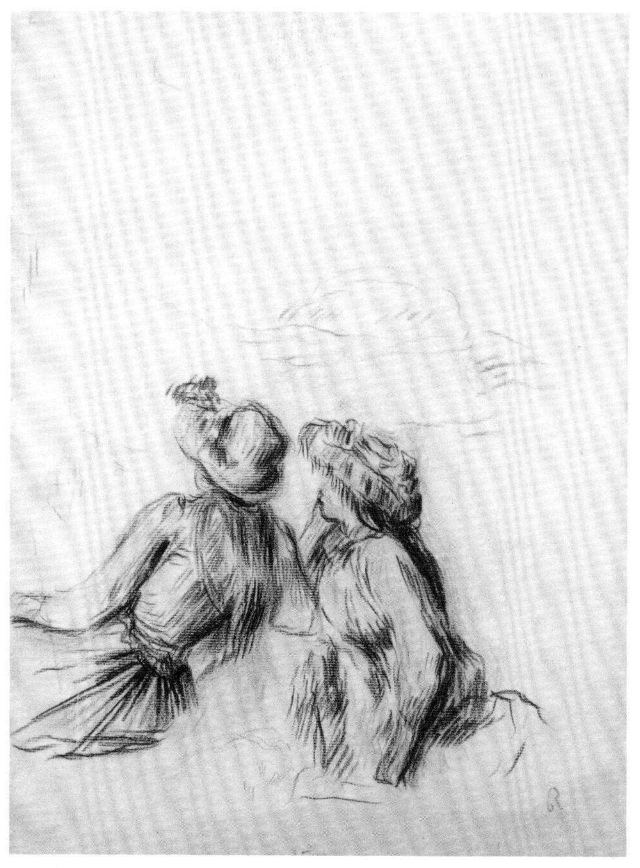

82   Two Girls, Seated Outside

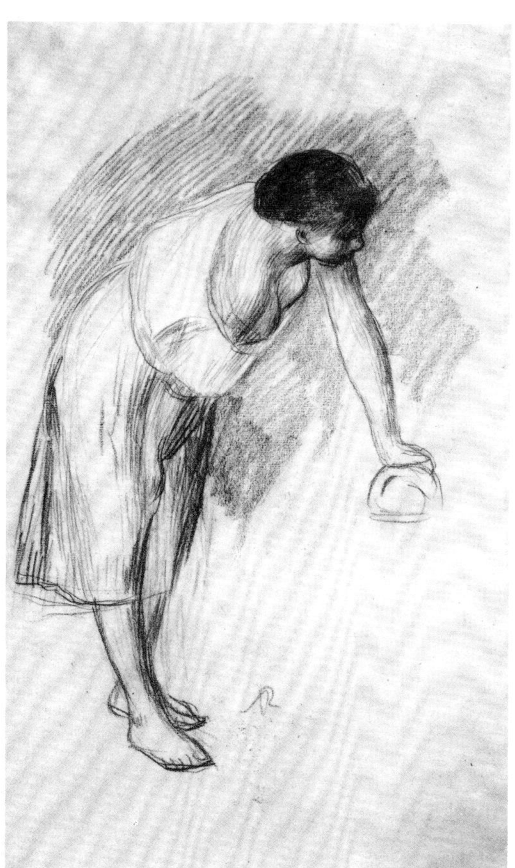

83   Woman with an Iron

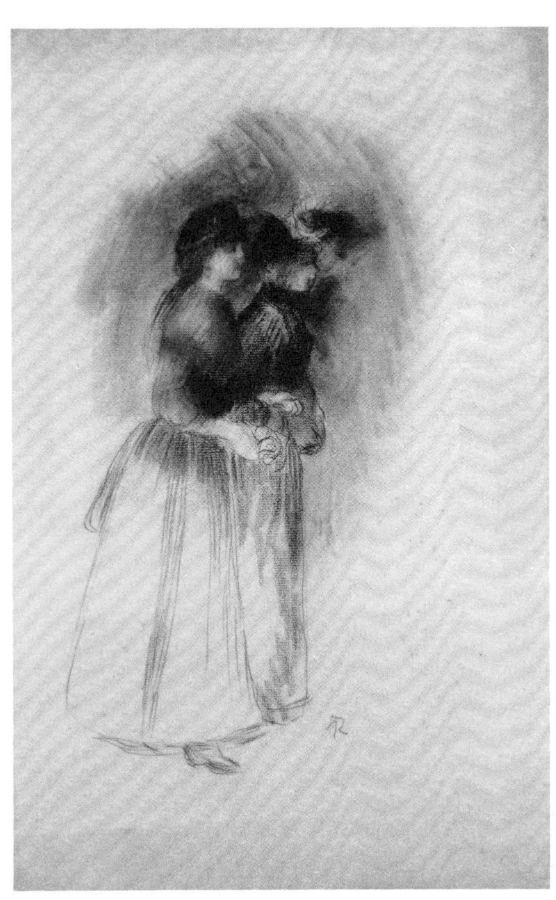

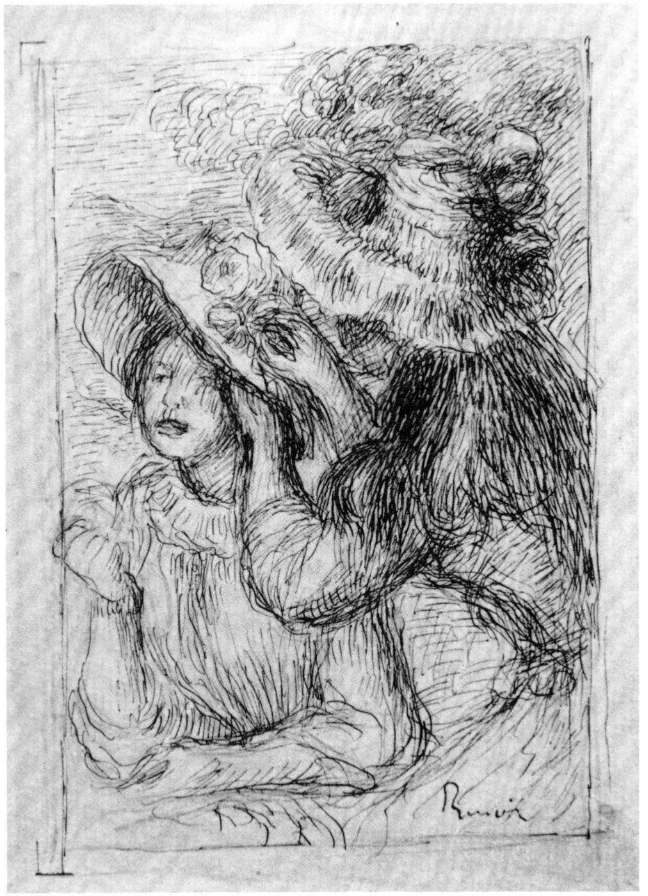

85   Two Girls

84
Women Walking to the Right

F II 23
Black chalk and pastel on vergé paper; 477 × 310 mm
Provenance: F. Koenigs; given by D. G. van Beuningen to the Museum Boymans Foundation, 1940
Literature: Rotterdam 1968, no. 224 (ill.)

Two young women are shown walking arm in arm toward the right side of this sheet. The woman on the left has reddish hair and a dark hat; she wears a reddish yellow dress. The woman on the right wears a darker dress and has a feather in her hat. A third woman is barely discernible just beyond them. The Rotterdam sheet is related to a red and black chalk drawing in a British collection, in which the third woman walks in front of the other two (see Chr. Lloyd and R. Thomson, *Impressionist Drawings from British Public and Private Collections,* London 1986, no. 71, ill. 77).

Vollard reproduced two of Renoir's drawings of two young women strolling to the right (A. Vollard, *La Vie & l'Oeuvre de Pierre-Auguste Renoir,* Paris 1919, ill. pp. 66, 243; and auction cat., New York, Parke-Bernet, 17 April 1951, no. 196 [ill.]). These drawings may be considered preparatory studies for the 1890 painting *La Promenade,* now in London (see Daulte 1971, I, no. 627 [ill.]), which depicts Miss Alexis, a daughter of the journalist and novelist Paul Alexis, and the Misses Lefèvre, who were Renoir's neighbors in Montmartre at that time (Daulte 1971, I, pp. 409, 415).
J.P.

85
Two Girls

MB 1976/T28
Pen and black ink, over pencil; 145 × 117 mm
Signed with pen in brown ink: *Renoir*
Provenance: Vitale Bloch bequest, 1976
Literature: Rotterdam 1978, cat. no. 31 (ill.)

This drawing shows two girls wearing large hats, one arranging flowers on the hat of the other. The drawing resembles a painting from 1893, formerly in Chicago, and a pastel, also dated around 1893 (see W. Gaunt, *Renoir Paintings,* London 1952, no. 72 [ill.]; J. Rewald, *Renoir Drawings,* New York 1946, ill. 68). It also recalls several etchings and lithographs, both in the same direction and in reverse to this drawing (see Delteil 1923, Renoir nos. 6–8, 29, 30, and 36 [ill.]). The lines and hatchings on the Rotterdam sheet are most like those on one of the etchings (Delteil 1923, Renoir no. 8 [ill.]).

The girls have been identified as Julie Manet—a daughter of painter Berthe Morisot and Eugène Manet, a brother of Edouard Manet—and her cousin Paule Goubillard. These girls, and Paule's sister Jeannie, were regular guests at Renoir's home, particularly after Berthe Morisot's death (see exhib. cat., London 1985/86, pp. 306, 307).
J.P.

AUGUSTE RODIN
Paris 1840–1917

86
Study of a Nude

MB 155
Pencil and watercolor; 322 × 247 mm
Signed with pencil: *AR*
Provenance: Unknown
Literature: Rotterdam 1968, cat. no. 229 (ill.)

This drawing shows a nude woman with blond hair sitting on the floor and reaching forward with both hands toward her extended right foot. The sheet is characteristic of the "life drawings" made by Rodin after 1900, especially those drawn directly after a nude model moving freely through the studio. The artist kept his eyes on the model while drawing, anxious to capture the essence of an attitude or movement; this explains the sketchy quality of the image (Elsen/Varnedoe 1971, p. 85). Watercolor washes were added later.

In pose, technique, and color, this sheet resembles the drawing *Femme nue couchée,* dated around 1900 (Daulte, 1969, ill. p. 101). The figure in these drawings recalls Rodin's sculpted *Danaïde* from 1885, now in Paris (see Elsen 1981, ill. 4.18, p. 94), but the drawings cannot be considered studies for the sculpture. Rodin's style of drawing was entirely different in 1885 (Elsen/Varnedoe 1971, ill. 55, 58).

J.P.

87
Cambodian Dancers

F II 111
Pencil, pen and brown ink, black chalk, and watercolor on smooth white paper; 298 × 199 mm
Signed with pencil: *A. Rodin*
Inscribed with pen and gray ink: *très beau* (?)
Provenance: F. Koenigs; given by D. G. van Beuningen to the Museum Boymans Foundation, 1940
Literature: Rotterdam 1968, cat. no. 231 (ill.); Elsen/Varnedoe, New York 1971, no. 87 (ill.); *Rodin Drawings: True and False,*
    exhib. cat., The Solomon R. Guggenheim Museum, New York 1972, no. 110

Six studies of a female dancer are dispersed over this sheet, and a study of two female dancers appears at the top right corner. The last-mentioned sketch is executed in pen and brown ink only, but the other pen and ink studies have been strengthened with black chalk and watercolor washes; bodies are rendered in brown and four of the garments in yellow. A blue-gray wash covers much of the sheet.

In these drawings Rodin focuses on external form and movement; details of anatomy, jewelry, or decoration are of little interest. Adornments appear only on the shoulders of the woman at the bottom left and in the barely discernible headdress of the woman next to her.

The dancers depicted here were members of the Royal Ballet of Cambodia, who traveled to Paris via Marseilles in 1906 in the retinue of their king (exhib. cat., Paris 1979, nos. 93–192 [ill.]). They gave performances at the *Exposition Coloniale de Marseilles* and then in Paris, where Rodin attended. Rodin followed the dancers to Marseilles on their trip home, where some of them posed for him in the garden of the Villa des Glycines (exhib. cat., Paris 1979, p. 67, ill. 140, and no. 130 [ill.]; E. G. Guse, *Auguste Rodin: Zeichnungen und Aquarelle,* Stuttgart 1984, nos. 165, 170 [ill.]; Cl. Judrin, *Inventaire des dessins, Musée Rodin,* Paris [1985], III, no. 4494 [ill.]). Rodin sketched Javanese dancers at the *World's Fair* in Paris in 1889/90 (Elsen/Varnedoe 1971, p. 84).

J.P.

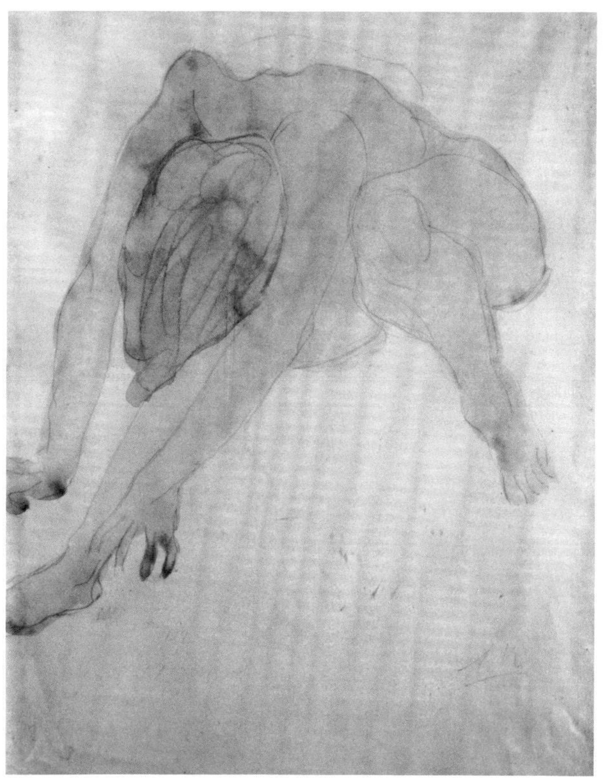

86   *Study of a Nude*

87   *Cambodian Dancers*

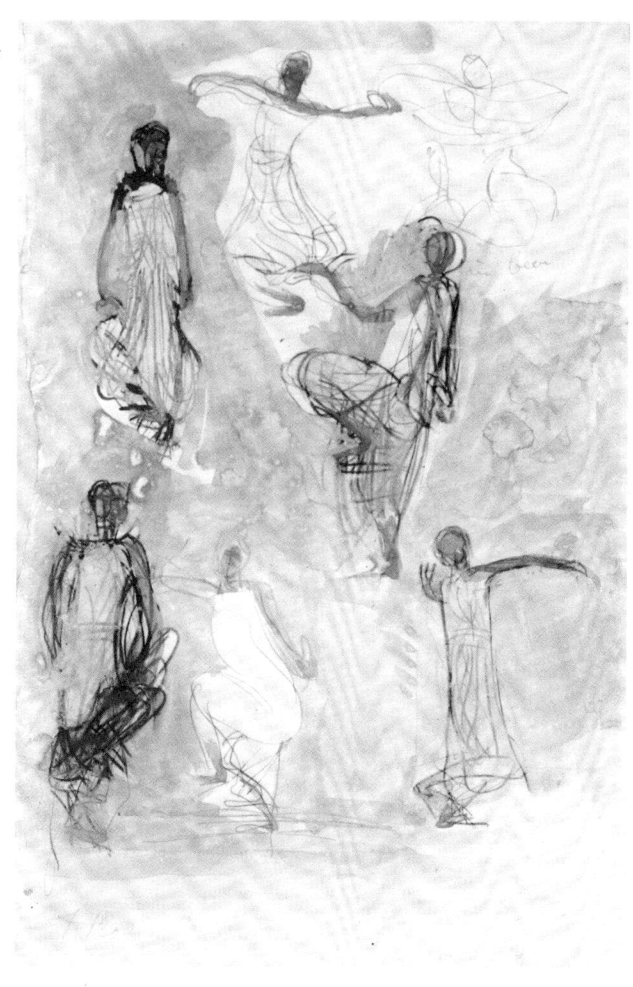

THÉODORE ROUSSEAU
Paris 1812–Barbizon 1867

88

View of Thiers in the Auvergne

> F II 93
> Pencil on vergé paper; 283 × 425 mm
> Inscribed on verso: *chemise* [portfolio] *119–740*
> *Provenance:* F. Koenigs; given by D. G. van Beuningen to the Museum Boymans Foundation, 1940
> *Literature:* Rotterdam 1968, cat. no. 238 (ill.)

89

View of Maringue in the Auvergne

> F II 224
> Pencil; laid down; 247 × 374 mm
> *Provenance:* F. Koenigs; given by D. G. van Beuningen to the Museum Boymans Foundation, 1940
> *Literature:* Rotterdam 1968, cat. no. 239 (ill.)

Both of these landscapes were drawn during a trip that Rousseau made to Auvergne in 1830 at the age of eighteen. He traversed the Limagne region of Clermont-Ferrand, making the first of these drawings from Coagne, southwest of Thiers (letter from A. Bigay, Thiers, dated 25 February 1964), and the second from a point overlooking Maringue, 15 kilometers northeast of Thiers.

After his return to Paris, Rousseau did several paintings of the scenery around Auvergne (*Théodore Rousseau,* exhib. cat., Louvre, Paris 1967/68, nos. 4, 5 [ill.]), among them, a view of Thiers from a somewhat greater distance; this painting is now in the Gulbenkian Foundation in Lisbon (*Collection de la Fondation Calouste Gulbenkian,* exhib. cat., Porto 1964, no. 55 [ill.]). Rousseau's sojourn in Auvergne and his ensuing predilection for painting rough and inhospitable terrain implied a break from his academic training.

In their style of drawing, both of these sheets recall Corot's landscapes from approximately the same period (see, for instance cat. nos. 19, 20, and 21), where topographical precision is emphasized.
A.M.

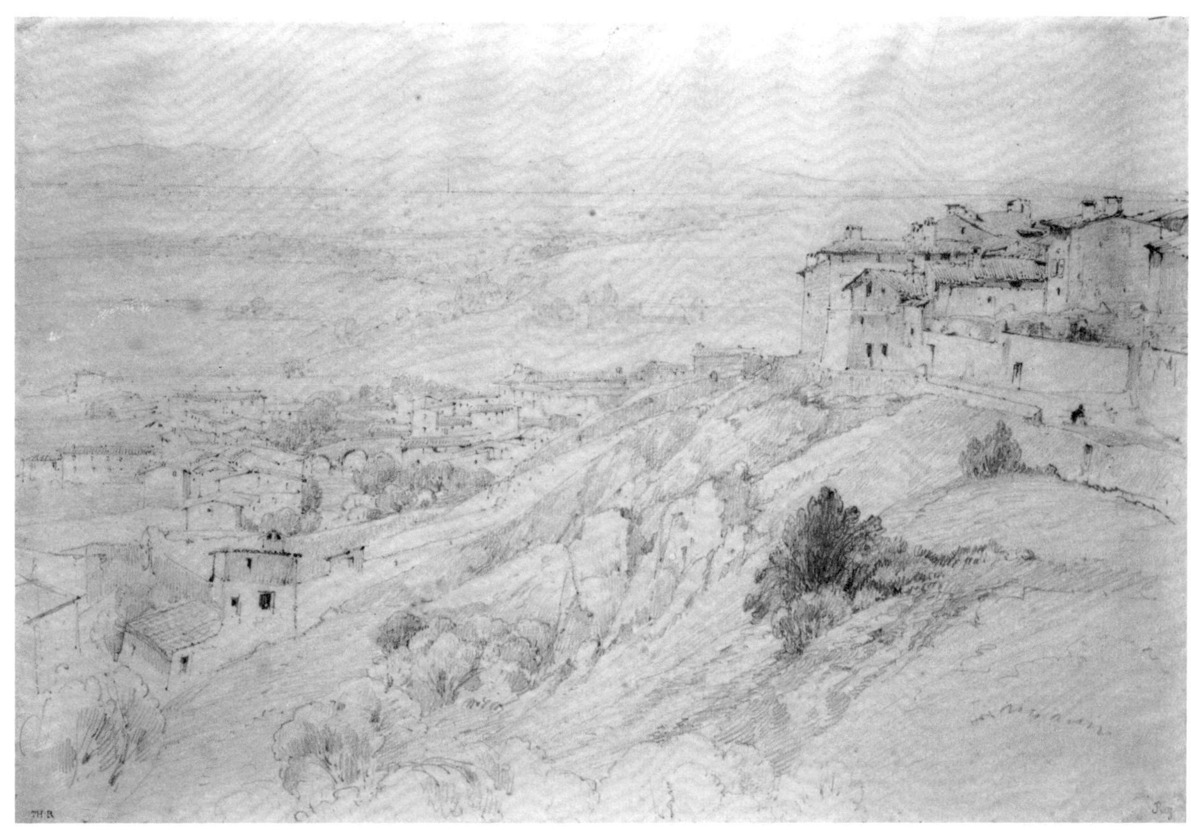

88   *View of Thiers in the Auvergne*

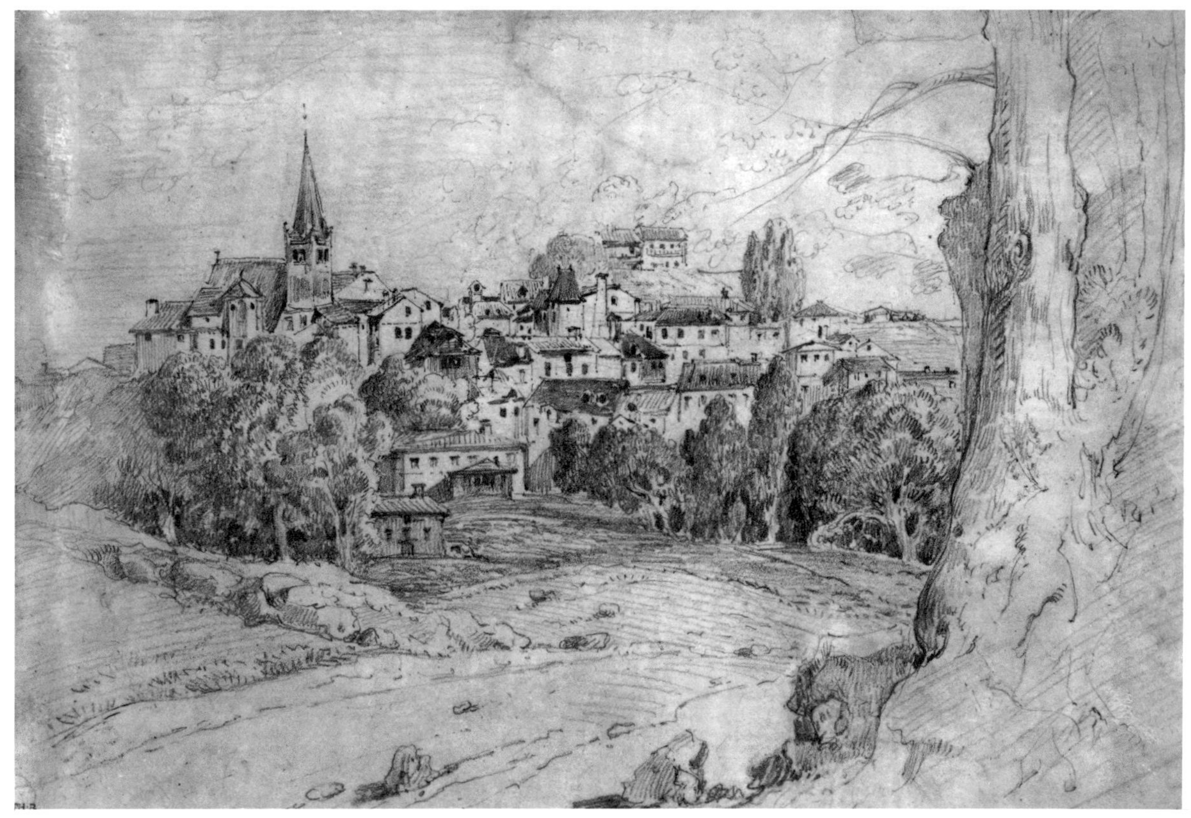

89   *View of Maringue in the Auvergne*

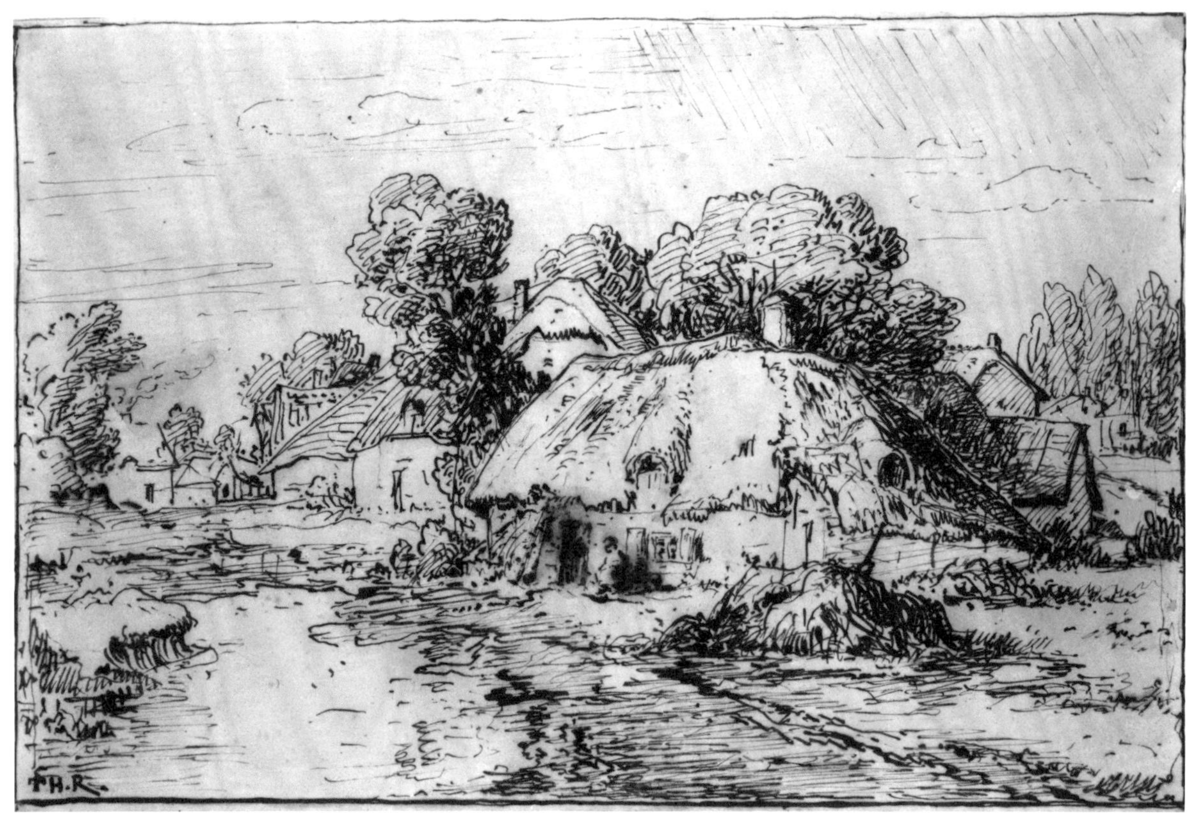

90 *Farmhouses*

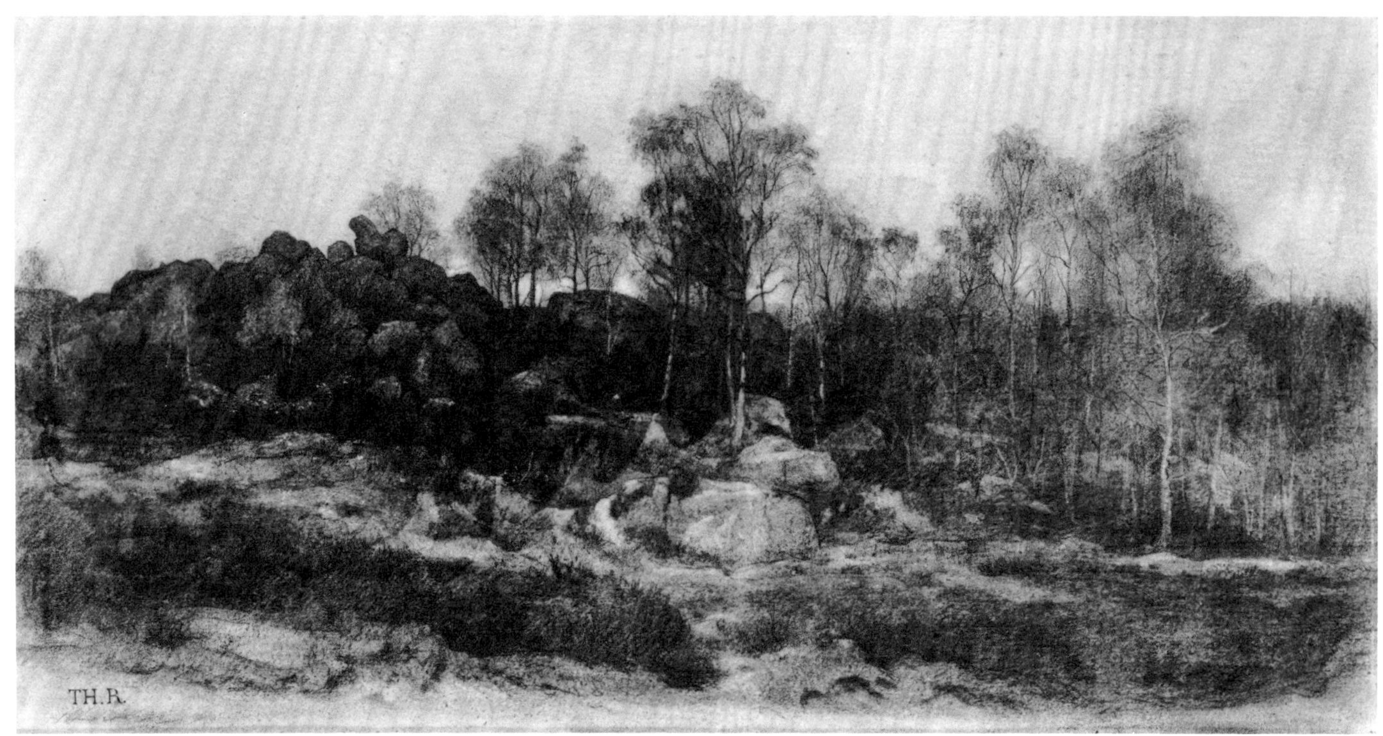

91 *View in the Forest of Fontainebleau*

90
Farmhouses

F II 92
Pen and brown ink; laid down; 193 × 286 mm
Signed with pen in brown ink: *TH.R.*
Provenance: F. Koenigs; given by D. G. van Beuningen to the Museum Boymans Foundation, 1940
Literature: Rotterdam 1968, cat. no. 237 (ill.)

This drawing shows some thatched farmhouses on the bank of a small river, with a woman sitting beside the open door of the farmhouse in the foreground, and a dunghill to the right with an upright pitchfork stuck in the top.

According to Claude Aubry (letter dated 20 September 1965), this scene was sketched in Berry, the region around the town of Bourges in France. Rousseau stayed there from June until December 1842 on the advice of his friend, the painter Jules Dupré. During his sojourn in Berry, Rousseau made numerous drawings with the intention of later using them as a basis for paintings. The borders around this image, drawn by the artist himself, confirm the intention, but thus far no painting has been found. Another painting with a very similar composition exists, however, based on the countryside around Berry (Cincinnati Art Museum; see *Barbizon Revisited,* exhib. cat., California Palace of the Legion of Honor, San Francisco 1962/63, no. 93 [ill.]). This painting is made up of the same elements that appear in the Rotterdam drawing, even arranged in the same manner.

A sheet in Cologne is also closely related to the Rotterdam drawing: it has the same kind of farmhouses, typical of Berry; and the artist has drawn borders around the composition as well (H. Robels, *Katalog Ausgewählter Handzeichnungen und Aquarelle im Wallraf-Richartz-Museum,* Cologne 1967, p. 95, ill. 49).
A.M.

91
View in the Forest of Fontainebleau

MB 1941/T15
Black chalk, heightened with white, on brown paper; 180 × 356 mm
Provenance: Unknown; entered the Museum in 1941
Literature: Rotterdam 1968, cat. no. 240 (ill.); exhib. cat., Bremen 1977, no. 121

In 1847 Rousseau rented a house in Barbizon and had the shed made into a studio. Although he had stayed regularly in Barbizon during previous summers, he now settled there more permanently. Two years later, Jean-François Millet rented the house just next to Rousseau's, and the two artists became close friends. They are generally considered founding fathers of what came to be called the "School of Barbizon."

Claude Aubry dates this drawing of "La Mare-aux-Fées" (Elfin's Pond) to around 1850 (letter dated 20 September 1965); an oil sketch after the drawing formerly belonged to the Gauthier collection in Paris, but its present location is not known. This pond, in the southern part of the Bois de Fontainebleau, was a favorite spot with the Barbizon painters. It appears again in an oil sketch on panel (Mesdag Museum in The Hague) dating from the same time as the Rotterdam drawing. The monochromatic character of the latter sketch reflects Rousseau's admiration for the seventeenth-century Dutch landscape painter Jan van Goyen, who was able to convey a striking impression of space without using much color. Rousseau, who owned a painting by Van Goyen, commented: "You might dispense with color, but you cannot get anywhere without harmony" (*L'Ecole de Barbizon,* exhib. cat., Institut Néerlandais, Paris 1986, no. 89). A monochrome tonality is achieved in the Rotterdam drawing by the use of brown paper, not discolored.
A.M.

GEORGES SEURAT
Paris 1859–1891

92

Landscape at Sunset

> MB 1951/T1
> Black chalk, crayon conté on vergé paper; 245 × 318 mm
> Signed on the verso with blue chalk: *seurat*
> *Provenance:* Acquired 1951
> *Literature:* Rotterdam 1968, cat. no. 241 (ill.); Franz/Grow 1983, no. 41 (ill.)

Two small houses on a hill are silhouetted sharply against the luminous sky on the left-hand side of this sheet. In the foreground the landscape is divided into lighter and darker horizontal zones.

Dusk is a time of the day often represented in works by Seurat: in the painting *Sunset* from 1881 now in Bristol, for instance; and more schematically, in the 1886 painting *Honfleur, Evening, Mouth of the Seine,* now in New York (exhib. cat., London 1979/80, nos. 194, 199 [ill.]). Dusk suited Seurat's great interest in light/dark contrasts, which he expressed in his drawings, particularly those from around 1882/83—the period in which the Rotterdam sheet is dated. See also the drawings *Coin d'Usine* in Zürich, and *Les deux Charrettes* and *La Péniche* in France (see C. M. de Hauke, *Seurat et son oeuvre,* Paris 1961, II, nos. 532, 533, 534 [ill.]). The division into light and dark zones in the Rotterdam drawing is similar to that in the drawing *Le Mur du Chemin* from approximately 1883, now in Wuppertal (see Franz/Growe 1983, no. 42 [ill.]). Strong contrasts between light and dark also appear in paintings from around 1882/83: see *Maison et Jardin* in New York, and *Ruines des Tuileries* in Switzerland, (J. Russell, *Seurat,* London 1965, ill. 35, 103).

After Seurat's death, most of his drawings were found in his studio; they were catalogued by the critic Felix Fénélon, and the Rotterdam sheet occurs in the list as no. 215. Seurat used a soft crayon conté for these sketches, not drawing lines but rubbing the crayon over the paper with varying degrees of pressure to achieve a light or dark effect; the paper was also of great importance (see *Seurat, Drawings and Oil Sketches from New York Collections,* exhib. cat., The Metropolitan Museum of Art, New York 1977, intro.).

J.P.

92   *Landscape at Sunset*

PAUL SIGNAC
Paris 1863–1935

93
The Port of Marseilles

> MB 156
> Bamboo pen and black ink over pencil on vergé paper; laid down; 270 × 420 mm
> Signed with pen in black ink: *P. Signac*
> *Provenance:* Gift from J. H. van Hasselt, 1928
> *Literature:* Rotterdam 1968, cat. no. 243 (ill.)

This drawing was originally thought to represent the harbor of La Rochelle, probably because of the incorrect identification of a similar scene in a 1913 painting in Essen—which in fact represents the harbor of Marseilles (see P. Vogt, *Das Museum Folkwang Essen,* Cologne 1965, ill. p. 55). A watercolor with the inscription "La Rochelle" (auction cat., New York, Sotheby's, 23 February 1984, no. 6 [ill.]) and a watercolor with the inscription "Marseilles," now in Mainz, confirm that the painting in Essen and the drawing in Rotterdam show views of the harbor of Marseilles. The Mainz watercolor resembles the Rotterdam drawing in both representation and dimensions (see *Französische Gemälde aus Mainzer Galeriebesitz,* exhib. cat., Haus am Dom, Mainz 1951, no. 29, ill. 16).

On the basis of the date of the painting in Essen, the Rotterdam drawing is usually dated around 1913 as well. The artist's signature, however, was added in a different ink around 1927 (see E. W. Kornfeld and P. A. Wick, *Catalogue raisonné de l'oeuvre gravé et lithographié de Paul Signac,* Berne 1974, signatures). The numeral "9" in the extreme lower right corner was added in the same ink and probably at the same time as the signature, but its function is uncertain. A watercolor dated 1907, showing a view of the port of Marseilles from another angle, bears a similar signature and the numeral "10" (auction cat., London, Sotheby's, 2 July 1970, no. 34a [ill.]).

Other annotations and pencil marks appear on the Rotterdam sheet, which is not unusual on drawings by Signac (see, for instance, two drawings of clouds, in Cachin 1971, ill. 66, 67). The arrow pointing to the sailboat at the bottom right suggests that it could represent Signac's own boat (see Cachin 1971, ill. pp. 52, 97, for several sailboats by Signac).

In 1892 Signac settled in St. Tropez, whence he sailed to many ports on the Mediterranean coasts, and also to Rotterdam; the Museum Boymans-van Beuningen owns a painting by Signac of Rotterdam's harbor (Cachin 1971, ill. 89). The artist painted watercolors and did pen and ink sketches during his trips, mostly to define the compositions. His choice of drawing materials—a bamboo pen and black ink—was probably influenced by Japanese art. Later in his studio, he produced finished paintings in the pointillist style, based on these sketches and watercolors.

J.P.

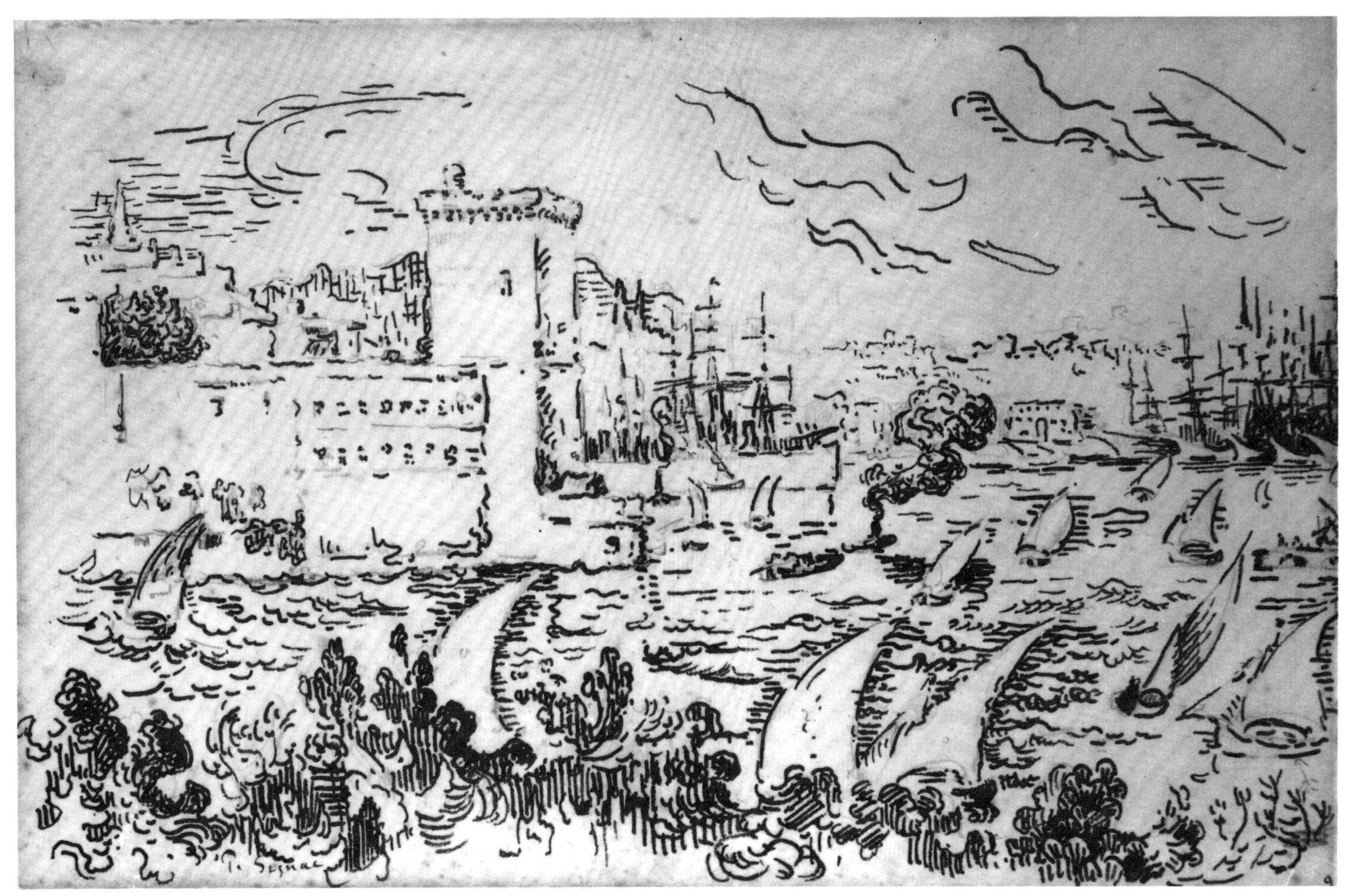

93   The Port of Marseilles

HENRI DE TOULOUSE-LAUTREC
Albi 1864–Château de Malromé 1901

94

Man on a Galloping Horse

F II 200
Pencil on note paper, corners rounded; 140 × 217 mm
Provenance: F. Koenigs; given by D. G. van Beuningen to the Museum Boymans Foundation, 1940
Literature: Rotterdam 1968, cat. no. 252 (ill.); Dortu 1971, V, no. D3036 (ill.); exhib. cat., Ixelles 1973, no. 29, ill. p. 67

A man in a coat and top hat is shown on a galloping horse, directed toward the right side of the sheet. Both horse and rider are defined in strong contours, and the pose and shading of the horse are similar to those of horses in the lithographs *Tandem Team* from 1897 and *The Jockey* from 1899 (*Toulouse-Lautrec* 1985, nos. 189 and 232–234 [ill.]). The scenery in the background of the Rotterdam drawing is very roughly indicated with broad pencil hatchings.

Toulouse-Lautrec was bedridden in 1879/80, recuperating from the leg fractures that would so radically influence his appearance and his future. To divert his thoughts, he filled his sketchbooks with drawings of horses and riders, a reflection of the importance of equestrian sports in the life of his family (Dortu 1971, IV; D. Cooper, *H. de Toulouse-Lautrec,* London 1955, ill. p. 18). Riders on galloping horses appear often, pointed to the right or to the left of the sheet, usually accompanied by a small dog running alongside; the dog, however, is missing in the Rotterdam drawing. See also the 1879 painting *Cavalier au trot avec un petit chien* in Albi (Dortu 1971, II, no. P. 20 [ill.]).

The shape of the sheet, with its perforated upper edge and rounded sides, is similar to that of another drawing in Rotterdam with a caricature of a man on horseback (Rotterdam 1968, cat. no. 246 [ill.]). Probably both drawings came from the same sketchbook and can be dated around the same time, approximately 1880.

J.P.

95

Sleeping Woman

F II 160
Red chalk on blue vergé paper (Ed. & Cie); 377 × 480 mm
Signed with red chalk: *HTLautrec*
Provenance: F. Koenigs; given by D. G. van Beuningen to the Museum Boymans Foundation, 1940
Literature: Rotterdam 1968, cat. no. 251 (ill.); Dortu 1971, VI, no. D.4.100 (ill.); *Henri de Toulouse-Lautrec: Dormeuses,* ed. M. G. Dortu and J. A. Meric, Paris 1976, no. 3; *Lautrec: "Elles,"* exhib. cat., Musée d'Albi, 1976, no. 48, ill. p. 19; Thomson 1977, ill. 63

This drawing—of a nude woman asleep on her back in a bed—is a preparatory study for a 1896 lithograph in red of a sleeping woman (see Delteil 1920, X, no. 170 [ill.]). Several other preparatory studies for this lithograph are known: for instance, a drawing in Paris, also in red chalk on blue paper, where the woman has turned to the left (Dortu 1971, VI, no. D.4.265 [ill.]). Another drawing in Rotterdam in red chalk on white transparent paper is a direct preparatory study for this lithograph (Rotterdam 1968, cat. no. 253 [ill.]). On this last-mentioned drawing and on the lithograph, the woman has turned her head somewhat to the right, and her right arm is partly covered by the blankets.

These drawings and the lithograph are related to the series of lithographs entitled "Elles" (1896), for which prostitutes served as models. Toulouse-Lautrec spent a great deal of time in the brothel at no. 5, Rue du Moulin, during the period 1894/96; the painting *Au Salon* in Albi originated here (*Toulouse-Lautrec* 1985, ill. 18).

J.P.

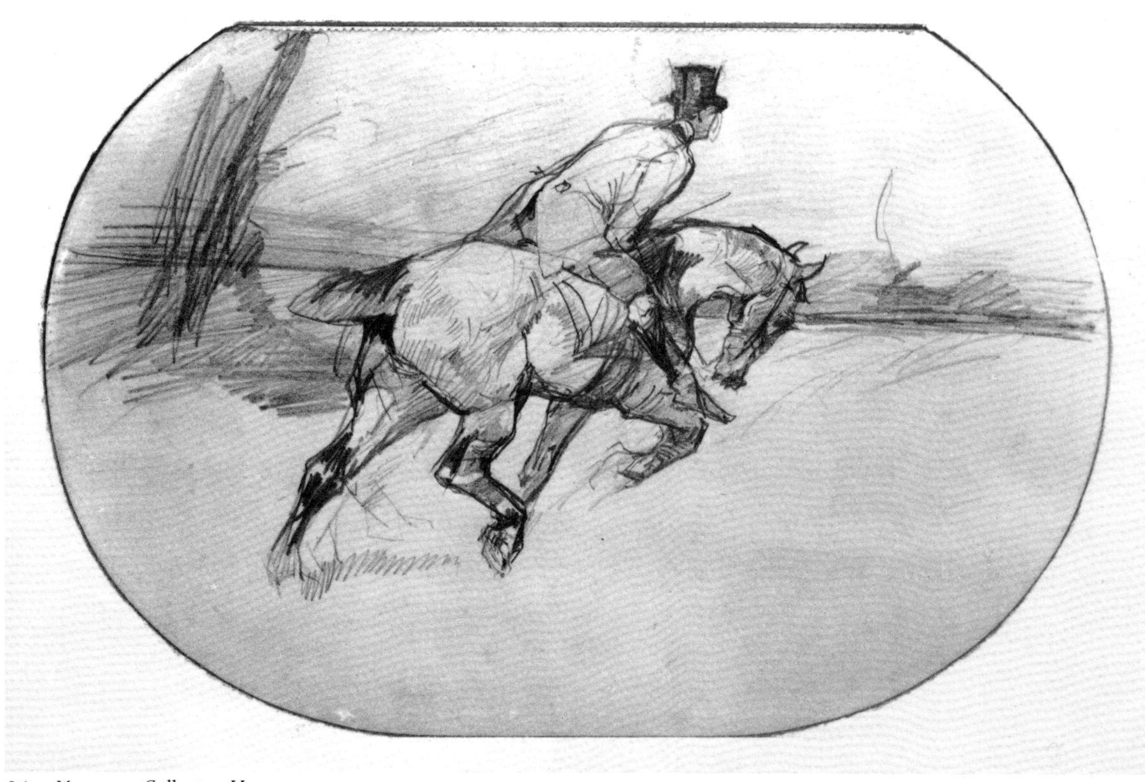

94   *Man on a Galloping Horse*

95   *Sleeping Woman*

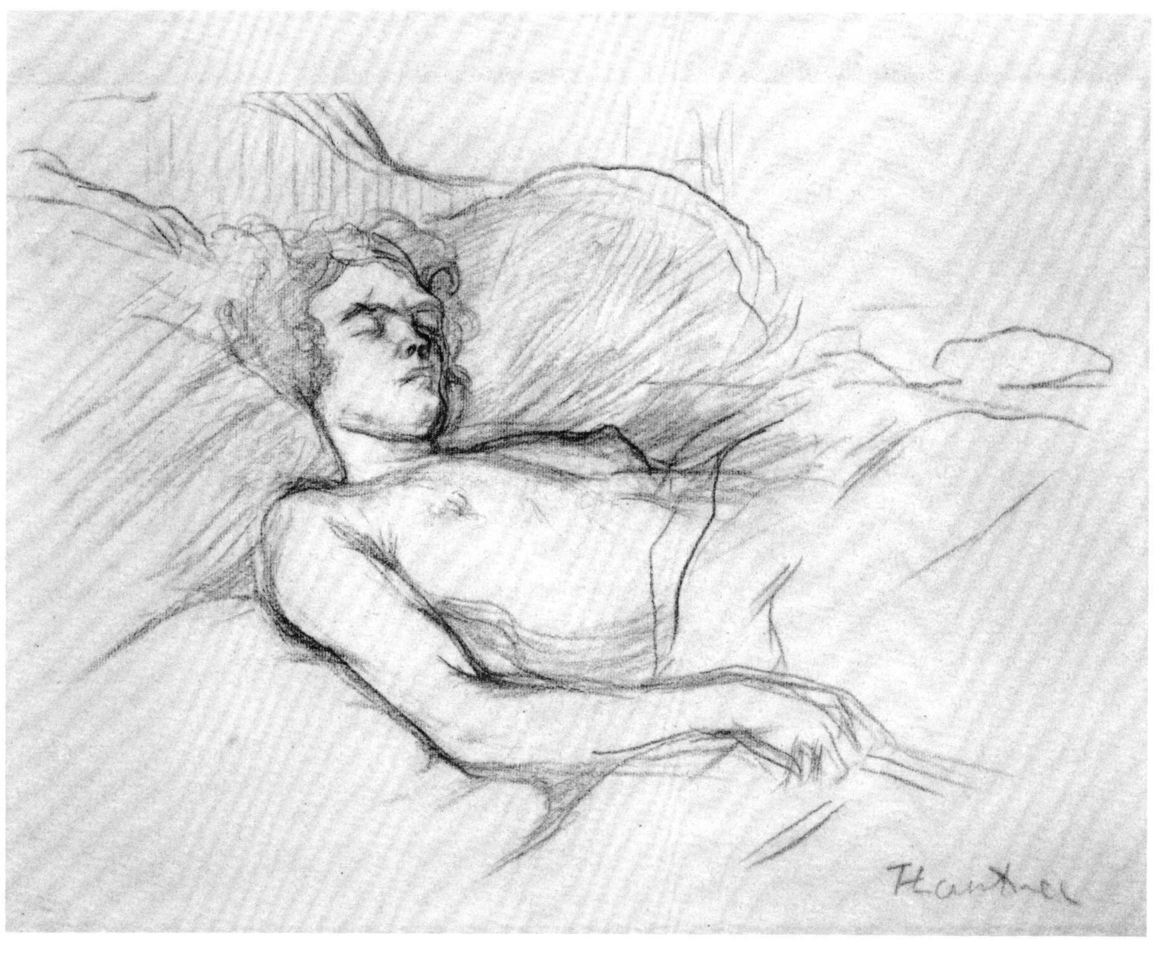

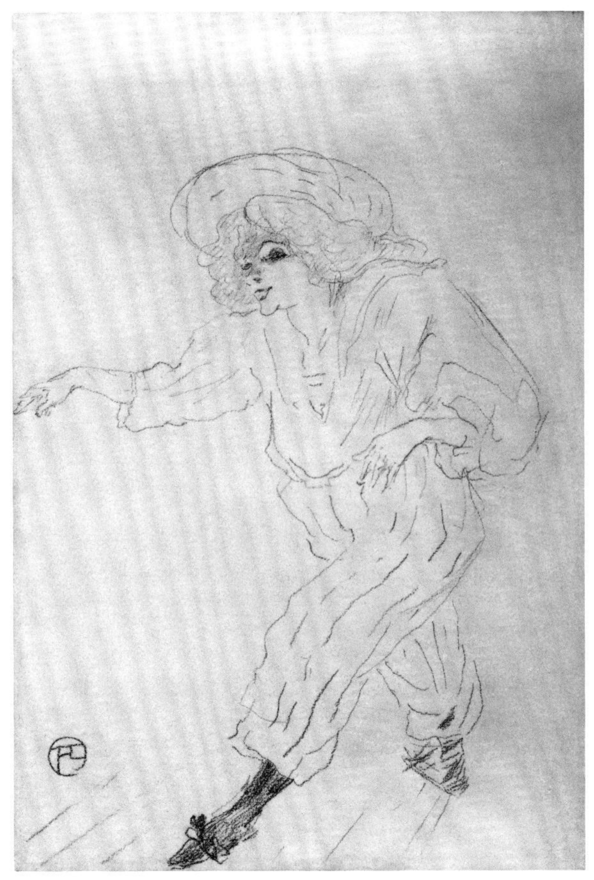

96   Chansonnière in a Sailor's Suit

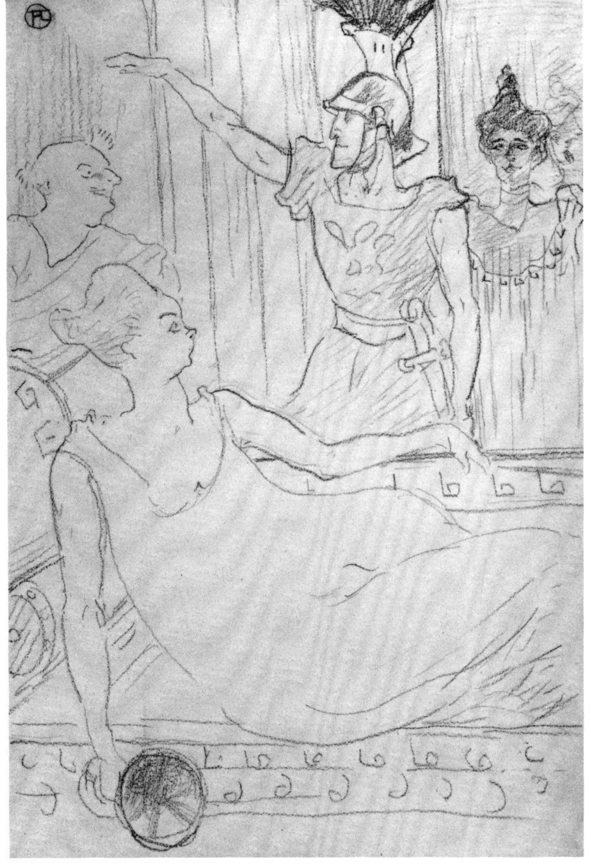

97   Comedy After the Classics

96
Chansonnière in a Sailor's Suit

F II 62
Black chalk on white watercolor paper; 505 × 355 mm
Signed with black chalk: *HTL* (monogram)
Provenance: F. Koenigs; given by D. G. van Beuningen to the Museum Boymans Foundation, 1940
Literature: Rotterdam 1968, cat. no. 248 (ill.); Dortu 1971, VI, no. D.4.451 (ill.)

The woman in this drawing, in a wide striped sailor suit and large hat, curtsies to the left. She has luxuriant hair, and wears shoes with a small bow. The drawing is related to several lithographs made by Toulouse-Lautrec on the occasion of his visit to *Le Star,* a sailors' bar in Le Havre where English bar girls performed (Delteil 1920, XI, nos. 269, 274, 275, 276 [ill.]). Other drawings are also known that relate to this visit (Dortu 1971, VI, nos. D.4.445–D.4.450). The Rotterdam drawing probably represents the bar girl "Miss Dolly" during a performance, and it may have inspired the much more anecdotal color lithograph *La Chanson du Matelot: Miss X in the Alabamah Coons* from 1899 (Wittrock 1985, no. 326 [ill.]).

In July 1899 Toulouse-Lautrec boarded a ship in Le Havre for a trip to Bordeaux, accompanied by Paul Viaud, who had been hired by the artist's mother to keep her son from drinking.

J.P.

97
Comedy After the Classics

F II 33
Black chalk and blue pencil on white watercolor paper; 505 × 355 mm
Signed with black chalk: *HTL* (monogram)
Provenance: F. Koenigs; given by D. G. van Beuningen to the Museum Boymans Foundation, 1940
Literature: Rotterdam 1968, cat. no. 247 (ill.); exhib. cat., Ixelles 1973, no. 45 (ill.)

A woman in a long, low-necked garment reclines on a chaise longue *à l'antique* in the foreground of this drawing; she holds an empty goblet in her right hand. Behind her stand a balding man in classical garb; a Roman warrior wearing a helmet, his right arm raised; and somewhat further behind, a woman with her hair piled high upon her head.

This drawing is related to a lithograph with an almost identical image—not reversed (Delteil 1920, X, no. 114 [ill.])—whose minor differences occur only in the figure of the woman in the background. In Delteil, the lithograph is dated 1895 and entitled *Madame Simon-Girard, Brasseur et Guy dans "La Belle Hélène."* But both the drawing and the lithograph should be dated around 1900, for they were inspired by Toulouse-Lautrec's visits to the opera at the Grand Théâtre de Louis in Bordeaux in 1899.

The opera from which this scene derives is not clear—operas and plays after antiquity were fashionable at the turn of the century—but the opera buffa *La Belle Hélène* (Jacques Offenbach, 1864) and the opera *Messaline* (Isidore di Lara, 1899) are both likely candidates. Toulouse-Lautrec was enthusiastic about both, and the latter was the inspiration for six paintings (Dortu 1971, III, nos. P. 704–706 [ill.]; P. Huisman and M. G. Dortu, *Lautrec par Lautrec,* Lausann 1964, ill. p. 233; Thomson 1977, ill. 77; *Toulouse-Lautrec,* Hasselt 1969, ill. 175, 176). The woman's garment and the armor of the Roman warrior in the Rotterdam drawing are similar to those of the figures in the paintings after *Messaline.*

J.P.

EDOUARD VUILLARD

Cuiseaux 1868–La Baule 1940

98
Design for a Program for the "Théâtre Libre"

MB 1978/T1
Brush and black ink, watercolor over pencil; 297 × 204 mm
Provenance: Two studio stamps: *E.V.* (Lugt 909c); gift from Felshafen Ltd., 1978
Literature: Henri de Toulouse-Lautrec: Images of the 1890s, ed. R. Castleman and W. Wittrock, New York 1985, ill. 40, p. 69

Like most artists of the group the "Nabis," who believed that art had a primarily decorative function, Vuillard was very involved in the contemporary theater. His interest in the design of sets, posters, and programs was stimulated by his friend and fellow lodger Lugné-Poe, a leading figure in avant-garde theater in Paris around 1900. In fact, Vuillard and Lugné-Poe co-founded the "Théâtre de l'Oeuvre" in Paris in 1893, for which Vuillard designed some sets but primarily programs (exhib. cat., Toronto 1971/72, ill. pp. 31, 32, 49, 53). And according to Lugné-Poe, "Vuillard was the best of advisers where the theatre was concerned" (exhib. cat., Toronto 1971/72, p. 85).

Earlier, Vuillard, through Lugné-Poe, had been asked to design a program for the "Théâtre Libre" (exhib. cat., Toronto 1971/72, p. 83), a theater founded by André Antoine in the spring of 1887. Antoine produced about 125 plays there between 1887 and 1890, most of them new; and he staged them in a naturalistic fashion. One of his greatest innovations was in forcing the audience to look at the stage by extinguishing the lights in the hall during performances (F. Hermann, "Vuillard und das Theater," *Neue Zürcher Zeitung,* edition for abroad, 8 October 1964, p. 16).

Vuillard's design for the program of the 1890/91 season of the "Théâtre Libre" was probably not used: we have no record of its having appeared in print; and its figures—a woman in a long white garment, a faintly drawn figure on the left, and a newspaper boy—bear no relationship to plays performed in the "Théâtre Libre" during the 1890/91 season. Vuillard's program designs may not have been meant to refer to the upcoming plays, however, but to theater activities in general. The only one of Vuillard's program designs for the "Théâtre Libre" that actually appeared in print shows a farmer working his field; it was probably intended for the play *L'Amant de sa Femme: Scènes de la Vie Parisienne,* by Amélien Scholl (exhib. cat., Toronto 1970, p. 25 [ill.]).

The style of the Rotterdam drawing is reminiscent of watercolors painted by Vuillard around 1892 of the actor Coquelin Cadet (exhib. cat., Toronto 1971/72, ill. 15–25). Two watercolors are known of another program design by Vuillard for the "Théâtre Libre," one of which is signed. On top, to the right, a woman with a large hat appears together with a newspaper boy and a man in a top hat (auction cat., London, Sotheby's, 12 April 1972, no. 63 [ill.]; and *Edouard Vuillard und die Nabis,* exhib. cat., Graphischez Kabinett, Bremen 1983, no. 5 [ill.]).
J.P.

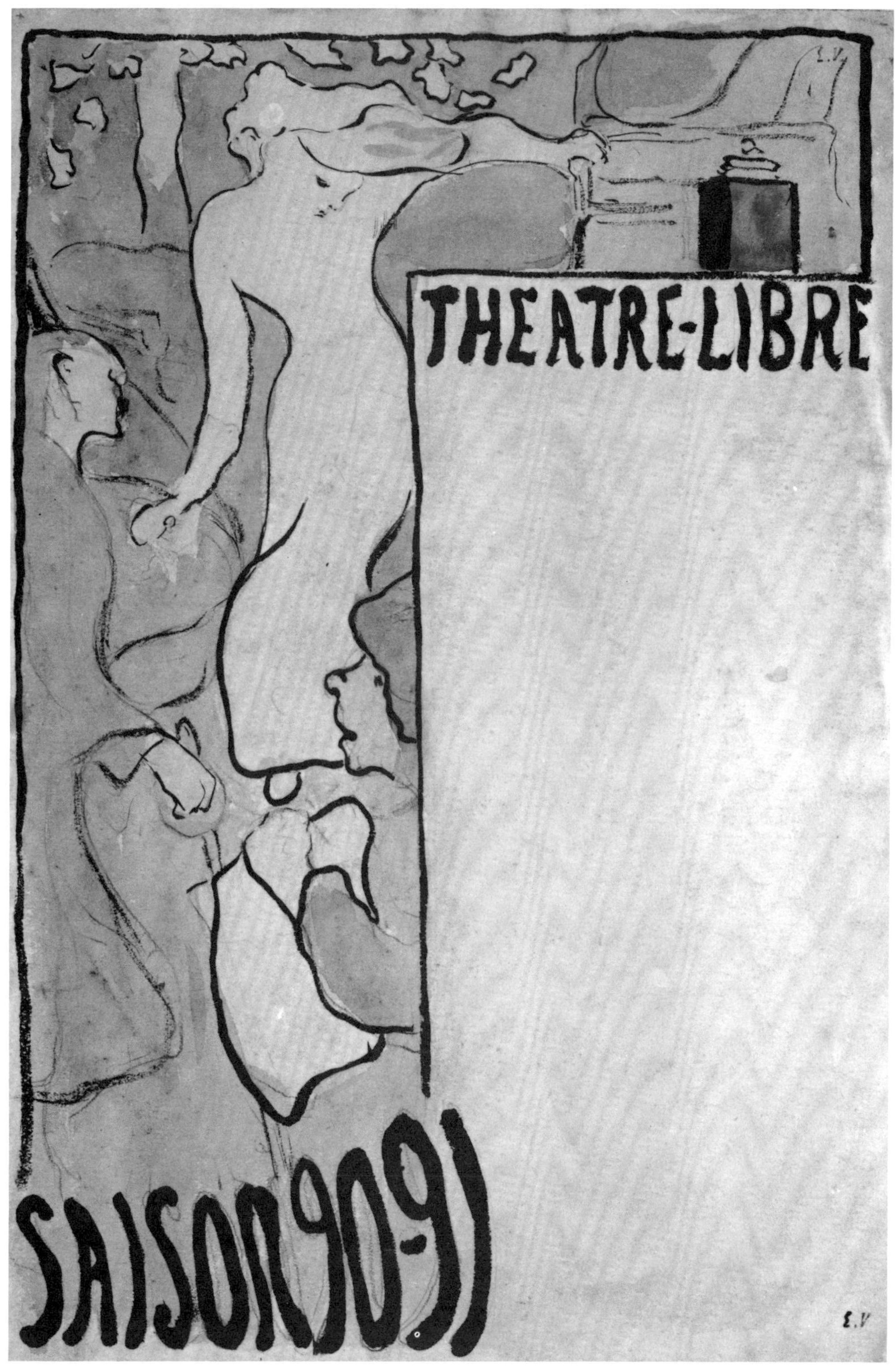

98   *Design for a Program for the "Théâtre Libre"*

SELECT BIBLIOGRAPHY

Adriani 1984 — G. Adriani, *Edgar Degas: Pastelle, Oelskizzen, Zeichnungen*, Köln 1984

Andersen 1970 — W. Andersen, *Cézanne's Portrait Drawings*, Cambridge, Mass., and London, 1970

Baden Baden 1978 — *Maillol*, Staatliche Kunsthalle, Baden Baden 1978

Baden Baden/Zürich 1984 — *Les Voyages secrets de Monsieur Courbet: Unbekannte Reiseskizzen aus Baden, Spa und Biarritz*, Staatliche Kunsthalle, Baden Baden, Kunsthaus, Zürich, 1984

Bremen 1977 — *Zurück zur Natur*, Kunsthalle, Bremen 1977

Bremen 1977/78 — *Zurück zur Natur*, Kunsthalle, Bremen 1977/1978, no. 29, ill. no. 37

Brettell, Lloyd 1980 — R. R. Brettell and Chr. Lloyd, *A Catalogue of the Drawings by Camille Pissarro in the Ashmolean Museum Oxford*, Oxford 1980

Brettell/McCullaugh 1984 — R. R. Brettell and S. Folds McCullagh, *Degas in The Art Institute of Chicago*, Chicago 1984

Boston 1984 — A. R. Murphy, *Jean-François Millet*, Museum of Fine Arts, Boston 1984

Cachin 1971 — F. Cachin, *Paul Signac*, Paris 1971

Chappuis 1962 — A. Chappuis, *Die Zeichnungen von Paul Cézanne, Kupferstichkabinett der Oeffentlichen Kunstsammlung Basel*, 2 vols., Olten, Lausanne 1962

Chappuis 1973 — A. Chappuis, *The Drawings of Paul Cézanne: Catalogue Raisonné*, 2 vols., London 1973

Cologne/Frankfurt am Main, 1972/73 — *Die schwarze Sonne des Traums: Radierungen, Lithographien und Zeichnungen von Rodolphe Bresdin, 1822–1885*, Wallraf-Richartz-Museum, Cologne (Frankfurt am Main, Städelsches Kunstinstitut), Köln 1972

Daulte 1969 — F. Daulte, *L'Aquarelle française au XIXe siècle.* Fribourg 1969

Daulte 1971 — F. Daulte, *Auguste Renoir: Figures (1860–1890)*, vol. I, Lausanne 1971

de Leiris 1969 — A. de Leiris, *The Drawings of Edouard Manet*, Berkeley/Los Angeles 1969

Delteil 1913 — L. Delteil, *Eugène Carrière (Le Peintre-graveur illustré*, vol. 8), Paris 1913

Delteil 1920 — L. Delteil, *H. de Toulouse-Lautrec (Le Peintre-graveur illustré*, vols. 10, 11), Paris 1920

Delteil 1921 — L. Delteil, *Charles-François Daubigny (Le Peintre-graveur illustré*, vol. 13), Paris 1921

Delteil 1923 — L. Delteil, *Camille Pissarro, Alfred Sisley, Auguste Renoir (Le Peintre-graveur illustré*, vol. 17), Paris 1923

Dortu 1971 — M. G. Dortu, *Toulouse-Lautrec et son oeuvre*, 6 vols., New York 1971

Edinburgh 1979 — *Degas 1879*, National Gallery of Scotland, Edinburgh 1979

Elsen 1981 — *Rodin Rediscovered*, ed. A.E. Elsen, Washington 1981

Elsen/Varnedoe 1971 — A. Elsen and J.K.T. Varnedoe, *The Drawings of Rodin*, New York 1971

Fernier 1969 — R. Fernier, *Gustave Courbet: Peintre de l'Art vivant*, Paris 1969

Fernier 1978 — R. Fernier, *La Vie et l'oeuvre de Gustave Courbet*, 2 vols., Lausanne, Paris, 1978

Finsen 1983 — H. Finsen, *Degas og familien Bellelli*, Kobenhavn 1983

Fraun/Growe 1983 — E. Fraun and B. Growe, *Georges Seurat: Zeichnungen*, Munchen 1983

Gobin 1960 — M. Gobin, *L'Art expressif au XIXe siècle français*, Paris 1960

Guillaud 1984 — *Degas: Le Modelé et l'espace*, ed. J. Guillaud and M. Guillaud, Paris 1984

Hamburg 1978 — *Courbet und Deutschland*, Kunsthalle, Hamburg 1978

Hellebranth 1976 — R. Hellebranth, *Charles-François Daubigny, 1817–1878*, Morges 1976

Hoetink 1963 — H. R. Hoetink, "Mediterrane Meditaties," Bulletin Museum Boymans-van Beuningen, XIV (1963), pp. 29–55

Hofmann 1985	W. Hofmann, *Edouard Manet: Das Fruhstuck im Atelier,* Frankfurt am Main 1985
Ixelles 1973	*Henri de Toulouse-Lautrec,* Musée d'Ixelles 1973, no. 29, ill. p. 67
Joachim 1974	J. Joachim, *The Helen Regenstein Collection of European Drawings,* The Art Institute of Chicago, 1974
Lapauze 1911	Henry Lapauze, *Ingres,* Paris 1911
Lemoisne 1946/48	P. A. Lemoisne, *Degas et son oeuvre,* 4 vols., Paris 1946–1948
Liège 1982	*Cézanne,* Musée Saint-Georges, Liège; Musée Granet, Aix-en-Provence, 1982
London 1976	R. L. Herbert, *Jean-François Millet,* Hayward Gallery, London 1976
London 1979/80	*Post-Impressionism: Crosscurrents in European Painting,* Royal Academy of Arts, London 1979/80
London 1980/81	*Camille Pissarro, 1830–1903,* Hayward Gallery, London 1980/81
London 1985/86	*Renoir,* Hayward Gallery, London 1958/86
Los Angeles 1971	L. Eitner, *Géricault,* Los Angeles County Museum of Art; The Detroit Institute of Arts; Philadelphia Museum of Art, 1971/72
Lugt	F. Lugt, *Les Marques de collections de dessins & d'estampes,* Amsterdam 1921; supplement, La Haye 1956
Madrid 1984	*Paul Cézanne,* Museo Espanol de Arte Contemporaneo, Madrid 1984
Maison 1968	K. E. Maison, *Honoré Daumier: Catalogue Raisonné of the Paintings Watercolours and Drawings,* 2 vols., Paris 1968
Naef	H. Naef, *Die Bildniszeichnungen J.–A.–D. Ingres,* 5 vols., Bern 1977–1980
New York 1975/76	*Aristide Maillol: 1861–1944,* The Solomon R. Guggenheim Museum, New York 1975/76
New York 1985	Ph. Grunchec, *Master Drawings by Géricault,* The Pierpont Morgan Library, New York; San Diego Museum of Art; The Museum of Fine Arts, Houston, 1985/86
Newcastle-upon-Tyne 1973	Robert Ratcliffe, *Watercolours and Pencil Drawings by Cézanne,* Laing Art Gallery, Newcastle-upon-Tyne, and Hayward Gallery, London, 1973
Northampton 1979	*Degas and the Dance,* Smith College Museum of Art, Northampton, Mass., 1979, pp. 6–14
Ottawa 1977	*Puvis de Chavannes,* Grand Palais, Paris; The National Gallery of Canada, Ottawa, 1976/77
Paris 1967	*Ingres,* Petit Palais, Paris 1967/68
Paris 1975	R. L. Herbert, *Jean-François Millet,* Grand Palais, Paris 1975
Paris 1978	*Cézanne: Les Dernières Années (1895–1906),* Grand Palais, Paris 1978
Paris 1979	*Rodin et l'Extrême Orient,* Musée Rodin, Paris 1979
Paris/New York, 1983	*Manet, 1832–1883,* Galeries Nationales du Grand Palais; Metropolitan Museum of Art, New York, 1983
Passeron 1979	R. Passeron, *Daumier,* Fribourg 1979
Pignatti 1981	T. Pignatti, *Il Disegno: Da Altamira a Picasso,* Milano 1981
Philadelphia/Chicago 1966/67	*Edouard Manet, 1832–1883,* Philadelphia Museum of Art; The Art Institute of Chicago, 1966–1967
Pissarro 1943	C. Pissarro, *Letters to His Son Lucien,* ed. J. Rewald, London 1943
Pissarro/Venturi 1939	L. R. Pissarro and L. Venturi, *Camille Pissarro: Son Art, Son Oeuvre,* 2 vols., Paris 1939
Poe	*Edgar Allan Poe: The Works of . . .,* vol. V, Philadelphia, 1974
Pontoisc 1980/81	*Pissarro & Pontoise,* Musée Pissarro, Pontoise 1980/81
Rewald 1961	J. Rewald, *The History of Impressionism,* New York 1961

Rewald 1983 J. Rewald, *Paul Cézanne: The Watercolours,* London 1983

Robaut A. Robaut, *L'Oeuvre de Corot,* 4 vols., Paris (1905), 1965

Robaut 1885 A. Robaut, *L'Oeuvre complet de Eugène Delacroix,* Paris 1885

Rome 1968 *Ingres in Italia,* Villa Medici, Rome 1968

Rome 1980 *Constantin Guys: Il Pittore della vita moderna,* Palazzo Braschi, Rome 1980

Rotterdam 1968 Hans R. Hoetink, *Franse tekeningen uit de 19e eeuw: Catalogus van de Verzameling in het Museum Boymans-van Beuningen,* Rotterdam 1968

Rotterdam 1978 *Legaat Vitale Bloch,* Museum Boymans-van Beuningen, Rotterdam 1978

Rouart/Wildenstein 1975 D. Rouart and D. Wildenstein, *Edouard Manet: Catalogue raisonné,* 2 vols., Lausanne/ Paris 1975

Shackelford 1984 G.T.M. Shackelford, *Degas: The Dancers,* Washington 1984

Siblík 1984 J. Siblík, *Cézanne: Drawings and Watercolors,* St. Paul, Minn., 1984

Thomson 1977 R. Thomson, *Toulouse-Lautrec,* London 1977

Toronto 1971/72 John Russell, *Edouard Vuillard,* Art Gallery of Ontario, Toronto 1971/72

Toulouse-Lautrec 1985 *Henri de Toulouse-Lautrec: Images of the 1890's,* ed. R. Castleman and W. Wittrock, New York 1985

Tübingen 1978 Götz Adriani, *Paul Cézanne: Zeichnungen,* Kunsthalle, Tübingen, Köln 1978

Tübingen 1982 Götz Adriani, *Paul Cézanne: Aquarelle,* Kunsthalle, Tübingen, Köln 1982

van Gelder 1976 D. van Gelder, *Rodolphe Bresdin,* La Haye 1976

van Gelder/Sillevis 1978 D. van Gelder and J. Sillevis, *Rodolphe Bresdin, 1822–1885,* Den Haag 1978

Venturi 1936 L. Venturi, *Cézanne: Son Art, Son Oeuvre,* 2 vols., Paris 1936

Venturi 1978 L. Venturi, *Cézanne,* Geneve 1978

Washington 1971 Anne d'Harnoncourt, *Cézanne,* The Phillips Collection, Washington; Museum of Fine Arts, Boston; The Art Institute of Chicago; Boston 1971

Weisberg 1980 G. P. Weisberg, *The Realist Tradition: French Painting and Drawing, 1830–1900,* Cleveland 1980

Wildenstein 1954 G. Wildenstein, *Ingres,* London 1954

Wildenstein 1974 D. Wildenstein, *Claude Monet: Bibliographie et catalogue raisonné,* 2 vols., Lausanne/ Paris 1974

Wilson Bareau 1986 J. Wilson Bareau, "The Hidden Face of Manet: An Investigation of the Artist's Working Processes," *The Burlington Magazine,* CXXVII (1986), supplement to issue 997

Wittrock 1985 W. Wittrock, *Toulouse-Lautrec: The Complete Prints,* London 1985